# STUDY GUIDE

The Economics

*of*

Money, Banking,

*and*

Financial Markets

*Sixth*
*Edition*

# John McArthur
# Frederic S. Mishkin

Addison
Wesley

Boston  San Francisco  New York
London  Toronto  Sydney  Tokyo  Singapore  Madrid
Mexico City  Munich  Paris  Cape Town  Hong Kong  Montreal

Study Guide to accompany Mishkin, *The Economics of Money, Banking, and Financial Markets*, Sixth Edition

Copyright © 2001 Addison Wesley Longman, Inc.

ISBN: 0-321-08542-6

2 3 4 5 6 7 8 9 10-VG-04030201

# Contents

## *How to Use this Study Guide and Workbook*

The only way to effectively learn the economics of money, banking, and financial markets is by continual, and active, application of the basic concepts in this field. To assists in this endeavor, we have written this Study Guide and Workbook as a tool to help you learn the material contained in *The Economics of Money, Banking, and Financial Markets*. This Study Guide and Workbook has one chapter for every chapter in the textbook, and it contains the following learning tools.

**Chapter Synopsis/Completions.** Rather than just providing you with a conventional chapter synopsis that briefly covers all the material in a textbook chapter, the chapter synopsis here requires you to fill in blanks with key words and phrases. This will make your review of a chapter a more active enterprise, one that presents you with a challenge.

**Exercises.** Following the chapter synopsis are a series of exercises that give you hands-on practice with the basic concepts taught in this course. The exercises are intended to provide you with a healthy workout. By pushing your way through them, you are strengthening your ability to make use of the concepts that are essential to learning the material in the textbook. The exercises vary in their approach in order to keep you interested (and awake!); some ask you to do calculations; others, to connect items in different columns; some to fill in key words; and others, to draw graphs. Each exercise comes with a heading that tells you what material is covered so that you can pick exercises on topics where you need the most work.

**Self-Test.** Each chapter ends with a self-test that allows you to gauge how well you are mastering the material. Typically, the self-test includes 10 true-false questions, which function as a warmup, and then 15 multiple-choice questions. If your performance on the self-test is strong, then you should have no problem with the exam in the course.

**Answers.** The answers to the chapter synopsis/completions, exercises, and self-test are all provided in the back of the book so that you can readily check your progress. The answers to the exercises are sufficiently detailed so that even when you have trouble with an exercise, the answer should help you to learn the necessary concepts.

**Strategies for Studying with the Study Guide and Workbook**

There are many possible strategies to improve your course performance with the Study Guide and Workbook. One is to first loosen up by filling in the blanks of the chapter synopsis and then to look up the answers. If you feel comfortable with the material, then you might want to go directly to the self-test. If your self-test performance is good, then you can rest easy and proceed to the next chapter. On the other hand, if you find that you are weak in some areas, then you can do those exercises which cover the topics you are having trouble with.

Alternatively, you might not feel very comfortable with the material after working your way through the chapter synopsis/completions. In this case, you might be better off to go right to the exercises and work your way through all of them. Then, when you think you are in better control of the material, you can take the self-test and evaluate your performance.

Some students may even find that taking the self-test alone is enough practice for them. Feel free to experiment with the Study Guide and Workbook. It is a flexible tool that should help you learn the material without too much strain and pain.

## Acknowledgements

Special thanks are extended to Professor Athanasios G. Noulas of Seaton Hall University, Linda L. Wilson of the University of Texas at Arlington, and Carole Endres of Wright State University for helpful comments on the third edition supplements. We believe they will find this edition to be better for their advice. We extend thanks to Dawn M. Saunders, and Professors Marc Bremer and King Banaian for their suggestions on earlier editions. Finally, we thank Sheryl Nelson at OffCenter Concepts who updated the artwork for this new edition.

John McArthur
Frederic S. Mishkin

# Chapter 1

## *Why Study Money, Banking, and Financial Markets?*

### CHAPTER SYNOPSIS/COMPLETIONS

The study of money is an extremely important part of both economics and finance. Research has found money to play an important role in the determination of aggregate output, the aggregate price level, the rate of inflation, and the level of interest rates.

Without the services provided by financial intermediaries, Americans could not enjoy the present high standard of living to which they have become accustomed. (1)___financial___ markets such as the bond market, the stock market, and foreign exchange market have become increasingly important areas of study. Small movements in bond and stock prices can have significant effects, and changes in (2)___Exchange___ ___rates___ – the price of one country's currency in terms of another's – not only affect those individuals involved in international trade, but all consumers and producers. The bond market is important since interest rates are determined in this market, while the (3)___stock___ ___Market___ is the most widely followed financial market in the United States.

Exchange rates are determined in foreign currency markets and have important effects on international trade. For example, a (4)___strong___ dollar means that the value of the dollar rises relative to foreign currencies and foreign goods become less expensive to Americans – good news for consumers. Unfortunately, a stronger dollar means that goods produced in the United States become more (5)___exspensive___ to foreign purchasers, who are now likely to purchase fewer American goods – bad news for producers. Thus we see that a stronger dollar is a double-edged sword.

Another major area of study in this course is the business of banking. Banks play an important role in determining the quantity of money in an economy. At one time, banks were unique among financial institutions in their roles as monetary policy players. Now a large number of (6)_____ _____ can have important effects on the nation's money supply. However, since the financial intermediary that people deal with most frequently is a commercial (7)_____, that will be the institution most discussed throughout the book.

Financial intermediaries are an important part of a modern industrial economy. They play an important role in transferring funds from those who wish to save to those who wish to (8)_____, thereby ensuring that resources are put to more productive uses. This process of channeling funds by way of an intermediary or middleman is known as (9)_____ _____.

The upward and downward movements in economic activity, commonly referred to as the (10)_____ _____, also have exhibited a close relationship to money growth. Indeed, every recession in the United States in the twentieth century has been preceded by a decline in the rate of money growth.

(11)_____, the condition of a continually rising price level, has exhibited a close relation to the money supply over so many countries and so many time periods that Nobel Laureate Milton Friedman has stated that "Inflation is always and everywhere a monetary phenomenon." Evidence indicates that those countries with the highest rates of inflation are also the ones with the highest money growth rates.

Moreover, economic theory suggests, and historical evidence indicates, that money has an important influence on the level of interest rates. Since interest rates play such an important role in people's (12)_____ and (13)_____ decisions, it should not be surprising that this has been one of the more intensively studied relationships in economics. For example, (14)_____ interest rates are typically blamed for the depressed conditions experienced by the housing industry from time to time. Thus, high interest rates may cause people to put off buying a house, but it may encourage them to save in hopes of buying one in the future.

Also of concern to economists has been the recent volatility of interest rates. In the 15-year period 1970 to 1985, interest rates became much more volatile than they had in the previous 15 years. Concern that these substantial fluctuations might reduce investment has led to additional research of this relationship. A related area concerns the interconnection between (15)_____ growth, interest rates, and budget deficits. Clearly, the study of money is diverse and intimately related to many important economic events.

## EXERCISES

### Exercise 1: Bond, Stock, and Foreign Exchange Markets

Some of the most important financial markets are discussed briefly in Chapter 1. The statements below refer to three of these markets in the United States: the bond market, the stock market, and the foreign exchange market. Indicate to which of the three markets the statement refers. Let B = bond market, S = stock market, and F = foreign exchange market.

_____1. The market where interest rates are determined.

_____2. The market where claims on the earnings of corporations are traded.

_____3. The market that made major news when the Dow-Jones industrial average fell 508 points on October 19, 1987.

_____4. Individuals trying to decide whether to vacation in California or France might be influenced by the outcomes in this market.

_____5. The most widely followed financial market in America.

_____6. The prices of Japanese video cassette recorders sold in the United States is affected by trading in this market.

### Exercise 2: Money and Inflation

Money growth and inflation rates are reported for a number of selected countries in the table below. Graph the money growth-inflation coordinate for each country, creating a scatter diagram in Figure 1A. Sketch a single line to illustrate the general relationship between money growth and inflation depicted in the scatter diagram. Does the line slope upward to the right?

| Country | Average Annual Rate of Money Growth (1975-1984) | Average Annual Rate of Inflation (1975-1984) |
| --- | --- | --- |
| Chile | 59.4 | 54.4 |
| Ecuador | 24.5 | 19.0 |
| France | 11.9 | 10.5 |
| Germany | 6.3 | 4.2 |
| Italy | 17.3 | 16.1 |
| Mexico | 39.2 | 40.1 |
| Portugal | 15.3 | 22.8 |
| Turkey | 39.5 | 45.3 |
| United Kingdom | 13.0 | 11.4 |
| United States | 7.5 | 7.6 |

Source: *International Financial Statistics*

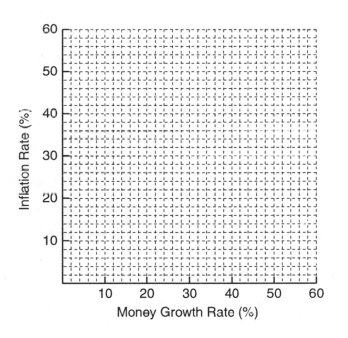

**Exercise 3: Money and Business Cycles**

A.  At the time the Second Bank of the United States closed its doors in 1836, the money supply in the United States was approximately $280 million.  By 1843, the money supply had fallen by more than $100 million.  Predict what happened to the price level and economic activity during the period 1836 to 1843.

_____

_____

B.  Referring to the effects of an expansion in the quantity of currency in 1723, the governor of colonial Pennsylvania said, "It is inconceivable to think what a prodigious good Effect immediately ensued on all the Affairs of the Province."  What do you suppose he means by "all the Affairs of the Province"?

_____

**SELF-TEST**

**Part A: True-False Questions**
Circle whether the following statements are true (T) or false (F).

T  F  1.  Empirical evidence suggests that the price level and the money supply move closely together over long periods of time.

T  F  2.  The condition of a continually rising price level is known as a recession.

T  F  3.  There is a strong negative association between inflation and the growth rate of money.

T  F  4.  Economists frequently talk about "the interest rate" because most interest rates move up and down together.

T  F  5.  The budget deficit is the excess of government tax revenues over government expenditures.

T  F  6.  Monetary policy is defined as the management of money and interest rates.

T  F  7.  Some economists express concern that huge government budget deficits cause the money supply to grow more rapidly, causing inflation.

T  F  8.  One can reasonably assume that financial intermediaries would not exist unless they provided services that people valued.

T  F  9.  Economists tend to disregard events in the stock market since stock prices tend to be extremely stable and are therefore of little interest.

T  F  10.  A stronger dollar means that American goods become more expensive in foreign countries and so foreigners will buy fewer of them.

**Part B: Multiple-Choice Questions**

Circle the appropriate answer.

1. Money appears to have a major influence on

    a. inflation.
    b. the business cycle.
    c. interest rates.
    d. each of the above.
    e. only (a) and (c) of the above.

2. Budget deficits are important to study in a money and banking class because

    a. budget deficits cause banks to fail.
    b. without budget deficits banks would not exist.
    c. budget deficits may influence the conduct of monetary policy.
    d. of each of the above.
    e. of none of the above.

3. An increase in the growth rate of the money supply is most likely to be followed by

    a. a recession.
    b. a decline in economic activity.
    c. inflation.
    d. all of the above.

4. A sharp decrease in the growth rate of the money supply is most likely to be followed by

    a. a decline in economic activity.
    b. an upswing in the business cycle.
    c. inflation.
    d. all of the above.

5. The process of channeling funds from individuals with surplus funds to those desiring additional funds in which the security issued by the borrower is not purchased by the saver is known as

    a. theft.
    b. redistribution.
    c. barter.
    d. financial intermediation.

6. Banks are an important part of the study of how money affects the economy since

    a. banks play a critical role in the creation of money.
    b. banks have been important in the rapid pace of financial innovation.
    c. both (a) and (b) are correct.
    d. neither (a) nor (b) are correct.

7. Suppose that due to a fear that the United States is about to enter a long period of stagnant growth, stock prices fall by 50% on average. Predict what would happen to spending by consumers.

   a. Spending would probably increase.
   b. Spending would probably fall.
   c. Spending would probably be unaffected.
   d. The change in spending would be ambiguous.

8. An increase in interest rates is likely to cause spending on houses to

   a. fall.
   b. rise.
   c. rise in the short run if interest rates are expected to fall in the future.
   d. remain unchanged.

9. Assume that large budget deficits have significant impacts on the level of interest rates. In which market will budget deficits have their biggest impact directly?

   a. The stock market
   b. The bond market
   c. The wheat market
   d. The gold market

10. An increase in the value of the dollar relative to all foreign currencies means that the price of foreign goods purchased by Americans

   a. increases.
   b. falls.
   c. remains unchanged.
   d. There is not enough information to answer.

11. If the price level is 100 in year 1 and 110 in year 2, then the rate of inflation from year 1 to year 2 is

   a. 10%.
   b. 9%.
   c. 11%.
   d. 110%.

12. Budgets deficits can be a concern because they might

   a. ultimately lead to lower inflation.
   b. lead to lower interest rates.
   c. lead to a higher rate of money growth.
   d. cause all of the above to occur.
   e. cause both (a) and (b) of the above to occur.

13. Which of the following is most likely to result from a stronger mark?

    a.  U.S. goods exported aboard will cost less in Germany, and so Germans will buy more of them.
    b.  U.S. goods exported aboard will cost more in Germany, and so Germans will buy more of them.
    c.  U.S. goods exported abroad will cost more in Germany, and so Germans will buy fewer of them.
    d.  Americans will purchase more foreign goods.

14. Which of the following are true statements?

    a.  Inflation is defined as a continual increase in the money supply.
    b.  Inflation is a condition of a continually rising price level.
    c.  The inflation rate is measured as the rate of change in the aggregate price level.
    d.  All of the above are true statements.
    e.  Only (b) and (c) of the above are true statements.

15. From 1971 to 1973 the dollar depreciated in value, thereby, benefiting _____ and harming _____.

    a.  American businesses; American consumers
    b.  American businesses; foreign consumers
    c.  foreign consumers; American businesses
    d.  foreign businesses; American consumers

# Chapter 2

## *An Overview of the Financial System*

### CHAPTER SYNOPSIS/COMPLETIONS

The financial system is a critical element in a well-functioning economy. Chapter 2 examines the general structure and operation of financial markets and institutions.

Financial markets perform the essential function of channeling funds from savers who have excess funds to spenders who have insufficient funds. In (1)_____ finance, borrowers obtain funds directly from lenders in financial markets through the sale of securities. In indirect finance, funds move from lenders to borrowers with the help of middlemen called (2)_____ _____.
Financial markets improve the economic welfare of the society because they move funds from those without productive investment opportunities to those with such opportunities. They also directly improve the well-being of consumers by allowing them to make their purchases when they desire them most. When the financial system breaks down, sever economic hardship results.

Financial markets can be classified as debt or (3)_____ markets, primary or secondary markets, organized exchanges or (4)_____-_____-_____ markets, and money or (5)_____ markets.

A debt instrument is a contractual agreement by the borrower to pay the holder of the instrument fixed dollar amounts at regular intervals. A debt instrument is (6)_____ term if its maturity is a year or less, is intermediate term if its maturity is from one to 10 years, and is long term if its maturity exceeds 10 years. An (7)_____ is a claim to share in the net income and the assets of a business firm.

A primary market is a financial market in which new issues of a security are sold to initial buyers by the corporation or government agency borrowing the funds. A secondary market is a financial market in which the securities that have been previously issued can be resold. Secondary markets can be organized in two ways. One is to organize (8)_____ , where buyers and sellers of securities meet in one central location to conduct trades. The other is to have an over-the-counter market, in which dealers at different locations buy and sell securities. The (9)_____ market is a financial market in which only short-term debt instruments are traded, while the capital market is the market in which longer-term debt and equity instruments are traded.

Financial intermediaries are financial institutions that acquire funds from lenders-savers by issuing (10)_____ and then, in turn, use the funds to make loans to borrowers-spenders. Financial intermediaries allow small savers and borrowers to benefit from the existence of financial markets, thus extending the benefits of these markets to nearly everyone in the economy.

Two factors help to explain the dominant role played by financial intermediaries in our financial structure: transactions costs and problems that arise from information asymmetries. Banks reduce transactions costs by bundling the funds they attract from small savers into loans large enough to finance business undertakings. The bargaining, contracting, and administrative costs – that is, transaction costs – decline as a percentage of the loan amount as the size of the loan increases. Therefore, the administration of loans is subject to economies of scale.

Because borrowers know better the potential returns and associated risks of their investment alternatives than do lenders, financial markets are characterized by asymmetries of information. This informational disadvantage can create problems both before and after the financial transaction is made. (11)_____ _____ is the problem created by asymmetric information before the transaction occurs; moral hazard is the problem created by asymmetric information after the deal has been made.

Adverse selection in financial markets occurs when bad credit risks are the ones who most actively seek financing and are thus the ones most likely to be financed. Moral hazard occurs when borrowers have incentives to engage in activities that are undesirable (i.e., immoral) from the lenders point of view.

The principal financial intermediaries fall into three categories: depository institutions (banks), contractual savings institutions, and investment intermediaries. (12)_____ institutions are financial intermediaries that accept deposits from individuals and institutions and use the acquired funds to make loans. They include commercial banks, savings and loan associations, mutual savings banks, and credit unions. Contractual savings institutions – life insurance companies, fire and casualty insurance companies, and pension funds – are financial intermediaries that acquire funds at periodic intervals on a contractual basis. Investment intermediaries include finance companies, mutual funds, and money market mutual funds.

The principal money market instruments (debt instruments with maturities of less than (13)_____ _____ ) are commercial paper, bankers' acceptances, repurchase agreements, and federal funds. The principal capital market instruments (instruments with maturities greater than one year) are U.S. government securities, mortgages, corporate bonds, U.S. government agency securities, state and local government bonds, and consumer and bank commercial loans.

The financial system is among the most heavily regulated sectors of the American economy. A combination of economic and political forces have shaped past and current government regulatory policy, explaining governments' active role in: (a) providing information to investors, (b) ensuring (14)_____ of the financial system, (c) improving control of monetary policy, and (d) encouraging home ownership. Regulations include: requiring disclosure of information to the public, restrictions on who can set up a financial intermediary, restrictions on what assets financial intermediaries can hold, the provision of deposit insurance, the requirement that depository institutions maintain minimum levels of capital, and the requirement that depository institutions keep a certain fraction of their deposits in accounts at the Federal Reserve (called (15)_____).

In the 1960s, 1970s and early 1980s, volatile interest rates made for dynamic financial markets as new types of financial instruments emerged in response to investor demands. Change in the financial markets since the early 1980s has come primarily from a different source: the internationalization of financial markets. Nothing illustrates this trend more than the growth in Eurobonds and Euroequities. Eurobonds are bonds denominated in a currency other than that of the country in which it is sold. Growth in Eurobonds has been so strong that the Eurobond market exceeds the U.S. corporate bond market as a source of new funds.

Euroequities are new stock issues that are sold primarily to institutional traders abroad. Trading volume in Euroequities has risen at a time when interest in foreign stocks also has increased greatly, as evidenced by the growth in trading activity on various foreign stock exchanges. For instance, until quite recently, the stock market in the United States was by far the largest in the world. Beginning in the mid-1980s, however,

Euroequities are new stock issues that are sold primarily to institutional traders abroad. Trading volume in Euroequities has risen at a time when interest in foreign stocks also has increased greatly, as evidenced by the growth in trading activity on various foreign stock exchanges. For instance, until quite recently, the stock market in the United States was by far the largest in the world. Beginning in the mid-1980s, however, the value of stocks traded in Japan has at times exceeded the value of stocks traded in the United States. Importantly, the internationalization of financial markets has facilitated the financing of domestic corporate and government debt; without these funds, the United States economy would be far less healthy.

## EXERCISES

### Exercise 1: Structure of Financial Markets

Put the following instruments in the appropriate box or boxes below:

U.S. Treasury bills             Federal funds
U.S. Treasury bonds           Common stocks
Corporate bonds                Commercial paper
Negotiable CDs

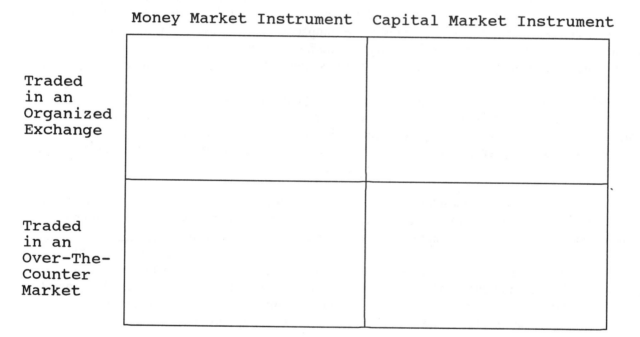

### Exercise 2: Direct versus Indirect Finance

For each of the following financial transactions indicate whether it involves direct finance or indirect finance by writing in the space provided a D for direct finance and an I for indirect finance.

_____ 1. You take out a car loan from a finance company.

_____ 2. You buy a U.S. savings bond.

_____ 3. You buy a share of GM stock.

_____ 4. You buy a share of a mutual fund.

_____ 5. You borrow $1000 from your father.

_____ 6. You obtain a $50,000 mortgage from your local S&L.

_____ 7. You buy a life insurance policy.

_____ 8. GM sells a share of its stock to IBM.

_____ 9. Chase Manhattan Bank issues commercial paper to AT&T.

_____ 10. AT&T issues commercial paper to Mobil Oil Corp.

## Exercise 3: Financial Intermediaries

A. Next to each of the following financial intermediaries, write the letter corresponding to its primary assets.

| Intermediary | Primary Assets |
| --- | --- |
| _____ 1. Commercial banks | a. mortgages |
| _____ 2. Savings and loans | |
| _____ 3. Mutual savings banks | b. consumer loans |
| _____ 4. Credit unions | c. money market instruments |
| _____ 5. Life insurance companies | |
| _____ 6. Pension funds | d. business loans |
| _____ 7. Fire and casualty insurance companies | e. corporate bonds |
| _____ 8. Mutual funds | f. U.S. government securities |
| _____ 9. Money market mutual funds | g. corporate stock |
| _____ 10. Finance companies | h. municipal bonds |

**B.** Next to each of the following financial intermediaries, write the letter corresponding to its primary liabilities.

| Intermediary | Primary Liabilities |
| --- | --- |
| _____ 1. Commercial banks | a. checkable deposits |
| _____ 2. Savings and loans | |
| | b. premiums from policies |
| _____ 3. Mutual savings banks | |
| _____ 4. Credit unions | c. savings deposits |
| _____ 5. Life insurance companies | |
| | d. employer and employee contributions |
| _____ 6. Pension funds | |
| _____ 7. Fire and casualty insurance companies | e. corporate bonds |
| _____ 8. Mutual funds | f. shares |
| _____ 9. Money market mutual funds | g. corporate stock |
| _____10. Finance companies | h. commercial paper |

## Exercise 4: Financial Regulation

Match the regulatory agency to whom it regulates.  Remember that some financial institutions are regulated by more than one agency.

| Regulatory Agency | Who it Regulates |
|---|---|
| _____1. Office of the Comptroller of the Currency | a. Savings and loans |
| _____2. National Credit Union Association | b. Commercial banks |
| _____3. State Banking and Insurance Commissions | c. Organized exchanges |
| _____4. Federal Reserve System | |
| _____5. Federal Deposit Insurance Corporation (FDIC) | d. Mutual savings banks |
| _____6. Office of Thrift Supervision | e. Credit unions |
| _____7. Securities and Exchange Commission | f. Insurance companies |
| _____8. Commodities Futures Trading Commission (CFTC) | g. Futures market traders |

## SELF-TEST

### Part A: True-False Questions

Circle whether the following statements are true (T) or false (F).

T F 1. When financial markets enable a consumer to buy a refrigerator before she has saved up enough funds to buy it, they are helping to increase economic welfare.

T F 2. Direct finance does not involve the activities of financial intermediaries.

T F 3. The difference between a primary and a secondary market is that in a primary market new issues of a security are sold, while in a secondary market previously issued securities are sold.

T  F  4.  An over-the-counter market has the characteristic that dealers in securities conduct their trades in one central location.

T  F  5.  Financial intermediaries only exist because there are substantial information and transactions costs in the economy.

T  F  6.  Liquidity of assets is as important a consideration for contractual savings institutions as it is for depository institutions.

T  F  7.  Money market mutual funds to some extent function as depository institutions.

T  F  8.  The volume of new corporate bonds issued in the United States is substantially greater than the volume of new stock issues.

T  F  9.  The Office of the Comptroller of the Currency is the chartering agency for all commercial banks.

T  F  10.  The primary role of the Securities and Exchange Commission is to make sure that adequate and accurate information can be obtained by investors.

## Part B: Multiple-Choice Questions

Circle the appropriate answer.

1.  Which of the following cannot be described as indirect finance?

   a.  You take out a mortgage from your local bank.
   b.  An insurance company lends money to General Motors Corporation.
   c.  You borrow $1000 from your best friend.
   d.  You buy shares in a mutual fund.
   e.  None of the above.

2.  Which of the following is a short-term financial instrument?

   a.  U.S. Treasury bill
   b.  Share of IBM stock
   c.  New York City bond with a maturity of 2 years
   d.  Residential mortgage

3.  Which of the following statements about the characteristics of debt and equity is true?

   a.  They can both be short-term financial instruments.
   b.  Bond holders are a residual claimant.
   c.  The income from bonds is typically more variable than that from equities.
   d.  Bonds pay dividends.
   e.  None of the above.

4. Which of the following markets in the United States is never set up as an organized exchange?

   a. Stock market
   b. Corporate bond market
   c. U.S. government bond market
   d. Futures market

5. Which of the following is traded in a money market?

   a. U.S. Treasury bonds
   b. Mortgages
   c. Common stocks
   d. Federal funds
   e. None of the above

6. Which of the following is a depository institution?

   a. Life insurance company
   b. Credit union
   c. Pension fund
   d. Finance company

7. The primary assets of a mutual savings bank are

   a. money market instruments.
   b. corporate bonds and stock.
   c. consumer and business loans.
   d. mortgages.

8. The primary liabilities of a savings and loan association are

   a. bonds.
   b. mortgages.
   c. deposits.
   d. commercial paper.

9. Savings and loan associations are regulated by the

   a. Office of the Comptroller of the Currency.
   b. Federal Home Loan Bank System and FSLIC.
   c. Securities and Exchange Commission (SEC).
   d. The Office of Thrift Supervision.

10. A bond denominated in a currency other than that of the country in which it is sold is called a(n)

    a. foreign bond.
    b. Eurobond.
    c. equity bond.
    d. currency bond.

11. Financial intermediaries promote efficiency and thereby increase people's wealth

    a.  by reducing the transaction costs of linking together lenders and borrowers.
    b.  to the extent that they help solve problems created by adverse selection and moral hazard.
    c.  by providing additional jobs.
    d.  because of all of the above.
    e.  because of only (a) and (b) of the above.

12. Contractual savings institutions include:

    a.  commercial banks and thrifts.
    b.  life insurance companies and pension funds.
    c.  finance companies and mutual funds.
    d.  all of the above.
    e.  only (a) and (b) of the above.

13. Typically, lenders have inferior information relative to borrowers about the potential returns and risks associated with any investment project. This difference in information is called _____, and it gives rise to the _____ problem.

    a.  asymmetric information; moral hazard
    b.  asymmetric information; adverse selection
    c.  adverse selection; moral hazard
    d.  adverse selection; asymmetric information

14. U.S. Treasury bills are

    a.  issued in three-, six-, nine-, and twelve-month maturities.
    b.  the most liquid of the money market instruments.
    c.  the safest of all the money market instruments.
    d.  all of the above.
    e.  are only (b) and (c) of the above.

15. Federal funds are loans made by the

    a.  Federal Reserve System to commercial banks.
    b.  one commercial bank to another.
    c.  the U.S. Treasury to the Federal Reserve.
    d.  the Federal Reserve to the U.S. Treasury.

# Chapter 3

## *What is Money?*

### CHAPTER SYNOPSIS/COMPLETIONS

Chapter 3 deals with a problem that has received increased attention among economists since the mid-1970s: just what is money or the money supply? This topic is given expanded treatment in a later chapter, but raising the issue here allows us to consider the importance of money, discovering why it evolves in all but the most primitive societies.

Economists define (1)_____ as anything that is generally accepted in payment for goods and services or in the repayment of debts. This usually means currency to most people, but to economists this definition is far too narrow. Economists include checking account deposits and travelers checks with currency to come up with a narrow definition of the (2)_____ _____ called M1.

Before discussing the significance of money, it is important that one distinguish money from income. Money is a stock; that is, it represents a measure at a point in time. For example the money stock, M1, was $1110.9 billion on May 8, 2000. Income is a (3)_____ of earnings per unit of time. Money serves a purpose, or in economists' jargon, it is productive. If money was not productive, we would abandon its use. Money's productivity results largely from its ability to reduce transaction costs and encourage (4)_____ and the division of labor.

Money has three primary functions: It is a medium of exchange, unit of account, and (5)_____ _____ _____, which all act to reduce transaction costs and encourage specialization. Generally regarded as its most important function, money's ability to serve as a medium of exchange is what distinguishes it from other assets, both financial and physical. Without money, exchanges would be strictly (6)_____ transactions. And while barter can be an efficient system for small groups of people, transaction costs rise significantly as the population grows because people find it increasingly difficult to satisfy a double coincidence of wants. Money reduces the high search costs that are characteristic of barter exchanges.

Money also lowers information and exchange costs by serving as a unit of account. Comparison shopping is extremely time-consuming and costly when goods are not priced in a common unit, whether the units be dollars, cigarettes, or beaver pelts.

Finally, money serves as a store of value. This function of money facilitates the exchange of goods over (7)_____. Although money is not unique as a store of value, it is the most (8)_____ of all assets, and thus it tends to be the preferred store of value for most people most of the time. To illustrate just how strong this tendency is, consider that people did not completely abandon the use of German currency even during the hyperinflationary 1920s, though barter did become much more prevalent.

Money's evolution over time has been driven by efforts designed to reduce transaction costs further. The introduction and subsequent acceptance of (9)_____ _____ and checks greatly reduced transportation costs and the loss from theft, respectively. More recently, there has been progression toward a checkless society. Although concerns about fraud have slowed development of an (10)_____ _____ _____ _____ (EFTS), one continues to observe movements in this direction.

Unfortunately, it is much easier to identify the virtues of money than it is to identify which assets actually function as money. For example, in a discussion among Federal Reserve Board members in the early 1980s, someone commented that money market mutual funds should not be included within the narrow money definition because most funds required a $500 minimum on all their checks. Then-chairman Paul Volker's response was to the effect that the minimum requirement had not often prevented his wife from spending from their account. Volcker's comment, though lighthearted, illustrates one problem to measuring money.

Because it is not clear what assets should be considered money, the Fed monitors closely the movements of several (11)_____ _____. Most important are the two narrowest definitions, M1 and M2. If both measures moved together and exhibited a high degree of correlation with economic activity, the Fed's job would be much easier. Such is not the case, however, and there seems little optimism among economists that a solution will be found soon to the measurement problem.

Further complicating matters is the unreliability of (12)_____ money statistics. Given all these problems, it is no wonder that some commentators refer to monetary policymaking as an art rather than a science. At the same time, it is this kind of controversy and uncertainty that makes the study of money and banking so interesting.

## EXERCISES

### Exercise 1: Medium of Exchange

Assume that there are three students on campus named Allen (A), Barbi (B), and Clyde (C). They live in the same dorm and know each other well. Allen owns a CD by R.E.M. (R), Barbi owns a Sugar Ray (S) CD, and Clyde has a CD by Shania Twain (T). Further assume that Allen prefers the Sugar Ray CD to the one by R.E.M. and that he prefers the R.E.M. CD to the one by Shania Twain. Barbi prefers the Shania Twain CD to her Sugar Ray CD, but likes R.E.M. the least. Clyde prefers the R.E.M. CD to his Shania Twain CD, liking the Sugar Ray CD the least. If we rank each student's preferences for the CDs, representing preference with the ">" symbol, we get the following table:

| Individual | Preferences | Initial CD |
|------------|-------------|------------|
| A | S > R > T | R |
| B | T > S > R | S |
| C | R > T > S | T |

Now assume an economy with no money, so that all trades are barter transactions. Note that when Allen (because he likes Sugar Ray better than R.E.M.) approaches Barbi about trading CDs, Barbi will be unwilling to trade since she will be worse off (she prefers Sugar Ray to R.E.M.). The same happens when any two individuals try to trade directly. Allen will be unwilling to give R.E.M. for Shania Twain in a trade with Clyde, and Clyde will be unwilling to trade away Shania Twain in an exchange with Barbi.

Thus we see from in this example that barter between any two individuals – because there is not a double coincidence of wants – prevents the three individuals from getting their most preferred musical artist.

However, if we assume that Barbi is aware of Clyde's willingness to trade his Shania Twain for the R.E.M. CD, then Barbi will be willing to accept the R.E.M. CD in exchange for her Sugar Ray since she knows that she will be able to exchange with Clyde at a later date.

Finish filling in the table below showing the movement of the CDs among Allen, Barbi, and Clyde.

| Individual | Initial CD | Intermediate CD | Final CD |
|------------|-----------|-----------------|----------|
| A | R | _____ | _____ |
| B | S | _____ | _____ |
| C | T | _____ | _____ |

What has the R.E.M. CD functioned as? _____.

## Exercise 2: The Functions of Money

Money has three primary functions: It is a medium of exchange, a store of value, and a unit of account. The statements below provide examples of these three functions. Indicate which of the three primary functions of money is illustrated by each statement. Let M = medium of exchange, S = store of value, and U = unit of account.

_____1. Erin purchases tickets to the Pearl Jam concert by writing a check.

_____2. Christopher drops the change from his pocket into the wine bottle bank on his study desk.

_____3. So that they might avoid calculating relative prices of goods in terms of all other goods, the traders at the trading post agreed to value their wares in terms of beaver pelts.

_____4. Everyone understood, including nonsmokers, that the prices of commodities traded in the prisoner-of-war camp were to be stated in terms of cigarettes.

_____5. Although he loved to smoke, Andrew saved cigarettes for he would be able to purchase chocolate bars on more favorable terms as the supply of cigarettes dwindled in the POW camp.

_____6. Anthony calculates that the opportunity cost of his time is $15.00 per hour.

_____7. Meghan purchases for $9.95 the videotape she plans to give to her parents for Christmas.

_____8. This function of money is important if people are to specialize at what they do best.

_____9. Function of money that reduces transaction costs in an economy by reducing the number of prices that need to be considered.

_____10. The role of money that would not be provided if bananas were to serve as money.

## Exercise 3: Functions of Money – Unit of Account

The price of one good in terms of another is referred to as the barter price or exchange rate. The benefits of using money are best appreciated by thinking of a barter economy. Between any two goods there is one barter price or exchange rate. But as the number of goods increases, the number of barter prices or exchange rates grows more rapidly. Complete the following table which dramatically illustrates the virtues of a unit of account.

Number of Prices in a Barter Versus a Money Economy

| Number of Goods | Number of Prices in a Barter Economy | Number of Prices in a Money Economy |
|---|---|---|
| 5 | _____ | 5 |
| 25 | _____ | 25 |
| 50 | _____ | _____ |
| 500 | 124,750 | _____ |
| 5000 | _____ | _____ |

## Exercise 4: Measuring Money – The Federal Reserve's Monetary Aggregates

After each asset, indicate in the space provided which monetary aggregate – M1, M2, M3, or L – includes the asset. As an aid, the first one has already been completed.

1. Currency   <u>M1, M2, M3, L</u>

2. Savings bonds _____

3. Overnight repurchase agreements _____

4. Checkable deposits _____

5. Short-term Treasury securities _____

6. Small-denomination time deposits _____

7. Money market deposit accounts _____

8. Money market mutual fund balances (institutional) _____

9. Savings deposits _____

## SELF-TEST

### Part A: True-False Questions

Circle whether the following statements are true (T) or false (F).

T  F  1.  Since checks are accepted as payment for purchases of goods and services, economists consider checking account deposits as money.

T  F  2.  Of its three functions, it is as a unit of account that distinguishes money from other assets.

T  F  3.  Money is a unique store of value, since physical goods depreciate over time.

T  F  4.  Money can be traded for other goods quickly and easily compared to all other assets. Thus money is said to be liquid.

T  F  5.  Money proves to be a good store of value during inflationary episodes, since the value of money is positively related to the price level.

T  F  6.  Paper currency evolved because it is less costly to transport than is commodity money.

T  F  7.  Inflation may reduce economic efficiency if it induces people to resort to barter.

T  F  8.  The major impetus behind the move to expand the EFTS is the relatively high cost of transporting and processing checks.

T  F  9.  In times past when only currency functioned as money, measuring money would have been conceptually much easier.

T  F  10.  The past behavior of M1 and M2 indicates that using only one monetary aggregate to guide policy is sufficient, since they move together very closely.

### Part B: Multiple-Choice Questions

Circle the appropriate answer.

1.  When an economist talks about the impossibility of barter, she really is not saying that barter is impossible. Rather, she means to imply that

    a.  barter transactions are relatively costly.
    b.  barter has no useful place in today's world.
    c.  it is impossible for barter transactions to leave the parties to an exchange better off.
    d.  each of the above is true.

2. The resources expended trying to find potential buyers or sellers and negotiating over price and terms are called

   a. barter costs.
   b. transaction costs.
   c. information costs.
   d. enforcement costs.

3. If cigarettes serve as a medium of exchange, a unit of account, and a store of wealth, cigarettes are said to function as

   a. bank deposits.
   b. reserves.
   c. money.
   d. loanable funds.

4. Because money reduces both the time it takes to make exchanges and the necessity of a double coincidence of wants, people will find that they can more easily pursue their individual comparative advantages. Thus money

   a. encourages nonproductive pursuits.
   b. encourages specialization.
   c. forces people to become too specialized.
   d. causes a waste of resources due to the duplication of many activities.

5. The narrowest meause of money, called M1, consists of

   a. currency.
   b. currency, checking account deposits, and money market mutual funds.
   c. currency, checking account deposits, and money market deposit account funds.
   d. currency, checking account deposits, and traveler's checks.

6. As the transaction costs of selling an asset rise, the asset is said to become

   a. more valuable.
   b. more liquid.
   c. less liquid.
   d. more moneylike.

7. Which of the following are problems with a payments system based largely on checks?

   a. Checks are costly to process.
   b. Checks are costly to transport.
   c. Checks take time to move through the check-clearing system.
   d. All of the above.
   e. Only (a) and (b) of the above.

8. Starting January 1, 1999

   a. the exchange rates of countries entering the European Union were fixed permanently to the euro.
   b. the European Central Bank took over monetary policy from the individual national central banks.
   c. the governments of the member countries began issuing debt in euros.
   d. all of the above occurred.
   e. only (a) and (b) of the above occurred.

9. Which of the following is not included in the money aggregate M2?

   a. Currency
   b. Money market deposit accounts
   c. Overnight repurchase agreements
   d. Savings bonds

10. Which of the following best describes the behavior of the money aggregates M1 and M2?

    a. While both M1 and M2 tend to rise and fall together, they often grow at very different rates.
    b. M1 tends to grow at a much faster rate than M2.
    c. While both M1 and M2 tend to move closely together over periods as short as a year, in the long run they tend to move in opposite directions.
    d. While both M1 and M2 tend to move closely together over periods as short as a year, in the long run their growth rates are vastly different.

11. The conversion of a barter economy to one that uses money

    a. increases efficiency by reducing the need to exchange goods.
    b. increases efficiency by reducing transaction costs.
    c. has no effect on economic efficiency since efficiency is a production concept, not an exchange concept.
    d. decreases efficiency by reducing the need to specialize.

12. Which of the following are true about the evolution of the payments system?

    a. The evolution of the payments system from barter to precious metals, then to fiat money, then to checks can best be understood as a consequence of innovations that allowed traders to more easily escape oppressive taxes on exchange.
    b. Precious metals had the advantage of being widely accepted, being divisible into relatively small units, and being durable, but had the disadvantage of being difficult to carry and transport from one place to another.
    c. Paper money has the advantage of being easy to transport, but has the disadvantage of being less accepted than checks.
    d. Only (a) and (b) of the above are true.

13. Generally, the problem of defining money becomes _____ troublesome as the pace of financia.
    innovation _____.

    a. less; quickens
    b. more; quickens
    c. more; slows
    d. more; stops

14. If an individual "cashes in" a U.S. savings bond for currency,

    a. M1 increases and M2 stays the same.
    b. M1 stays the same and M2 increases.
    c. M1 stays the same and M2 stays the same.
    d. M1 increases and M2 increases.

15. Generally speaking, the initial data on the monetary aggregates reported by the Fed are

    a. not a reliable guide to the short-run behavior of the money supply.
    b. a reliable guide to the long-run behavior of the money supply.
    c. a reliable guide to the short-run behavior of the money supply.
    d. both (a) and (b) of the above.
    e. both (b) and (c) of the above.

# Chapter 4

## *Understanding Interest Rates*

### CHAPTER SYNOPSIS/COMPLETIONS

Interest rates are among the most important variables in the economy. This chapter explains how interest rates are measured and shows that the interest rate on a bond is not always an accurate measure of how good an investment it will be.

Credit market instruments generally fall into four types: a simple loan, a fixed-payment loan, a coupon bond, and a discount bond. A simple loan provides the borrower with an amount of funds that must be repaid at the maturity date along with an interest payment. A (1)_____-_____ loan requires the borrower to make the same payment every period until the maturity date. A coupon bond pays the owner a fixed coupon payment every year until the maturity date when the face value is repaid. Its (2)_____ _____ equals the coupon payment expressed as a percentage of the face value of the bond. A (3)_____ bond is bought at a price below its face value, but the face value is repaid at the maturity date.

The concept of (4)_____ _____ tells us that a dollar in the future is not as valuable as a dollar today; that is, a dollar received *n* years from now is worth $1/(1 + i)^n$ today. The yield to maturity, the economists' preferred measure of the interest rate, is the interest rate that equates the present value of future payments of a debt instrument with its value (or price) today. Applications of this principle reveal that bond prices and interest rates are (5)_____ related; when the interest rate rises, the price of the bond falls, and vice versa.

Two less accurate measures of interest rates that are commonly used to quote interest rates. The current yield, which equals the (6)_____ payment divided by the price of the coupon bond, is a better measure of the interest rate the closer the bond's price is to the bond's par value and the (7)_____ is the maturity of the bond. The yield on a discount basis (also called a discount yield) understates the yield to maturity; and the longer the maturity of the discount bond, the greater this understatement becomes. Even when either of these measures is a misleading guide to the level of the interest rate, a rise in either of these rates signals a (8)_____ in the yield to maturity, and a fall signals a fall in the yield to maturity.

How well you have done by holding a security over a period of time is measured by the security's (9)_____ – the payments to the owner plus the change in its value, expressed as a percentage of the purchase price. The return is equal to the yield to maturity in only one special case: when the holding period is equal to the (10)_____ of the bond. For bonds with maturities greater than the holding period, capital gains and losses can be substantial when (11)_____ _____ change. Returns can therefore differ greatly from the yield to maturity. This is why long-term bonds are not considered to be safe assets with a certain return over short holding periods.  The real interest rate is defined as the nominal interest rate minus the expected rate of inflation.  It is a better measure of the incentives to borrow and lend than is the nominal interest rate, making it a better indicator of the tightness of (12)_____ _____ conditions than is the nominal interest rate.

## EXERCISES

### Exercise 1: Present Discounted Value

Calculate the present discounted value for the following payments:

1.  $500 two years from now when the interest rate is 5%.          _____

2.  $500 two years from now when the interest rate is 10%.        _____

3.  $500 four years from now when the interest rate is 10%.       _____

4.  What do the calculations indicate about the present value of a payment as the interest rate rises?

_____

5.  What do the calculations indicate about the present value of a payment as it is paid further in the future?

_____

### Exercise 2: Yield to Maturity

A.  Suppose you are offered a $1000 fixed-payment car loan that requires you to make payments of $600 a year for the next two years.

1.  Write down the equation that can be solved for the yield to maturity on this loan: that is, the equation that equates the present value of the payments on the loan to the amount of the loan.

    _____

2.  Calculate the present value of the loan payments when the interest rate is 10%.

    _____

3.  Must the yield to maturity be above or below 10%? _____

4.  Calculate the present value of the loan payments when the interest rate is 15%.

    _____

5.  Must the yield to maturity be above or below 15%? _____

Verify that the present value of the loan payments is approximately $1000 when the interest rate is 13%, indicating that this is the yield to maturity.

B.  Suppose you are thinking of buying a $1000 face-value coupon bond with a coupon rate of 10%, a maturity of 3 years, and a price of $1079.

1.  Is the yield to maturity going to be above or below 10%? _____ Why?

_____

2.  Write down the equation that can be solved for the yield to maturity of this bond: that is, the equation that equates the present value of the bond payments to the price of the bond.

_____

3.  Calculate the present value of the bond when the interest rate is 8%.

_____

4.  Must the yield to maturity be above or below 8%? _____

5.  Calculate the present value of the bond when the interest rate is 5%.

_____

6.  Must the yield to maturity be above of below 5%? _____

Verify that the present value of the loan payments is approximately $1079 when the interest rate is 7%, indicating that this is the yield to maturity.

## Exercise 3: Yield to Maturity and Yield on a Discount Basis

For discount bonds with a face value of $1000, fill in the yield to maturity (annual rate) and the yield on a discount basis in the following table.

| Price of the Discount Bond | Maturity | Yield on a Discount Basis | Yield to Maturity |
|---|---|---|---|
| $900 | 1 year (365 days) | | |
| $950 | 6 months (182 days) | | |
| $975 | 3 months (91 days) | | |

Note: For bonds with a maturity of 6 months, the yield to maturity at an annual rate equals $[(1 + i_{six})^2 - 1]$, where $i_{six}$ is the return over 6 months; for bonds with a maturity of 3 months, the yield to maturity at an annual rate equals $[(1 + i_{three})^4 - 1]$, where $i_{three}$ is the return over 3 months.

What does the preceding table indicate about the degree of understatement of the  yield to maturity by the yield on a discount basis as the maturity of a discount bond shortens?

_____

_____

## Exercise 4: Current Yield

For the five U.S. Treasury bonds on May 16, 2000 fill in the value of the current yield in the following table:

| Coupon Rate | Maturity Date | Price | Yield to Maturity | Current Yield |
|---|---|---|---|---|
| 10 3/4s | May 2003 | 110 11/32 | 6.87% | |
| 12 3/8s | May 2004 | 118 31/32 | 6.86% | |
| 6 3/4s | May 2005 | 100 5/32 | 6.71% | |
| 6 1/2s | Nov 2026 | 101 12/32 | 6.39% | |
| 6 1/4s | May 2030 | 101 26/32 | 6.12% | |

For which of these bonds is the current yield a good measure of the interest rate?  Why?

_____

_____

## Exercise 5: The Rate of Return

1. For a consol with a yearly payment of $100, calculate the return for the  year if its yield to maturity at the beginning of the year is 10% and at the end of the year is 5%. (Hint: Calculate the initial price and end-of-year price first; then calculate the return.)

_____

2. For a 10% coupon bond selling at par with 2 years to maturity, calculate the return for the year if its yield to maturity at the beginning of the year is 10% and at the end of the year is 5%. (Hint: Calculate the initial price and end-of-year price first; then calculate the return.)

_____

Which of the bonds is a better investment? _____

Why do you think that this has happened? _____

_____

**Exercise 6: Real Interest Rates**

Calculate the real interest rate in the following situations:

1. The interest rate is 3% and the expected inflation rate is -3%          _____

2. The interest rate is 10% and the expected inflation rate is 20%.          _____

3. The interest rate is 6% and the expected inflation rate is 3%.          _____

4. The interest rate is 15% and the expected inflation rate is 15%.          _____

In which of these situations would you prefer (everything else equal) to be a lender?

_____ A borrower? _____

## SELF-TEST

**Part A: True-False Questions**

Circle whether the following statements are true (T) or false (F).

T  F  1. A bond that pays the bondholder the face value at the maturity date and makes no interest payments is called a discount bond.

T  F  2. The yield to maturity of a coupon bond that is selling for less than its face value is less than the coupon rate.

T  F  3. You would prefer to own a security that pays you $1000 at the end of 10 years than a security that pays you $100 every year for 10 years.

T  F  4. The yield to maturity on a coupon bond can always be calculated as long as the coupon rate and the price of the bond are known.

T  F  5. The current yield is the most accurate measure of interest rates, and it is what economists mean when they use the term interest rates.

T  F  6. You would prefer to hold a 1-year Treasury bond with a yield on a discount basis of 10% to a 1-year Treasury bond with a yield to maturity of 9.9%.

T  F  7. A 5-year $1000 coupon bond selling for $1008 with a 9% current yield has a higher yield to maturity than a 1-year discount bond with a yield on a discount basis of 8.9%.

T  F  8. When interest rates rise from 4 to 5%, bondholders are made better off.

T  F  9. If interest rates on all bonds fall from 8 to 6% over the course of the year, you would rather have been holding a long-term bond than a short-term bond.

T  F  10. Business firms are more likely to borrow when the interest rate is 2% and the price level is stable than when the interest rate is 15% and the expected inflation rate is 14%.

**Part B: Multiple-Choice Questions**

Circle the appropriate answer.

1.  A discount bond

    a.  pays the bondholder the same amount every period until the  maturity date.
    b.  at the maturity date pays the bondholder the face value of the bond plus an interest payment.
    c.  pays the bondholder a fixed interest payment every period and repays the face value at the maturity date.
    d.  pays the bondholder the face value at the maturity date.

2.  A $5000 coupon bond with a coupon rate of 5% has a coupon payment every year of

    a.  $50.
    b.  $500.
    c.  $250.
    d.  $100.
    e.  none of the above.

3.  With an interest rate of 5%, the present value of a security that pays $52.50 next year and $110.25 two years from now is

    a.  $162.50.
    b.  $50.
    c.  $100.
    d.  $150.

4.  The present value of a security that pays you $55 next year and $133 three years from now is $150 if the interest rate is

    a.  10%.
    b.  5%.
    c.  15%.
    d.  20%.

5.  If a security pays you $105 next year and $110.25 the year after that, what is its yield to maturity if it sells for $200?

    a.  4%
    b.  5%
    c.  6%
    d.  7%

6.  The yield to maturity on a $20,000 face value discount bond that matures in one year's time and currently sells for $15,000 is

    a.  20 percent.
    b.  25 percent.
    c.  33 1/3 percent.
    d.  66 2/3 percent.

7. Which of the following $1000 face value securities has the lowest yield to maturity?

   a. 5% coupon bond selling for $1000
   b. 5% coupon bond selling for $1200
   c. 5% coupon bond selling for $900
   d. 10% coupon bond selling for $1000
   e. 10% coupon bond selling for $900

8. Which of the following $1000 face value securities has the highest yield to maturity?

   a. 5% coupon bond selling for $1000
   b. 5% coupon bond selling for $1200
   c. 5% coupon bond selling for $900
   d. 10% coupon bond selling for $1000
   e. 10% coupon bond selling for $900

9. If a $5000 face value discount bond maturing in 1 year is selling for $4000, its yield to maturity is

   a. 5%.
   b. 10%.
   c. 25%.
   d. 50%.

10. The current yield on a $5000 10% coupon bond selling for $4000 is

    a. 5%.
    b. 10%.
    c. 12.5%.
    d. 15%.

11. The yield on a discount basis _____ the yield to maturity, and the _____ the maturity of the discount bond the greater is the _____.

    a. overstates; longer; overstatement
    b. overstates; shorter; overstatement
    c. understates; longer; understatement
    d. understates; shorter; understatement

12. The current yield is a

    a. more accurate approximation of the yield to maturity, the nearer the bond's price is to the par value and the shorter the maturity of the bond.
    b. less accurate approximation of the yield to maturity, the nearer the bond's price is to the par value and the longer the maturity of the bond.
    c. more accurate approximation of the yield to maturity, the nearer the bond's price is to the par value and the longer the maturity of the bond.
    d. more accurate approximation of the yield to maturity, the farther the bond's price is to the par value and the shorter the maturity of the bond.

13.  The yield on a discount basis of a 180-day $1000 Treasury bill selling for $975 is

    a.  5%.
    b.  10%.
    c.  20%.
    d.  50%.

14.  What is the return on a 15% coupon bond that initially sells for $1000 and sells for $700 next year?

    a.  15%
    b.  10%
    c.  -5%
    d  -15%

15.  In which of the following situations would you rather be borrowing?

    a.  the interest rate is 20% and expected inflation rate is 15%
    b.  the interest rate is 4% and expected inflation rate is 1%
    c.  the interest rate is 13% and expected inflation rate is 15%
    d.  the interest rate is 10% and expected inflation rate is 15%

# Chapter 5

## *The Behavior of Interest Rates*

### CHAPTER SYNOPSIS/COMPLETIONS

Chapter 5 examines how interest rates are determined and the factors that influence their behavior. The supply and demand analysis developed here explains why interest rates have had such substantial fluctuations in recent years. The supply and demand analysis for bonds, known as the loanable funds framework, provides one theory of how interest rates are determined. The (1)_____ for bonds is the relationship between the quantity demanded and the bond price (which is (2)_____ related to the interest rate) when all other economic variables are held constant.

With the bond price plotted on the left-hand vertical axis, the demand curve is downward sloping because a declining bond price means a (3)_____ interest rate, thereby causing the expected return on bonds to rise, resulting in an increase in the quantity of bonds demanded. If the interest rate is plotted on the right-hand vertical axis, the interest rate *decreases* as one moves (4)_____ the axis because of the inverse relationship between bond prices and interest rates.

The supply curve for bonds is upward sloping because a rising bond price means a (5)_____ interest rate, thereby reducing the cost of borrowing funds (issuing bonds), resulting in an increase in the quantity of bonds supplied. The market interest rate is the market (6)_____, which occurs when the quantity of bonds demanded equals the quantity supplied; that is, at the intersection of the supply and the demand curves.

The theory of asset demand portfolio choice indicates that there are four factors that cause the demand curve for bonds to shift. Specifically, the demand curve shifts to the right when wealth (7)_____, when the expected return on bonds relative to alternative assets (8)_____, when the riskiness of bonds relative to alternative assets (9)_____ or when the liquidity of bonds relative to alternative assets (10)_____.

There are three factors that cause the supply curve for bonds to shift. Specifically, the supply curve shifts to the right when the expected profitability of investment opportunities increases, as in a business cycle boom, when expected inflation (11)_____, or when the government increases the supply of debt by running high budget deficits. Changes in any of these factors cause interest rates to change. This supply and demand analysis indicates, for example, that a rise in expected inflation leads to a rise in interest rates, a phenomenon known as the (12)_____ effect.

An alternative theory of how interest rates are determined is provided by the liquidity preference framework, which analyzes the supply and demand for money. The demand curve for money slopes downward because, with a lower interest rate, the expected return on bonds falls relative to the expected return on money. According to the theory of asset demand, this causes the quantity of money demanded to

(13)_____. The demand curve for money shifts to the right when income
(14)_____, when the price level increases, or when inflation is expected to increase.

The central bank is assumed to control the quantity of money supplied at a fixed amount, meaning that the supply curve for money is a vertical line. The equilibrium interest rate occurs at the intersection of the supply and demand curves for money. The supply and demand analysis of the money market indicates that the interest rate rises when either income or the price level rises, or when the money supply
(15)_____.

The liquidity preference and loanable funds frameworks indicate that there are four possible effects of an increase in the rate of money supply growth on interest rates: (a) the liquidity effect, (b) the income effect, (c) the price-level effect, and (d) the expected inflation effect. The liquidity effect indicates that higher money supply growth leads to a (16)_____ in interest rates; the other effects work in the (17)_____ direction. The evidence seems to indicate that the income, price-level, and expected inflation effects dominate the liquidity effect, implying that an increase in money supply growth leads to permanently (18)_____ interest rates. Whether interest rates initially fall rather than rise when money growth is increased depends critically on how fast people's expectations about inflation adjust.

## EXERCISES

### Exercise 1: Factors that Shift Supply and Demand Curves for Bonds

For each of the following situations (holding everything else constant), indicate in the space provided how the supply and demand curves for bonds shift: D → for demand curve to the right, ← D for demand curve to the left, S → for supply curve to the right, and ← S for supply curve to the left.

_____ 1. A decline in brokerage commission on bonds.

_____ 2. Expected inflation rises.

_____ 3. There is a new tax on purchases and sales of gold.

_____ 4. There is a large federal budget deficit.

_____ 5. Businessmen become more optimistic about the success of their investments in new plant and equipment.

_____ 6. Bond prices become more volatile.

_____ 7. The economy booms and wealth rises.

_____ 8. Stock prices become more volatile.

_____ 9. People suddenly expect a bear market (a decline in prices) for stocks.

_____10. People suddenly expect interest rates to rise.

## Exercise 2: Theory of Asset Demand

In the second column of the following table indicate with an arrow whether the quantity demanded of the asset will increase (↑) or decrease (↓):

| Variable | Change in Variable | Change in Quantity Demanded |
|---|---|---|
| Wealth | ↓ | |
| Liquidity of asset | ↓ | |
| Riskiness of asset | ↓ | |
| Expected return of asset | ↓ | |
| Riskiness of other assets | ↓ | |
| Liquidity of other assets | ↓ | |
| Expected return of other assets | ↓ | |

## Exercise 3: Analyzing a Change in the Equilibrium Interest Rate

Suppose the supply and the demand for long-term bonds are as marked in Figure 5A and market equilibrium is at point 1. Suppose that, as occurred in the 1980s and for much of the 1990s, the federal government begins to run a large budget deficit and at the same time the volatility of interest rates increases. Draw in the new supply and demand curves in Figure 5A.

**FIGURE 5A**

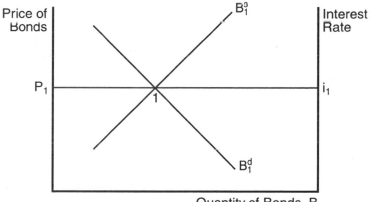

What happens to the interest rate? _____

**Exercise 4: Supply and Demand Analysis of the Money Market**

Suppose the supply and the demand for money are as drawn in Figure 5B.  Now the Federal Reserve decreases the money supply and as a result income falls.  Draw the new supply and demand curves in Figure 5B.

**FIGURE 5B**

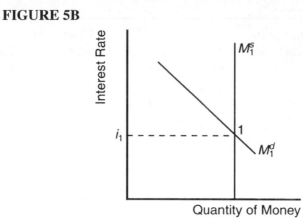

What happens to the interest rate? _____


**Exercise 5: Money Growth and Interest Rates**

Plot in Figure 5C the path of the interest rate, if at time T the rate of money growth is slowed from 10 to 7% and the liquidity effect is greater than the income, price-level, and expected inflation effects.


**FIGURE 5C**

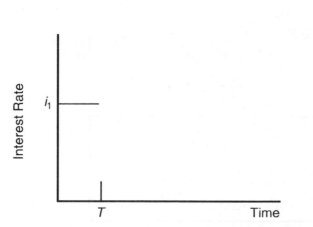

Plot in Figure 5D the path of the interest rate, if at time T the rate of money growth is slowed from 10 to 7%, while the liquidity effect is smaller than the income, price-level, and expected inflation effects, and there is slow adjustment of inflation expectations.

**FIGURE 5D**

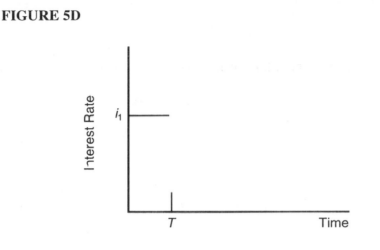

**SELF-TEST**

**Part A: True-False Questions**

Circle whether the following statements are true (T) or false (F).

T  F  1. The demand curve for bonds slopes downward because at a lower bond price, the expected return on the bonds is higher and the quantity demanded is higher.

T  F  2. The loanable funds terminology relabels the demand curve for bonds as one for loanable funds and the supply curve for bonds as the one for loanable funds.

T  F  3. A rise in the price of a bond shifts the demand curve for bonds to the left.

T  F  4. When businessmen become optimistic about the future health of the economy, the supply curve for bonds shifts to the left.

T  F  5. A rise in the expected future price of long-term bonds shifts the demand curve for long-term bonds to the right.

T  F  6. A federal budget surplus will shift the supply curve for bonds to the right.

T  F  7. The Fisher effect suggests that periods of high interest rates will also tend to be periods of high inflation.

T  F  8. In Keynes's view of the world in which there are only two assets, an excess demand in the money market implies that there is an excess demand in the bond market.

T  F  9. If the stock market becomes riskier, the demand curve for money shifts to the right.

T  F  10.  The reason that Milton Friedman is unwilling to accept the view that lower interest rates will result from higher money growth is that he disagrees with Keynes's liquidity preference analysis.

## Part B: Multiple-Choice Questions

Circle the appropriate answer.

1.  When the interest rate is below the equilibrium interest rate, there is an excess _____ for (of) bonds and the interest rate will _____.

    a.  supply; fall
    b.  supply; rise
    c.  demand; rise
    d.  demand; fall

2.  When brokerage commissions in the housing market are raised from 6 to 7% of the sales price, the _____ curve for bonds shifts to the _____.

    a.  demand; right
    b.  demand; left
    c.  supply; left
    d.  supply; right

3.  When rare coin prices become less volatile, the _____ curve for bonds shifts to the _____.

    a.  demand; right
    b.  demand; left
    c.  supply; left
    d.  supply; right

4.  When the expected inflation rate decreases, the demand for bonds shifts to the _____, the supply of bonds shifts to the _____, and the interest rate _____.

    a.  right; right; rises
    b.  right; left; falls
    c.  left; left; falls
    d.  left; right; rises

5.  When people revise downward their expectations of next year's short-term interest rate, the demand for long-term bonds shifts to the _____ and their interest rates _____.

    a.  right; rises
    b.  right; falls
    c.  left; falls
    d.  left; rises

6. In a recession, normally, the demand for bonds shifts to the _____, the supply of bonds shifts to the _____ and the interest rate _____.

    a. right; right; rises
    b. right; left; falls
    c. left; left; falls
    d. left; right; rises

7. In the money market, when the interest rate is below the equilibrium interest rate, there is an excess _____ for (of) money, people will try to sell bonds, and the interest rate will _____.

    a. demand; rise
    b. demand; fall
    c. supply; fall
    d. supply; rise

8. If the price level falls, the demand curve for money will shift to the _____ and the interest rate will _____.

    a. right; rise
    b. right; fall
    c. left; rise
    d. left; fall

9. If the Fed wants to permanently lower interest rates, then it should raise the rate of money growth if

    a. there is a fast adjustment of expected inflation.
    b. there is slow adjustment of expected inflation.
    c. the liquidity effect is smaller than the expected inflation effect.
    d. the liquidity effect is larger than the other effects.

10. When the growth rate of the money supply is increased, interest rates will rise immediately if the liquidity effect is _____ than the other money supply effects and there is _____ adjustment of expected inflation.

    a. larger; fast
    b. larger; slow
    c. smaller; slow
    d. smaller; fast

11. When the interest rate on a bond is _____ the equilibrium interest rate, in the bond market there is excess _____ and the price of bonds will _____.

   a.  below; demand; rise
   b.  above; demand; fall
   c.  below; supply; fall
   d.  above; supply; rise

12. In the Keynesian liquidity preference framework, when income is _____ during a business cycle contraction, interest rates will _____.

   a.  rising, rise
   b.  rising, fall
   c.  falling, rise
   d.  falling, fall

13. In the liquidity preference framework, the price level effect of a one-time increase in the money supply will have its maximum impact on interest rates

   a.  at the moment the price level hits its peak (stops rising) because both the price level and expected inflation effects are at work.
   b.  immediately after the price level begins to rise, because both the price level and expected inflation effects are at work.
   c.  at the moment the expected inflation rate hits its peak.
   d.  at the moment the inflation rate hits its peak.

14. In the liquidity preference framework, the difference between the price level and expected inflation effects of a one-time increase in the money supply can be stated as follows:

   a.  the increase in the interest rate caused by the rise in the price level remains once the price level has stopped rising, but the increase in the interest rate caused by expected inflation will be reversed once the price level stops rising.
   b.  the increase in the interest rate caused by the rise in the expected inflation rate remains once the price level has stopped rising, but the increase in the interest rate caused by the rise in the price level will be reversed once the price level stops rising.
   c.  once the price level stops rising, the interest rate declines because of the price level effect, but the expected inflation effect remains after the price level has stopped rising.
   d.  there is no difference, as both effects cause the interest rate to rise.

15. The most plausible explanation for why interest rates rose in the 1970s is

   a.  the contractionary monetary policy pursued by the Federal Reserve System.
   b.  the decline in the money supply caused by the many failures of savings and loan associations.
   c.  the rapidly rising level of income.
   d.  the continual increase in expected inflation.
   e.  the steady increase in the price level.

# Chapter 6

## *The Risk and Term Structure of Interest Rates*

### CHAPTER SYNOPSIS/COMPLETIONS

The supply and demand analysis of interest rate behavior in Chapter 5 examined the determination of just one interest rate, even though there are many different interest rates in the economy. This chapter completes the interest rate picture by examining the relationship among interest rates on securities that differ in their riskiness, liquidity, income tax treatment, and term to maturity.

The relationship among interest rates on different securities with the same term to maturity is called the (1)_____ structure of interest rates. One attribute of a bond that influences its interest rate is its (2)_____ _____, the chance that the issuer of the bond will default, that is, be unable to make interest payments or pay the face value when the bond matures. When default risk on a bond increases, the demand curve for this bond shifts to the left and the demand curve for default-free bonds shifts to the right. The result is that as default risk increases, the (3)_____ premium (the spread between this bond's interest rate and the interest rate on a default-free bond) rises.

Another attribute of a bond that influences its interest rate is its (4)_____, that is, how quickly and cheaply it can be converted into cash if the need arises. Supply and demand analysis reveals that the less liquid a bond is, the higher its interest rate will be relative to more liquid securities. Therefore, the lower liquidity of corporate bonds relative to U.S. government bonds (5)_____ the spread between the interest rates on these two bonds and thereby contributes to the risk premium of corporate bonds.

Income tax rules also have an impact on the risk structure of interest rates. The tax exemption of municipal bonds (6)_____ their interest rate relative to U.S. Treasury securities. The risk structure of interest rates is, therefore, explained by three factors: default risk, liquidity, and the income tax treatment of the bond.

The relationship among interest rates on bonds with different terms to maturity is called the (7)_____ structure of interest rates. It is graphed as the (8)_____ _____, a plot of the yields on default-free government bonds with differing terms to maturity. Three theories have been proposed to explain the term structure of interest rates. The first theory, the expectations theory, is derived using the assumption that bonds of different maturities are perfect substitutes, implying that their expected returns must be equal. It indicates, therefore, that the interest rate on a long-term bond will equal an average of short-term interest rates that people expect to occur over the life of the long-term bond. Although the expectations theory can explain the empirical fact that interest rates on bonds of different maturities tend to move together over time, it is unable to explain the fact that yield curves are usually (9)_____ sloping.

The (10)_____ _____ theory of the term structure sees markets as completely separated or segmented.  It assumes that bonds of different maturities are not substitutes at all.  Hence, the interest rate for each maturity bond is determined by the supply and demand for that maturity with no effects from expected returns on bonds with either shorter or longer maturities.  Although this theory can explain why yield curves usually slope upward, it cannot explain the empirical fact that interest rates on bonds of different maturities move together.

The liquidity premium theory of the term structure states the following: the interest rate on a long-term bond will equal an average of short-term interest rates expected to occur over the life of the long-term bond, plus a (11)_____ premium that responds to supply and demand conditions for that bond.  The theory takes the view that bonds of different maturities are (12)_____, so that the expected return on a bond of one maturity does influence the expected return of a bond with a different maturity, but it also allows investors to prefer one bond maturity over another.

The liquidity premium theory is able to explain the two empirical facts discussed above.  It explains why interest rates on different maturity bonds move together over time.  If short-term interest rates are expected, on average, be (13)_____ in the future, then long-term interest rates will rise along with them.  Moreover, it explains why yield curves are usually upward-sloping, suggesting that the risk premium is (14)_____ because of people's preference for short-term bonds.  Also, the theory explains a third empirical fact: when short-term interest rates are low, yield curves are more likely to have a steep upward slope; when short-term interest rates are high, yield curves are more likely to slope downward.

The liquidity premium theory has the additional attractive feature that it permits one to infer what the market is predicting for the movement of short-term interest rates in the future.  A steep upward slope of the yield curve means that short-term rates are expected to (15)_____; a mild upward slope means that short-term rates are expected to remain the same; a flat slope means that short-term rates are expected to fall moderately; and a downward slope means that short-term rates are expected to fall sharply.

## EXERCISES

### Exercise 1: Default Risk and Liquidity Effects on the Risk Structure

Figure 6A plots the supply and demand curves in the corporate bond market and the Treasury bond markets.  If the health of the economy improves so that the probability of bankruptcy decreases, draw the new supply and demand curves in Figure 6A.

1.  What happens to the interest rate on corporate bonds? _____

2.  What happens to the interest rate on Treasury bonds? _____

3.  What happens to the size of the risk premium? _____

FIGURE 6A

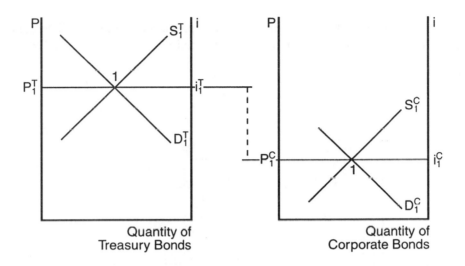

**Exercise 2: Tax Effects on the Risk Structure**

Suppose your income tax bracket is 25%.

1. What is your after-tax return from holding a 1-year municipal bond with an 8% yield to maturity?

_____

2. What is your after-tax return from holding a 1-year corporate bond with a 10% yield to maturity?

_____

3. If both these securities have the same amount of risk and liquidity, then which one of them would you prefer to own?

_____

4. What does this example suggest about the relationship found in the bond market between interest rates on municipal bonds and those on other securities?

_____

### Exercise 3: Deriving a Yield Curve

Given that the expectations theory of the term structure is correct, plot in Figure 6B the yield curve when the expected path of 1-year interest rates over the next 10 years is the following: 1%, 2%, 3%, 4%, 5%, 5%, 4%, 3%, 2%, 1%.

**FIGURE 6B**

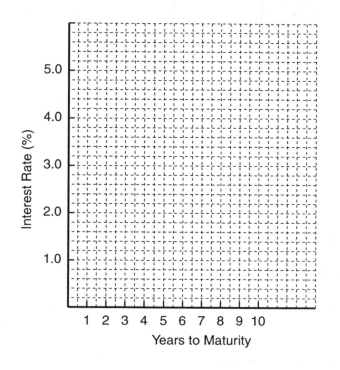

### Exercise 4: Expectations Theory of the Term Structure

An investor is presented with the following two alternative investment strategies: Purchase a 3-year bond with an interest rate of 6% and hold it until maturity, or purchase a 1-year bond with an interest rate of 7%, and when it matures, purchase another 1-year bond with an expected interest rate of 6%, and when it matures, purchase another 1-year bond with an interest rate of 5%.

1.  What is the expected return over the 3 years for the first strategy?

_____

2.  What is the expected return over the 3 years for the second strategy?

_____

3. What is the relationship between the expected returns of the two strategies?

_____

4. Why does our analysis of the expectations theory indicate that this is exactly what you should expect to find?

_____

**Exercise 5: Inferring Market Predictions of Future Interest Rates**

A. What is the market predicting about the movement of future short-term interest rates (assuming there is a mild preference for shorter maturity bonds) if the yield curve looks like the one in Figure 6C?

_____

_____

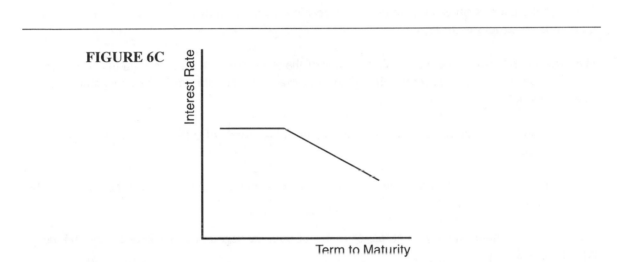

**FIGURE 6C**

B. What is the market predicting about the movement of future short-term interest rates (assuming there is a mild preference for shorter maturity bonds) if the yield curve looks like the one in Figure 6D?

_____

_____

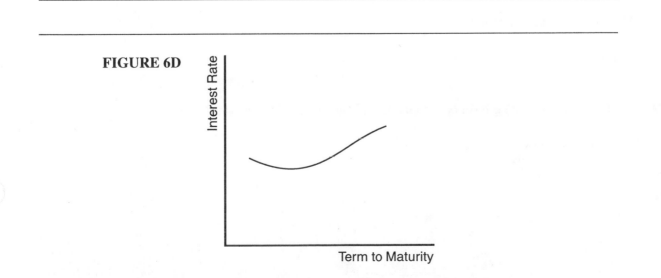

**FIGURE 6D**

## SELF-TEST

### Part A: True-False Questions

Circle whether the following statements are true (T) or false (F).

T  F  1. The term structure of interest rates is the relationship among interest rates of bonds with the same maturity.

T  F  2. The greater is a bond's default risk, the higher is its interest rate.

T  F  3. Negotiable certificates of deposit tend to have lower interest rates than Treasury bills.

T  F  4. The risk premium on a bond only reflects the amount of risk this bond has relative to a default-free bond.

T  F  5. A plot of the interest rates on default-free government bonds with different terms to maturity is called a term structure curve.

T  F  6. The difference between the expectations theory of the term structure and the liquidity premium theory is that the liquidity premium theory allows for a risk premium while the expectations theory does not.

T  F  7. The expectations theory of the term structure assumes that bonds of different maturities are perfect substitutes.

T  F  8. The segmented markets theory of the term structure is unable to explain why yield curves usually slope upward.

T  F  9. The liquidity premium theory combines elements of both the segmented markets theory and the expectations theory.

T  F  10. The liquidity premium theory assumes that bonds of different maturities are not substitutes.

### Part B: Multiple-Choice Questions

Circle the appropriate answer.

1. Which of the following long-term bonds tend to have the highest interest rate?

   a. corporate Baa bonds
   b. U.S. Treasury bonds
   c. corporate Caa bonds
   d. municipal bonds

2. When the default risk on corporate bonds increases, other things equal, the demand curve for corporate bonds shifts to the _____ and the demand curve for Treasury bonds shifts to the _____.

   a. right; right
   b. right; left
   c. left; right
   d. left; left

3. When the corporate bond market becomes less liquid, other things equal, the demand curve for corporate bonds shifts to the _____ and the demand curve for Treasury bonds shifts to the _____.

   a. right; right
   b. right; left
   c. left; left
   d. left; right

4. The risk premium on corporate bonds falls when

   a. brokerage commissions fall in the corporate bond market.
   b. a flurry of major corporate bankruptcies occurs.
   c. the Treasury bond market becomes more liquid.
   d. both (b) and (c) of the above occur.

5. The interest rate on municipal bonds rises relative to the interest rate on corporate bonds when

   a. there is a major default in the municipal bond market.
   b. income tax rates are raised.
   c. Treasury securities become more widely traded.
   d. corporate bonds become riskier.

6. If all taxes were abolished,

   a. the interest rate on flower bonds would fall.
   b. the interest rate on municipal bonds would fall.
   c. the interest rate on municipal bonds would rise.
   d. the interest rate on flower bonds would rise.
   e. both (c) and (d) of the above would occur.

7. Which of the following theories of the term structure is able to explain the fact that when short-term interest rates are low, yield curves are more likely to slope upward:

   a. expectations theory.
   b. segmented markets theory.
   c. liquidity premium theory.
   d. both (b) and (c) of the above.
   e. both (a) and (c) of the above.

8.  If the expected path of 1-year interest rates over the next 3 years is 4, 1, and 1% then the expectations theory predicts that today's interest rate on the 3-year bond is

    a.  1%.
    b.  2%.
    c.  3%.
    d.  4%.
    e.  none of the above.

9.  If the expected path of 1-year interest rates over the next 5 years is 2, 2, 4, 3, and 1%, the expectations theory predicts that the bond with the highest interest rate today is the one with a maturity of

    a.  1 year.
    b.  2 years.
    c.  3 years.
    d.  4 years.
    e.  5 years.

10. If the yield curve slopes upward mildly for short maturities and then slopes sharply upward for longer maturities, the liquidity premium theory (assuming a mild preference for short-term bonds) indicates that the market is predicting

    a.  a rise in short-term interest rates in the near future and a decline further out in the future.
    b.  constant short-term interest rates in the near future and a rise further out in the future.
    c.  a decline in short-term interest rates in the near future and a rise further out in the future.
    d.  a decline in short-term interest rates in the near future which levels off further out in the future.

11. Because municipal bonds bear substantial default risk, their interest rates

    a.  tend to be higher than interest rates on default-free U.S. Treasury bonds indicating that the default premium exceeds the tax advantages of municipal bonds.
    b.  tend to be higher than interest rates on default-free U.S. Treasury bonds indicating that the default premium falls short of the tax advantages of municipal bonds.
    c.  tend to be lower than interest rates on default-free U.S. Treasury bonds indicating that the default premium exceeds the tax advantages of municipal bonds.
    d.  tend to be lower than interest rates on default-free U.S. Treasury bonds indicating that the default premium falls short of the tax advantages of municipal bonds.

12. When income tax rates are _____, the interest rates on Treasury bonds _____ relative to the interest rate on state and local bonds.

    a.  lowered; fall
    b.  lowered; rise
    c.  raised; fall
    d.  raised; do not change

13. The risk structure of interest rates is explained by three factors:

    a.  default risk, liquidity, and the income tax treatment of the security.
    b.  default risk, maturity, and the income tax treatment of the security.
    c.  liquidity, maturity, and the income tax treatment of the security.
    d.  default risk, maturity, and the liquidity of the security.

14. According to the liquidity premium theory

    a.  a steeply rising yield curve indicates that short-term interest rates are expected to rise in the future.
    b.  a moderately rising yield curve indicates that short-term interest rates are expected to decline in the future.
    c.  interest rates on bonds of different maturities need not move together over time.
    d.  only (a) and (b) of the true.

15. The _____ of the term structure states the following: the interest rate on a long-term bond will equal an average of short-term interest rates expected to occur over the life of the long-term bond but investors do not prefer short-term over long-term bonds.

    a.  segmented markets theory
    b.  expectations theory
    c.  liquidity premium theory
    d.  liquidity preference theory

# Chapter 7

## *The Foreign Exchange Market*

### CHAPTER SYNOPSIS/COMPLETIONS

Exchange rate movements are extremely important to our economy. Chapter 7 develops a modern analysis of exchange rate determination that explains both recent behavior in the foreign exchange market, and why exchange rates are so volatile from day to day.

The exchange rate is the price of one country's (1)_____ in terms of another's. Trades in the foreign exchange market typically involve the exchange of bank (2)_____ denominated in different currencies. Spot exchange rates involve the immediate exchange of bank deposits, while (3)_____ exchange rates involve the exchange of deposits at some specified future date. When a currency increases in value, it has (4)_____; when a currency falls in value and is worth fewer U.S. dollars, it has depreciated. Exchange rates are important because when a country's currency appreciates its exports become (5)_____ expensive and foreign imports become less expensive. Conversely, when a country's currency depreciates its goods become less expensive for foreigners, but foreign goods become more expensive (implying that net exports decline, all else constant).

The starting point for undertaking an investigation of how exchange rates are determined is the law of one price, which states the following: If two countries produce an identical good, the price of the good should be the same throughout the world no matter which country produces it. Applying the law of one price to countries' price levels produces the theory of (6)_____ _____ _____, which suggests that if one country's price level rises relative to another's, its currency should (7)_____.

The theory of purchasing power parity cannot fully explain exchange rate changes because goods produced in different countries are not identical and because many goods and services (whose prices are included in a measure of a country's price level) are not (8)_____ across borders. Other factors also affect the exchange rate in the long run, including trade barriers such as (9)_____ and quotas, the demand for imports and exports, and relative productivity.

The key to understanding the short-run behavior of exchange rates is to recognize that an exchange rate is the price of domestic bank deposits in terms of foreign bank deposits. Because the exchange rate is the price of one asset in terms of another, the natural way to investigate the short-run determination of exchange rates is through an asset-market approach using the theory of asset demand.

The theory of asset demand indicates that the most important factor affecting the demand for both domestic (dollar) and foreign deposits is the (10) _____ _____ on these assets relative to one another. According to the interest parity condition, however, the expected return on both domestic and foreign deposits is identical in a world in which there is (11) _____ _____. Because the interest parity condition is an equilibrium condition, it provides a framework for understanding short-run movements in exchange rates as a result of factors that cause the expected return on either domestic or foreign deposits to change temporarily.

Therefore, changes in foreign interest rates, the domestic (12)_____ _____, or a change in the expected future exchange rate will cause the exchange rate to change in the short run. Because long-run determinants of the exchange rate influence the expected future exchange rate, the five determinants of long-run exchange rates affect short-run exchange rates. For example, any factor that raises the expected return on domestic deposits relative to foreign deposits causes the domestic currency to appreciate. These factors include a (13)_____ in the domestic interest rate, a decline in the foreign interest rate, or any long-run factor that causes the expected future exchange rate to (14)_____.

A rise in domestic interest rates relative to foreign interest rates can result in either an appreciation or a depreciation of the domestic currency. If the rise in the domestic interest rate is due to a rise in expected inflation, then the domestic currency depreciates. If the rise in the domestic interest rate, however, is due to a rise in the real interest rate, then the domestic currency (15)_____, as happened to the dollar in the early 1980s. Higher domestic money growth leads to a (16)_____ of the domestic currency.

Exchange rates have been very volatile in recent years. The theory of asset demand explains this volatility as a consequence of changing expectations which are also volatile, and play an important role in determining the demand for domestic assets and, thereby, affects the value of the exchange rate.

## EXERCISES

### Exercise 1: Foreign Exchange Rates and Goods Prices

1. Suppose the exchange rate between the Swiss franc and the dollar is $0.50 per franc. What would be the exchange rate if it is quoted as francs per dollar? _____

2. If you are contemplating buying a fancy Swiss watch that costs 1000 francs, how much will it cost you in dollars? _____

3. If a Swiss is contemplating buying an American pocket calculator that costs $100, how much will it cost him in francs? _____

4. If the exchange rate changes to $.25 per Swiss franc, has there been an appreciation or depreciation of the Swiss franc? _____ Of the dollar? _____

5. Now if you buy the Swiss watch that costs 1000 francs, how much will it cost you in dollars? _____ Does the Swiss watch cost you more or less than before? _____

6. Now how much will it cost the Swiss in francs for the $100 pocket calculator? _____ Does it cost more or less than before? _____

7. What does the example here indicate about the effect on prices of foreign goods in a country and domestic goods sold abroad when the exchange rate appreciates? _____

**Exercise 2: Definitions and Terminology**

Match the following terms on the right with the definition or description on the left. Place the letter of the term in the blank provided next to the appropriate definition. Terms may be used once, more than once, or not all.

_____  1. The price of one country's currency in terms of another's.

    a. law of one price

_____  2. Condition in which exchange rate falls more in short run than long run when money supply increases.

    b. interest parity condition

_____  3. The current exchange rate regime in which exchange rates fluctuate from day to day, but central banks intervene to influence exchange rate movements.

    c. capital mobility

    d. devaluation

_____  4. States that the domestic interest rate equals the foreign interest rate plus the expected depreciation of the domestic currency.

    e. exchange rate

_____  5. Value of the domestic currency increases relative to one or more foreign currencies.

    f. quota

_____  6. Value of foreign currency increases relative to the domestic currency.

    g. managed float regime (dirty float)

_____  7. When two countries produce an identical good, the price of the good should be the same throughout the world no matter which country produces it.

    h. tariff

_____  8. Theory that exchange rates between any two countries will adjust to reflect changes in the price levels of the two countries.

    i. exchange rate overshooting

_____  9. Barrier to trade restricting the quantity of foreign goods that can be imported.

    j. spot exchange transaction

_____ 10. The predominant type of exchange rate transaction that involves the immediate exchange of bank deposits denominated in different currencies.

    k. forward exchange transaction

_____ 11. Americans can easily purchase foreign assets; foreigners can easily purchase American assets.

    l. purchasing power parity

_____ 12. An exchange rate transaction that involves the exchange of bank deposits denominated in different currencies at a specified future date.

    m. appreciation

    n. depreciation

**Exercise 3: Law of One Price and Purchasing Power Parity**

**Part A.**

Suppose that Polish wheat costs 3000 zloties per bushel and that American wheat costs $6 per bushel. In addition, assume that American wheat and Polish wheat are identical goods.

1. If the exchange rate is 300 Polish zloties per U.S. dollar, what is the price of Polish wheat in dollars?
   _____

2. What is the price of American wheat in zloties? _____

3. What will be the demand for Polish wheat? _____ Why?_____

   _____

4. If the exchange rate is 600 Polish zloties per U.S. dollar, what is the price of Polish wheat in dollars?
   _____

5. What is the price of American wheat in zloties? _____

6. What will be the demand for American wheat? _____ Why?_____

   _____

7. What does the law of one price indicate will be the exchange rate between the Polish zloty and the U.S. dollar? _____

   Why? _____

8. If the price of American wheat rises to $10 per bushel, what does the law of one price suggest will be the new exchange rate? _____

   Is this an appreciation or depreciation of the U.S. dollar? _____

**Part B.**

1. If the American price level doubles while that in Poland remains unchanged, what does the theory of purchasing power parity suggest will happen to the exchange rate which initially is at 500 zloties to the dollar?

   _____

2. If the American inflation rate is 5% and the Polish inflation rate is 7%, then what does the theory of purchasing power parity predict will happen to the value of the dollar in terms of zloties in one year's time?

   _____

**Exercise 4: Factors that Affect Exchange Rates**

In the second column of the following table indicate with an arrow whether the exchange rate will rise (↑) or fall (↓) as a result of the change in the factor. (Recall that a rise in the exchange rate is viewed as an appreciation of the domestic currency.)

| Change in Factor | | Response of the Exchange Rate |
|---|---|---|
| Domestic interest rate | ↓ | |
| Foreign interest rate | ↓ | |
| Expected domestic price level | ↓ | |
| Expected tariffs and quotas | ↓ | |
| Expected import demand | ↓ | |
| Expected export demand | ↓ | |
| Expected productivity | ↓ | |

# SELF-TEST

**Part A: True-False Questions**

Circle whether the following statements are true (T) or false (F).

T  F  1. Most trades in the foreign exchange market involve the buying and selling of bank deposits.

T  F  2. If the interest rate on euro-denominated assets is 5% and is 8% on dollar-denominated assets, then the expected return on dollar-denominated assets is higher than that on euro-denominated assets if the dollar is expected to depreciate at a 5% rate.

T  F  3. When a country's currency appreciates, its goods abroad become more expensive, and foreign goods in that country become cheaper, all else constant.

T  F  4. The interest parity condition does not hold if there is perfect capital mobility in international finance.

T  F  5. The model of foreign exchange rate behavior indicates that whenever the domestic interest rate rises relative to the foreign interest rate, the exchange rate appreciates.

T  F  6. If a central bank lowers the growth rate of the money supply, then its currency will appreciate.

T  F  7. If expected inflation in the U.S. rises from 5 to 8% and the interest rate rises from 7 to 9%, the dollar will appreciate.

T  F  8. Under the current exchange rate regime, central banks rarely intervene in the foreign exchange market.

T F 9. The phenomenon in which the exchange rate falls by more in the short run than it does in the long run when the money supply increase is called exchange rate overshooting.

T F 10. The high volatility of exchange rate movements indicates that participants in the foreign exchange market do not behave in a rational manner.

## Part B: Multiple-Choice Questions

Circle the appropriate answer.

1. When the Swiss franc appreciates (holding everything else constant), then

   a. Swiss watches sold in the United States become more expensive.
   b. American computers sold in Switzerland become more expensive.
   c. Swiss army knives sold in the United States become cheaper.
   d. American toothpaste sold in Switzerland becomes cheaper.
   e. Both (a) and (d) of the above are true.

2. The theory of purchasing-power parity indicates that if the price level in the United States rises by 5% while the price level in Mexico rises by 6%, then

   a. the dollar appreciates by 1% relative to the peso.
   b. the dollar depreciates by 1% relative to the peso.
   c. the exchange rate between the dollar and the peso remains unchanged.
   d. the dollar appreciates by 5% relative to the peso.
   e. the dollar depreciates by 5% relative to the peso.

3. If, in retaliation for "unfair" trade practices, Congress imposes a quota on Japanese cars, but at the same time Japanese demand for American goods increases, then in the long run

   a. the Japanese yen should appreciate relative to the dollar.
   b. the Japanese yen should depreciate relative to the dollar.
   c. the dollar should depreciate relative to the yen.
   d. it is not clear whether the dollar should appreciate or depreciate relative to the yen.

4. If the interest rate on dollar-denominated assets is 10% and it is 8% on euro-denominated assets, then if the euro is expected to appreciate at a 5% rate,

   a. dollar-denominated assets have a lower expected return than euro-denominated assets.
   b. the expected return on dollar-denominated assets in euros is 2%.
   c. the expected return on euro-denominated assets in dollars is 3%.
   d. none of the above will occur.

5. Of the following factors, which will not cause the expected return schedule for foreign deposits to shift?

    a.   A change in the expected future exchange rate.
    b.   A change in the foreign interest rate.
    c.   A change in the current exchange rate.
    d.   A change in the productivity of American workers.

6. A rise in the expected future exchange rate shifts the expected return schedule on foreign deposits to the
   _____ and causes the exchange rate to _____.

    a.   right; appreciate
    b.   right; depreciate
    c.   left; appreciate
    d.   left; depreciate

7. A rise in the domestic interest rate is associated with

    a.   a shift in the expected return schedule for domestic deposits to the right.
    b.   a shift in the expected return schedule for domestic deposits to the left.
    c.   a shift in the expected return schedule for foreign deposits to the right.
    d.   a shift in the expected return schedule for foreign deposits to the left.

8. If the foreign interest rate rises and people expect domestic productivity to rise relative to foreign
   productivity, then (holding everything else constant)

    a.   the expected return schedule for domestic deposits shifts left and the domestic currency appreciates.
    b.   the expected return schedule for domestic deposits shifts right and the domestic currency
         appreciates.
    c.   the expected return schedule for foreign deposits shifts left and the domestic currency depreciates.
    d.   the expected return schedule for foreign deposits shifts right and the domestic currency depreciates.
    e.   the effect on the exchange rate is uncertain.

9. When domestic real interest rates rise, the

    a.   the expected return schedule for dollar deposits shifts to the right, and the dollar appreciates.
    b.   the expected return schedule for dollar deposits shifts to the left, and the dollar appreciates.
    c.   the expected return schedule for dollar deposits shifts to the right, and the dollar depreciates.
    d.   the expected return schedule for dollar deposits shifts to the left, and the dollar depreciates.

10. If the interest rate on dollar deposits is 10 percent, and the dollar is expected to appreciate by seven
    percent over the coming year, then the expected return on the dollar deposit in terms of foreign
    currency is

    a.   3%.
    b.   17%.
    c.   -3%.
    d.   10%.

11. If the interest rate on dollar deposits is 10 percent, and the dollar is expected to appreciate by seven percent over the coming year, then the expected return on the dollar deposit in terms of dollars is

    a. 3%.
    b. 17%.
    c. -3%.
    d. 10%.

12. Reasons why the theory of purchasing power parity might not fully explain exchange rate movements include

    a. differing monetary policies in different countries.
    b. changes is the prices of goods and services not traded internationally.
    c. changes in the domestic price level that exceed changes in the foreign price levels.
    d. changes in the foreign price levels that exceed changes in the domestic price level.

13. An expected _____ in _____ productivity relative to _____ productivity (holding everything else constant) causes the domestic currency to _____.

    a. rise; foreign; domestic; depreciate
    b. rise; domestic; foreign; depreciate
    c. decline; foreign; domestic; depreciate
    d. rise; foreign; domestic; appreciate

14. When the domestic nominal interest rate falls because of a decrease in expected inflation, the expected appreciation of the dollar rises, $RET^F$ shifts in _____ than $RET^D$, and the exchange rate _____.

    a. less; falls
    b. less; rises
    c. more; falls
    d. more; rises

15. A lower domestic money supply causes the domestic currency to

    a. depreciate more in the short run than in the long run.
    b. depreciate more in the long run than in the short run.
    c. appreciate more in the short run than in the long run.
    d. appreciate more in the long run than in the short run.

# Chapter 8

## *An Economic Analysis of Financial Structure*

### CHAPTER SYNOPSIS/COMPLETIONS

Lending is risky. Borrowers with ill intentions may choose to skip town and fail to leave a forwarding address, and even those with honest intentions may undertake actions that increase the probability that they will be unable to meet their payment obligations. Given these hazards, individuals may be understandably reluctant to lend. Although lending is risky for the lender, the channeling of funds from individuals with savings to others with productive investment opportunities is essential for economic growth. Channeling funds from savers to investors is beneficial for the economy and the parties to the exchange, but only if investors have incentives to honor their promises and pay back the borrowed funds. The key to understanding the structure of financial markets is to ask how the observed financial arrangements (e.g., the dominance of financial (1)_____ and complicated loan contracts) help to reduce the risk of loan defaults and the uncertainty of lending, thereby encouraging the financing of worthwhile business activities.

Although our financial system is complex in both structure and function, a few simple but powerful economic concepts provide the key insights necessary to understand its complexity. A careful examination of financial markets and institutions reveals that eight basic puzzles require explaining. Economic analysis of the eight puzzles indicates that our financial structure is best understood as a response to the problems of (2)_____ _____ and (3)_____ _____.

The eight basic puzzles of financial markets throughout the world include:

1. Stocks are not an important source of finance for American businesses. Between 1970 and 1985, the stock market accounted for only a very small fraction of the financing of American businesses. Indeed, in the mid- to late-1980s, American corporations repurchased such large numbers of shares that stock market financing was negative.

2. Issuing marketable securities is not the primary way businesses finance their operations. In the United States, (4)_____ are a far more important source of finance than are stocks, yet, combined, bonds and stocks supply less than (5)_____-_____ of the external funds corporations use to finance their activities.

3. Indirect finance, which involves the activities of (6)_____ intermediaries, is many times more important than direct finance. If direct finance is defined as the sale to households of marketable securities such as stocks and bonds, then direct finance accounts for less than five percent of the external financing of American business.

4. Banks are the most important source of (7)_____ funds to finance businesses.

Indeed, bank loans provide twenty-five times more financing of corporate activities than does the stock market.

5.  The financial system is among the most heavily regulated sectors of the economy.

6.  Only large, well-established corporations have access to securities markets to finance their activities.

7.  Collateral is a prevalent feature of debt contracts for both households and businesses.

8.  Debt contracts are typically (8)_____ legal documents that place substantial restrictions on the behavior of the borrower.

Two factors help to explain the dominant role played by financial intermediaries in our financial structure: transaction costs and problems that arise from asymmetric (9)_____. Banks reduce transaction costs by bundling the funds they attract from small savers into loans large enough to finance business undertakings.  The bargaining, contracting, and administrative costs – that is, transaction costs – decline as the size of the loan increases.  Therefore, the administration of loans is subject to economies of scale.  Economies of scale in financial markets also helps to explain the popularity of mutual funds.

Financial intermediaries further reduce transactions cost through their expertise in computer technology so that they can make it easier for customers to conduct transactions.

Because borrowers know better the potential returns and associated risks of their investment alternatives than do lenders, financial markets are characterized by asymmetries of information.  This informational disadvantage can create problems both before and after the financial transaction is made.
(10)_____ _____ is the problem created by asymmetric information before the transaction occurs; moral hazard is the problem created by asymmetric information after the deal has been made.

Adverse selection in financial markets occurs when bad credit risks are the ones who most actively seek financing.  Moral hazard in financial markets occurs when borrowers have incentives to engage in activities that are undesirable from the lenders point of view.

Tools to help solve adverse selection include: the private production and sale of information (e.g., bond rating services), government regulation to increase information in securities markets, financial intermediation, requirements that collateral be pledged in loan contracts, and requirements that borrowers have sufficient net worth.

The concept of adverse selection explains the first seven of the eight puzzles about financial structure.  The first four puzzles emphasize the importance of financial intermediaries.  Financial intermediaries – because they have expertise in evaluating credit (11)_____ – are better able to identify and screen potential bad risks.  Moreover, since financial intermediaries such as banks hold mostly non-traded bank loans, they are better able to avoid the free-rider problem that would otherwise reduce their incentives to produce such information.  Puzzle five, that financial markets are heavily regulated, is explained by the problem of asymmetric information.  Puzzles six and seven can be understood as mechanisms by which lenders (1) screen on the basis of net worth, and (2) reduce their risk exposure by asking that collateral be pledged.  Borrowers who are good risks will neither want to lose their collateral nor have their net worth diminished, thus these requirements discourage bad risks from asking for loans and thereby reduce the "lemons problem" in financial markets.

Moral hazard in (12)_____ contracts is known as the principal-agent problem because the manager (the agent) has less incentive to maximize profits than do the stockholders (the principals). Because principals have an incentive to free-ride on others' information gathering efforts, it is likely that too few resources will be devoted to monitoring the agent.  Government regulations that force firms to adhere to standard accounting principles, venture capital firms, and debt contracts are financial market mechanisms that reduce principal-agent problems.

The prevalence of debt contracts, relative to equity contracts, does not, however, imply that the use of debt is the sole solution to moral hazard problems.  High net worth can reduce moral hazard problems in debt contracts by making them *incentive compatible*.  Lenders further reduce their risks by requiring that borrowers comply with a (sometimes lengthy) list of conditions called (13)_____ _____.  Finally, because of free-rider problems, financial intermediaries have a comparative advantage in reducing or avoiding moral hazard problems.

Although means have been devised for reducing adverse selection and moral hazard problems, (14)_____ _____ remind us that financial markets are not immune to the disruptions caused by the failure of a major financial or non-financial firm.  Financial crises occur when rising adverse selection and moral hazard problems prevent financial markets from channeling funds to those with productive investment opportunities, hastening the decline in economic activity.  There are four factors which lead to financial crises: (1) increases in interest rates, (2) increases in uncertainty, (3)stock market declines, and (4)deterioration of banks' balance sheets.

The important economic concepts of adverse selection and moral hazard help us to better understand the structure of our financial system.  In the next five chapters, we find that these two important concepts contribute additional insights to workings in financial markets and the behavior of financial market participants.

## EXERCISES

### Exercise 1: Adverse Selection and Moral Hazard

The eight basic puzzles of financial markets in the United States are listed below.  For each of the following puzzles indicate whether the puzzle is explained by adverse selection (A), moral hazard (M), or both (B).

_____ 1.  Stocks are not an important source of finance for American businesses.

_____ 2.  Issuing marketable securities is not the primary way businesses finance their operations.

_____ 3.  Indirect finance, which involves the activities of financial intermediaries, is many times more important than direct finance, in which businesses raise funds directly from lenders in financial markets.

_____ 4.  Banks are the most important source of external funds to finance businesses.

_____ 5.  The financial system is among the most heavily regulated sectors of the economy.

_____ 6.  Only large, well-established corporations have access to securities markets to finance their activities.

_____ 7.  Collateral is a prevalent feature of debt contracts for both households and businesses.

_____ 8. Debt contracts are typically extremely complicated legal documents that place substantial restrictions on the behavior of the borrower.

## Exercise 2: Financial Structure Definitions and Terminology

Match the terms on the right with the definition or description on the left. Place the letter of the term in the blank provided next to the appropriate definition or description.

_____ 1. Problem of too little information gathering and monitoring activity because the person undertaking the activity cannot prevent others from benefiting from the information and monitoring.

a. Adverse selection

_____ 2. Another term for equity capital, the difference between a firm's assets and its liabilities.

b. Moral hazard

_____ 3. Problem that results when the manager behaves contrary to the wishes of stockholders due to the separation of ownership and control.

c. Collateralized debt

_____ 4. Term describing the solution that high net worth provides to the moral hazard problem in debt contracts by aligning the incentives of the borrower to that of the lender.

d. Restrictive covenants

_____ 5. Major disruptions in financial markets characterized by sharp declines in asset prices and the failures of many financial and nonfinancial firms.

e. Collateral

_____ 6. Property that is pledged to the lender if a borrower cannot make his or her debt payments.

f. Financial crises

_____ 7. Clauses in bond and loan contracts that either proscribe certain activities that borrowers may have incentive to undertake, or requires certain activities that borrowers may not have incentive to undertake.

g. Incentive compatible

_____ 8. The predominant form of household debt contract, accounting for about 85 percent of household debt.

h. Principal-agent problem

_____ 9. The problem in which borrowers have incentives to use funds obtained from external sources to finance riskier projects than originally envisioned by the lender.

i. Net worth

_____10. The lemons problem.

j. Free-rider problem

_____11. The decline in firms' net worth because of the increased burden of indebtedness due to a substantial decline in the price level.

k. Debt deflation

**Exercise 3:  Financial Crises and Aggregate Economic Activity**

A.  Asset Market Effects on Balance Sheets

List the four factors in the economic environment that can lead to a substantial deterioration of firm's balance sheets that can worsen adverse selection and moral hazard problems in financial markets, eventually leading to a financial crises.

1. _____

2. _____

3. _____

4. _____

B.  Most financial crises in the United States have begun with the following four factors:

1. _____

2. _____

3. _____

4. _____

**SELF-TEST**

**Part A: True-False Questions**

Circle whether the following statements are true (T) or false (F).

T  F  1. Stocks are the most important source of external finance for American businesses.

T  F  2. In the United States, bonds are a more important source of external finance for business than are stocks.

T  F  3. Most American households own financial market securities.

T  F  4. Financial intermediaries benefit savers by reducing transactions costs.

T  F  5. Banks avoid the free-rider problem by primarily making private loans rather than purchasing securities that are traded in financial markets.

T  F  6. Collateral, which is property promised to the lender if the borrower defaults, reduces the consequences of adverse selection because it reduces the lender's losses in the case of default.

T  F  7. Firms with higher net worth are the ones most likely to default.

T  F  8. Venture capitalists, unlike banks, are able to reduce moral hazard problems by placing individuals on the board of directors of the firm receiving the loan.

T  F  9. One way of describing the solution that high net worth provides to the moral hazard problem is to say that it makes the debt contract incentive compatible.

T  F  10. The requirement that the borrower keep her collateral in good condition, as one of the conditions to receiving a loan, is called a restrictive covenant.


**Part B: Multiple-Choice Questions**

Circle the appropriate answer.


1. The recovery process from an economic downturn can be short-circuited by a substantial decline in the price level that reduces firms' net worth, a process called

   a. adverse selection.
   b. moral hazard.
   c. debt deflation.
   d. insolvency.

2. Which of the following statements concerning external sources of financing for nonfinancial businesses in the U.S. are true?

   a. In the mid- to late-1980s, American corporations in the aggregate did not issue shares to finance their activities.
   b. Issuing marketable securities is not the primary way businesses finance their operations.
   c. Direct finance is many times more important than indirect finance as a source of external funds.
   d. All of the above.
   e. Only (a) and (b) of the above.

3. Poor people have difficulty getting loans because

   a. they typically have little collateral.
   b. they are less likely to benefit from access to financial markets.
   c. of both (a) and (b) of the above.
   d. of neither (a) nor (b) of the above.

4.  Financial intermediaries provide their customers with

    a.   reduced transactions costs.
    b.   increased diversification.
    c.   reduced risk.
    d.   all of the above.
    e.   only (b) and (c) of the above.

5.  Because of the adverse selection problem,

    a.   lenders are reluctant to make loans that are not secured by collateral.
    b.   lenders may choose to lend only to those who "do not need the money."
    c    lenders may refuse loans to individuals with high net worth.
    d.   all of the above.
    e.   only (a) and (b) of the above.

6.  That most used cars are sold by intermediaries (i.e., used car dealers) provides evidence that these intermediaries

    a.   help solve the adverse selection problem in this market.
    b.   profit by becoming experts in determining whether an automobile is of good-quality or a lemon.
    c.   are unable to prevent purchasers from free-riding off the information they provide.
    d.   do all of the above.
    e.   do only (a) and (b) of the above.

7.  Mishkin's analysis of adverse selection indicates that financial intermediaries in general and banks in particular, because they hold a large fraction of non-traded loans,

    a.   play a greater role in moving funds to corporations than do securities markets as a result of their ability to overcome the free-rider problem.
    b.   provide better-known and larger corporations a higher percentage of their external funds than they do to newer and smaller corporations, which tend to rely on the new issues market for funds.
    c.   both (a) and (b) of the above.
    d.   neither (a) nor (b) of the above.

8.  The principal-agent problem arises because

    a.   principals find it difficult and costly to monitor agents' activities.
    b.   agents' incentives are not always compatible with those of the principals.
    c.   principals have incentives to free-ride off the monitoring expenditures of other principals.
    d.   of all of the above.
    e.   of only (a) and (b) of the above.

9.  Equity contracts

    a.   are agreements by the borrowers to pay the lenders fixed dollar amounts at periodic intervals.
    b.   have the advantage over debt contracts of a lower cost of state verification.
    c.   are used much more frequently to raise capital than are debt contracts.
    d.   are none of the above.

10. Factors that lead to worsening conditions in financial markets include

    a. declining interest rates.
    b. declining stock prices.
    c. unanticipated increases in the price level.
    d. only (a) and (c) of the above.
    e. only (b) and (c) of the above.

11. The "lemons problem" is a term used to describe the

    a. moral hazard problem.
    b. adverse selection problem.
    c. free-rider problem.
    d. principal-agent problem.

12. The _____ problem helps to explain why _____ cannot be eliminated solely by the private production and sale of information.

    a. free-rider; adverse selection
    b. free-rider; moral hazard
    c. principal-agent; adverse selection
    d. principal-agent; moral hazard

13. Equity contracts are subject to a particular example of _____ called the _____ problem.

    a. adverse selection; principal-agent
    b. moral hazard; principal-agent
    c. adverse selection; free-rider
    d. moral hazard; free-rider

14. Debt-deflation occurs when the price level _____, reducing the value of business firms' _____.

    a. rises; net worth
    b. rises; collateral
    c. falls; net worth
    d. falls; collateral

15. Important factors leading up to the financial crises in both Mexico and East Asia in the mid- to late 1990s include:

    a. weak supervision of banks by regulators.
    b. lack of expertise in screening and monitoring borrowers at banking institutions.
    c. an increase in indebtedness due to depreciation of their currencies.
    d. all of the above.
    e. only (a) and (b) of the above.

# Chapter 9

## *The Banking Firm and The Management of Financial Institutions*

### CHAPTER SYNOPSIS/COMPLETIONS

Banks are the most important financial intermediaries in the United States. In this chapter we examine the bank balance sheet and the basic principles of bank management in order to improve our understanding of how banks operate in our economy.

The bank balance sheet, which lists assets and liabilities, can be thought of as a list of the sources and uses of bank funds. It has the characteristic that total assets equal total liabilities plus bank equity (1)_____. The bank's liabilities are its (2)_____ of funds, which include: checkable deposits, nontransactions deposits, borrowings, and bank equity capital. The bank's assets are its uses of funds, and include: reserves, cash items in process of collection, deposits at other banks, securities, loans, and other assets (mostly physical capital). Reserves are either bank deposits held at the Fed or currency that is physically held by banks (called (3)_____ _____). Reserves are held for two reasons. First, by law a certain fraction of deposits must be held as reserves, called (4)_____ _____. Additional reserves, called *excess reserves*, can be used by a bank to meet obligations to depositors. Banks also hold U.S. government securities, sometimes referred to as secondary (5)_____ because of their high liquidity.

The basic operation of a bank is to make profits by engaging in the process of *asset transformation*. Banks issue liabilities such as deposits and use the proceeds to acquire income earning assets such as loans. An important consideration for a bank engaged in this process is that when it receives additional deposits it gains an equal amount of reserves, but when it loses deposits, it loses an equal amount of reserves.

Banks must ensure that they have enough ready cash to pay their depositors in the event of deposit (6)_____. To keep enough cash on hand, the bank must engage in (7)_____ management, the acquisition of sufficiently liquid assets to meet the obligations of the bank to depositors. Specifically, banks hold excess and secondary reserves to escape the costs of (a) borrowing from other banks in the federal funds market, (b) selling securities, (c) borrowing from the Fed, and (d) calling in or selling loans – the latter being the costliest way of acquiring reserves when there is a deposit outflow. Excess reserves are insurance against the cost of deposit outflows. Hence, the higher the cost, the more excess reserves banks will want to hold.

Banks manage their assets using the following four principles. First, they try to find borrowers who will pay high interest rates and are unlikely to (8)_____ on their loans. Second, banks try to purchase securities with high expected returns and low risk. Third, banks attempt to minimize risk by (9)_____ their holdings of both loans and securities. Fourth, banks must manage the liquidity of their assets so they can satisfy reserve requirements without incurring huge costs. This means that banks hold liquid assets even if they earn a somewhat lower return than other assets.

Before the 1960s, *liability management* was a staid affair.  For the most part, banks took their liabilities as fixed and spent their time trying to achieve an optimal mix of assets.  Starting in the 1960s, large banks in key financial centers began to explore ways in which liabilities on their balance sheets could provide them with reserves and liquidity.  This led to an expansion of overnight loan markets, such as the (10)_____ _____ market, and the development of new financial instruments such as negotiable CDs (introduced in 1961).  Large banks no longer took their sources of funds (liabilities) as given; instead, they aggressively set target goals for asset growth, acquiring funds by issuing liabilities as they were needed.

A bank must manage capital to reduce the chance that it will become insolvent and then fail, assure an adequate return to its stockholders, and satisfy minimum capital requirements.  A bank can raise capital by issuing equity or reducing its (11) _____ to shareholders.  Alternatively, a bank can respond to a shortage of capital by restraining asset growth.

Banks attempt to reduce their exposure to *credit risk* by (a) screening good from bad credit risks, (b) specializing in lending to particular firms, (c) monitoring and enforcing restrictive covenants, (d) fostering long-term relationships with loan customers, (e) requiring collateral and compensating balances, and (f) rationing credit.

With the increased volatility of interest rates that occurres in the 1980s, banks have become more concerned about their exposure to interest-rate risk – the riskiness of earnings and returns that is associated with changes in interest rates.  Interest rate fluctuations can significantly impact bank profits.  For example, if a bank has (12)_____ rate-sensitive liabilities than assets, a rise in interest rates will reduce bank profits, while a decline in interest rates will raise bank profits.

Bank managers can measure the sensitivity of bank profits to changes in interest rates using two techniques.  Under (13)_____ analysis, the difference of rate-sensitive assets and rate-sensitive liabilities (that is, the gap) is multiplied by the change in the interest rate to obtain the effect on bank profits.  Alternatively, duration analysis is based on Macauly's concept of duration, which measures the average lifetime of a security's stream of payments.  If the average duration of a bank's assets exceeds the average duration of its liabilities, then rising interest rates will reduce the bank's net worth.

Another important banking development to emerge in recent years has been the growth in *off-balance-sheet activities*.  Off-balance-sheet activities consist of trading financial instruments and the generation of income from fees, both of which affect bank profits but are not visible on bank balance sheets.  Although these activities can increase bank profitability, many believe that they expose banks to increased risk.

*Financial innovation* was little discussed only 30 years ago.  Since then it has received increasing attention from economists as they have come to realize that the financial structure of the economy and its institutions respond in ways that may nullify the intended effects of regulations and blur the distinctions among financial institutions.  For example, lenders discovered that adjustable-rate (14)_____ reduced interest-rate risk to the benefit of both lender and borrower.  Borrowers were able to get adjustable-rate mortgages at lower interest rates than fixed-rate mortgages, while lenders reduced their exposure to interest-rate risk.

Changes in computer technology have stimulated innovations by lowering the cost of supplying financial services.  Examples include the expansion of credit and debit cards, and the rapid growth of electronic banking.

Ironically, government financial regulations have spurred financial innovations designed to avoid the regulations, a process Edward Kane calls (15)_____ _____. For example, nonuniform reserve requirements and Regulation Q ceilings gave banks a strong incentive to create new accounts free of the requirements and ceilings in order to prevent (16)_____ when market interest rates rose above regulated ceilings. Eurodollars, bank commercial paper, overnight repurchase agreements, NOW accounts, and *sweep accounts* are some of the innovations either created or expanded in response to regulations that prevented an orderly adjustment to rising interest rates.

## EXERCISES

### Exercise 1: Definitions and Terminology

Match the terms on the right with the definition or description on the left. Place the letter of the term in the blank provided next to the appropriate definition.

_____ 1. An arrangement whereby any balances above a certain amount in a corporation's checking account is invested in overnight repos that pay the corporation interest.

    a. Gap and duration analysis

_____ 2. The riskiness of earnings and returns that is associated with changes in interest rates.

    b. Bank liabilities

_____ 3. Methods employed to measure interest-rate risk.

    c. Nontransaction deposits

_____ 4. Trading financial instruments and the generation of fee income, for example.

    d. Interest rate risk

_____ 5. Commercial banks' sources of funds.

    e. Negotiable CDs

_____ 6. Commercial banks' uses of funds.

    f. Off-balance-sheet activities

_____ 7. The primary source of bank funds.

    g. Bank assets

_____ 8. A simplified balance sheet that lists the changes that occur in balance sheet items.

    h. Liquidity management

_____ 9. The acquisition of sufficiently liquid assets to meet the obligations of the bank to depositors.

    i. T-account

_____ 10 Financial instruments developed in 1961 that enabled money center banks to quickly acquire funds.

    j. Sweep accounts

## Exercise 2: T-Accounts, and Deposits and Withdrawals

A.  Fill in the T-account of the First National Bank if Shirley Student deposits $2000 in cash into her checking account at this bank.

### FIRST NATIONAL BANK

| Assets | Liabilities |
|---|---|
|  |  |

B.  Fill in the T-accounts of the First National Bank and the Second National Bank when Shirley writes a $1000 check written on her account at the First National Bank to pay her tuition at State University, which in turn deposits the check in its accounts at the Second National Bank.

| First National Bank | | Second National Bank | |
|---|---|---|---|
| Assets | Liabilities | Assets | Liabilities |
|  |  |  |  |

C.  What is the net effect of the transactions in A and B on the reserve position at the two banks?

## Exercise 3: Bank Response to Deposit Outflows and Liquidity Management

Suppose that the First National Bank has the following balance-sheet position and that the required reserve ratio on deposits is 20%.  (In million dollars).

| Assets | | Liabilities | |
|---|---|---|---|
| Reserves | $25 | Deposits | $100 |
| Loans | 75 | Bank capital | 10 |
| Securities | 10 |  |  |

A.  If the bank suffers a deposit outflow of $6 million, what will its balance sheet now look like?  Show this by filling in the amounts in the following balance sheet.

| Assets | Liabilities |
|---|---|
| Reserves<br>Loans<br>Securities | Deposits<br>Bank capital |

Must the bank make any adjustment in its balance sheet? _____

Why? _____

B. Suppose the bank now is hit by another $4 million deposit outflow. What will its balance- sheet position look like now? Show this by filling in the amounts in the following balance sheet.

| Assets | Liabilities |
|---|---|
| Reserves<br>Loans<br>Securities | Deposits<br>Bank capital |

Must the bank make any adjustment in its balance sheet? _____

Why? _____

C. If the bank satisfies its reserve requirements by selling off securities, how much will it have to sell?

_____

Why? _____

D. After selling off the securities to meet its reserve requirements, what will its balance sheet look like? Show this by filling in the amounts in the following balance sheet:

| Assets | Liabilities |
|---|---|
| Reserves<br>Loans<br>Securities | Deposits<br>Bank capital |

E. If after selling off the securities the bank is now hit by another $10 million of withdrawals of deposits and it sells off all its securities to obtain reserves, what will its balance sheet look like? Again show this by filling in the amounts in the following balance sheet:

| Assets | Liabilities |
|---|---|
| Reserves<br>Loans<br>Securities | Deposits<br>Bank capital |

If the bank is now unable to call in or sell any of its loans and no one is  willing to lend funds to this bank, then what will happen to the bank and why?

_____

_____


## Exercise 4: Asset Management

List the four main concerns of bank asset management.

1. _____

2. _____

3. _____

4. _____


## Exercise 5: Liability Management

List three of the changes in the way banks operate as a result of the flexibility in liabilities management that occurred after 1960.

1. _____

2. _____

3. _____


## Exercise 6: Risk Management

List six management methods that banks use to reduce their exposure to credit risk.

1. _____

2. _____

3. _____

4. _____

5. _____

6. _____

## Exercise 7: Gap Analysis

Suppose that the First State Bank has the following balance sheet (in million dollars):

| Assets | | Liabilities | |
|---|---|---|---|
| Variable-Rate Loans | 20 | Variable-Rate CDs | 30 |
| Short-Term Securities | 10 | Money Market Deposits | 15 |
| Reserves | 10 | Federal Funds | 5 |
| Long-Term Loans | 40 | Checkable and Savings | |
| Long-Term Securities | 10 | Deposits | 30 |
| | | Long-term CDs | 20 |

A. Calculate the gap by subtracting the amount of rate-sensitive liabilities from rate-sensitive assets.

Gap = _____

B. If interest rates suddenly increase by two percentage points, will First State Bank's profits increase or decrease?

_____

C. By how much do profits change? _____

D. If, instead, interest rates were to drop by three percentage points, what will be the change in First State's profits?

_____

## SELF-TEST

### Part A: True-False Questions

Circle whether the following statements are true (T) or false (F).

T  F  1. A bank's assets are its sources of funds.

T  F  2. Bank capital equals the total assets of the bank minus the total liabilities.

T  F  3. Savings accounts are the most common type of nontransaction deposit.

T  F  4. Checkable deposits are usually the lowest-cost source of bank funds.

T  F  5. Checkable deposits are the primary source of bank funds.

T  F   6. Interest paid on deposits makes up over half of total bank operating expenses.

T  F   7. Banks are only able to borrow reserves from the Fed.

T  F   8. Loans provide banks with most of their revenue.

T  F   9. If a bank has more rate-sensitive assets than liabilities, a rise in interest rates will reduce bank profits.

T  F  10. The wider use of credit cards coincided with the decline in costs of computer technology.

## Part B: Multiple-Choice Questions

Circle the appropriate answer.

1.  Which of the following bank assets is the most liquid?

    a.  Consumer loans
    b.  State and local government securities
    c.  Physical capital
    d.  U.S. government securities

2.  Reserves

    a.  equal the deposits banks hold at the Fed.
    b.  include bank holdings of U.S. government securities.
    c.  can be divided up into required reserves plus excess reserves.
    d.  equal both (a) and (c) of the above.

3.  When a $1000 check written on the Chase Manhattan Bank is deposited in an account at the Bank of America, then

    a.  the liabilities of Chase Manhattan Bank increase by $1000.
    b.  the reserves of Chase Manhattan Bank increase by $1000.
    c.  the liabilities of Bank of America fall by $1000.
    d.  the reserves of Bank of America increase by $ 1000.

4.  When you deposit a $100 check in your bank account at the First National Bank of Chicago and you withdraw $50 in cash, then

    a.  the liabilities of First National Bank rise by $100.
    b.  the reserves of First National Bank rise by $100.
    c.  the assets of the First National Bank rise by $100.
    d.  the liabilities of the First National Bank rise by $50.
    e.  none of the above occurs.

5. If a bank has $1 million of deposits and a required reserve ratio of 5%, and it holds $100,000 in reserves, then it must rearrange its balance sheet if there is a deposit outflow of

   a. $51,000.
   b. $20,000.
   c. $30,000.
   d. $40,000.
   e. none of the above.

6. A bank will want to hold less excess reserves (everything else equal) when

   a. it expects to have deposit inflows in the near future.
   b. brokerage commissions on selling bonds rise.
   c. both (a) and (b) of the above occur.
   d. neither (a) nor (b) of the above occurs.

7. When a bank faces a reserve deficiency because of a deposit outflow, it will try to do which of the following first?

   a. Call in loans
   b. Borrow from the Fed
   c. Sell securities
   d. Borrow from other banks

8. A bank failure is more likely to occur when

   a. a bank holds more U.S. government securities.
   b. a bank suffers large deposit outflows.
   c. a bank holds more excess reserves.
   d. a bank has more bank capital.

9. When interest rates are expected to fall in the future, a banker is likely to

   a. make short-term rather than long-term loans.
   b. buy short-term rather than long-term bonds.
   c. buy long-term rather than short-term bonds.
   d. do both (a) and (b) of the above.

10. If Bruce the Bank Manager determines that his bank's gap is a positive $20 million, then a five percentage point increase in interest rates will cause bank profits to

   a. increase by $1 million.
   b. decrease by $1 million.
   c. increase by $10 million.
   d. decrease by $10 million.

11. Items listed on the liability side of banks' balance sheets include

    a.  bank capital.
    b.  loans.
    c.  reserves.
    d.  all of the above.
    e.  only (a) and (b) of the above.

12. Collectively, reserves, cash items in process of collection, and deposits at other banks, are referred to as _____ in a bank balance sheet.

    a.  secondary reserves
    b.  cash items
    c.  liquid items
    d.  compensating balances

13. Credit risk management tools include:

    a.  credit rationing.
    b.  collateral.
    c.  compensating balances.
    d.  all of the above.

14. For a given return on _____, the _____ is bank capital, the _____ is the return for the owners of the bank.

    a.  liabilities; lower; lower
    b.  assets; lower; higher
    c.  assets; higher; higher
    d.  liabilities; lower; higher

15. An improvement in technology stimulates financial innovations by

    a.  lowering the cost of providing new services.
    b.  raising the demand of providing new services.
    c.  reducing the competition from those providing financial services.
    d.  doing all of the above.

# Chapter 10

## *Banking Industry: Structure and Competition*

### CHAPTER SYNOPSIS/COMPLETIONS

This chapter starts by examining the commercial banking industry and then goes on to look at the thrift industry in the United States. Next, the chapter considers the forces behind the growth in international banking with special emphasis on developments that have affected us in the United States. The chapter concludes by examining how financial innovations have increased the competitive environment in banking, fundamentally changing this industry.

Modern commercial banking in America dates to 1781 when the Bank of North America was chartered in Philadelphia. At that time, debate centered on who should have authority to charter banks – the states or the federal government. Prior to 1863, the federal government chartered two commercial banks that possessed some of the functions of central banks. Both of these banks – the First and Second Banks of the United States – closed when their charters were not renewed because of populist political opposition.

The National Bank Act of 1863 created the Office of the (1)_____ of the Currency to charter and regulate (2)_____ banks. Beginning with this legislation, commercial banking in America became an industry regulated by many agencies with overlapping jurisdictions. For example, the Federal Reserve regulates bank holding companies and (3)_____ banks that are members of the Federal Reserve System; the Comptroller of the Currency regulates national banks; and the FDIC and state banking authorities jointly supervise (4)_____ banks that are not members of the Federal Reserve System.

The U.S. banking industry until a few years ago was characterized by many (5)_____ banks. This structure was best explained by the restrictions of both the federal government and many state governments to (6)_____ _____. Beginning in the mid-1980s, bank consolidation and, to a minor extent, bank failures changed the landscape of banking. Consolidation began to occur as states enacted legislation to relax barriers to interstate banking, leading to a new class of bank, the so-called (7)_____ banks.

Bank consolidation has been given additional stimulus with the passage in 1994 of legislation that establishes the basis for a nationwide banking system. Banking consolidation has been rapid, as the number of banks declined from about 10,000 in 1996 to about 8500 in 2000. Economists predict that once bank consolidation settles down, we are likely to be left with a banking system with several thousand banks.

Passage of the Financial Services Modernization Act of 1999 repealed the Glass-Steagall Act of 1933, which separated commercial and investment banking. This legislation promises to change the role that banks have traditionally played in financial markets. Eliminating the barriers between banking and the securities industries means that the financial structure in the United States will begin to resemble the structure in other countries more closely.

Since 1980, federally-chartered S&Ls have been permitted to branch statewide, and since 1981, mergers of troubled S&Ls with sound institutions, have led to branching of S&Ls across state lines. The impetus behind the more liberal branching laws came from the reluctance of thrift regulators to expend deposit insurance funds at a time when so many thrift institutions were in financial trouble.

The rapid expansion in international trade spurs the growth of (8)_____ banking. Contributing to this growth has been banks' desire to escape burdensome regulations, and to tap into the large pool of dollar-denominated deposits in foreign countries known as (9)_____. U.S. banks have most of their branches in Latin America, the Far East, the Caribbean, and London.

The growth of international trade has increased the presence of foreign banks in the U.S. With more than 500 offices operating in the United States, foreign banks now hold more than 20% of total bank assets in America, and do almost as much commercial lending as U.S.-owned banks.

Despite the growth in international banking, and the relaxation of branching and underwriting restrictions, the traditional role of the American banking industry has been in *decline* for thirty years. Several indicators document this decline. In 1974, banks provided about 35% of the total credit advanced, but by 1999 their share had declined to near 20%. Today, thrifts provide less than (10)_____ of total credit advanced, down from over 20% two decades ago.

The decline in the relative importance of banks and thrifts in the provision of financial services began when inflation of the late 1960s and early 1970s eroded their (11)_____ advantage in acquiring funds. Regulations, that had once virtually assured bank profitability, hindered their efforts to acquire funds by limiting what banks could pay for deposits. *Disintermediation* – the net withdrawal of deposits from financial intermediaries – crimped bank loan growth and profitability.

Compounding the loss of cost advantages, banks and thrifts have realized an erosion of their income advantages in financial markets. The growth of the (12)_____ paper market, the (13)_____ bond market, and securitization are the three most important developments that have eroded banks' income advantage over their competitors. The process of financial innovation that has eroded banks' cost advantages in acquiring funds and income advantages in making loans is the source of the decline in the industry's traditional banking business. Although it is of no consolation to U.S. bankers, banks in other industrialized countries have seen the similar declines in their market shares as financial deregulation and innovations have allowed firms direct access to securities markets.

## EXERCISES

### Exercise 1: Responses to Branching Restrictions

List the three financial innovations that banks have used to get around the restrictions to branch banking.

1. _____

2. _____

3. _____

## Exercise 2: Definitions and Terminology

Match the terms on the right with the definition or description on the left. Place the letter of the term in the blank provided next to the appropriate definition.

_____ 1. Deposits in banks outside the United States denominated in dollars.

a. International Banking Act of 1978

_____ 2. Bank subsidiary engaged primarily in international banking.

b. dual banking system

_____ 3. Legislation putting domestic and foreign banks on a more equal of the footing.

c. Comptroller of the Currency

_____ 4. Cannot make loans to domestic residents but can make loans to foreigners and accept their deposits.

d. superregional banks

_____ 5. System of bank regulation in which banks are supervised by both federal and state regulators.

e. Edge Act corporation

_____ 6. Bank holding companies that rival money center banks in size.

f. Eurodollars

_____ 7. Regulatory body that charters national banks.

g. central bank

_____ 8. Government institution responsible for supplying money and credit in economy.

h. international banking facilities

_____ 9. Limited service banks that either do not make commercial loans or alternatively do not acquire deposit liabilities.

i. nonbank banks

## Exercise 3: The Decline of Traditional Banking

A. List the four financial innovations that have contributed to the decline in traditional banking.

1. _____

2. _____

3. _____

4. _____

B. Explain why the rise of the junk bond market reduced the demand for bank loans.

_____

_____


## SELF-TEST

### Part A: True-False Questions

Circle whether the following statements are true (T) or false (F).


T  F  1.  Economic analysis suggests that banks will devise ways around regulations which restrict certain banking activities.

T  F  2.  Noting the lack of strong regulation, many economist argue that bank failures in the first half of the nineteenth century resulted from fraudulent practices.

T  F  3.  The Comptroller of the Currency has been granted the sole responsibility for supervising bank holding companies.

T  F  4.  Regulations that restrict competition in the banking industry, such as the Glass-Steagall Act before its repeal in 1999, are often justified by the desire to prevent bank failures.

T  F  5.  Periodic examinations of banks help regulators identify problems at banks before they have a detrimental effect on the financial soundness of the economy.

T  F  6.  It has been argued that the large number of banking firms in the United States—about 8,500 in early 2000—can be seen as an indication of the absence of competition rather than the presence of competition.

T  F  7.  One impetus in the early 1980s leading to greater branching of savings and loans was the merging of financially troubled S&Ls across state lines.

T  F  8.  Prior to 1978, foreign banks actually enjoyed an advantage over domestic banks in being able to branch across state lines.

T  F  9.  The rise of the junk market has contributed to the decline in banking.

T  F  10.  The same technological forces that have hurt the competitiveness of banks in the United States also seem to be at work abroad, helping to explain the decline of banking in other nations.

T  F  11.  The legislation that repealed the Glass-Steagal Act is the Gramm-Leach-Bliley Financial Services Modernization Act of 1999.

T  F  12.  Savings and loans are primarily regulated by the Office of Thrift Supervision.

## Part B: Multiple-Choice Questions

Circle the appropriate answer.

1.  Which of the following is a bank regulatory agency?

    a.  Comptroller of the Currency
    b.  Federal Reserve System
    c.  Federal Deposit Insurance Corporation
    d.  All of the above

2.  The bundling of a portfolio of mortgage or auto loans into a marketable capital market instrument is known as

    a.  "fastbacking."
    b.  arbitrage.
    c.  computerization.
    d.  securitization.
    e.  optioning the portfolio.

3.  Savings and loans are regulated by

    a.  the Office of Thrift Supervision.
    b.  the FDIC.
    c.  the FHLBS.
    d.  all of the above.
    e.  only (b) and (c) of the above.

4.  Which of the following factors explain the rapid growth in international banking in the past 25 years?

    a.  Rapid growth of world trade in this period
    b.  Decline in world trade since 1960
    c.  Creation of the League of Nations
    d.  None of the above

5.  When economists argue that banking regulations have been a mixed blessing, they are referring to the fact that

    a.  bank regulations foster competition at the expense of banking system safety.
    b.  bank regulations foster banking system safety at the expense of competition.
    c.  branch banking, while desired by consumers, leads to less competition.
    d.  bank regulations foster competition by limiting branching.

6   The U.S. banking system has been labeled a dual system because

    a.  banks offer both checking and savings accounts.
    b.  it actually includes both banks and thrift institutions.
    c.  it is regulated by both federal and state governments.
    d.  it was established during the Civil War, thus making it necessary to create separate regulatory bodies for the North and South.

7.  The Glass-Steagall Act, before it was repealed in 1999, prohibited

    a.  commercial banks from engaging in underwriting and dealing of corporate securities.
    b.  investment banks from engaging in commercial banking activities.
    c.  commercial banks from selling new issues of government securities.
    d.  only (a) and (b) of the above.

8.  The McFadden Act of 1927

    a.  effectively prohibited banks from branching across state lines.
    b.  created the dual banking system in the United States.
    c.  effectively prohibited banks from branching within states.
    d.  did all of the above.

9.  Rapid expansion of international banking has been caused by

    a.  McFadden Act restrictions against interstate banking.
    b.  McFadden Act restrictions against intrastate banking.
    c.  the rapid growth in international trade.
    d.  both (a) and (c) of the above.
    e.  both (b) and (c) of the above.

10. Commercial banks' importance as a source of funds for borrowers has _____ dramatically, from around _____ percent of total credit advanced in 1974 to _____ percent by 1999.

    a.  expanded; 40; 60
    b.  expanded; 35; 55
    c.  contracted; 35; 20
    d.  contracted; 60; 40

11. The recent consolidation in the banking industry, combined with many bank failures in the 1980s, has led to a shrinking number of commercial banks from around _____ in the 1970s to about _____ today.

    a.  12,000; 9,500
    b.  15,000; 8,500
    c.  20,000; 9,500
    d.  17,000; 7,500

12. Financial innovation has caused banks' cost advantages to _____, and their income advantages to _____.

    a.  increase; increase
    b.  increase; decrease
    c.  decrease; increase
    d.  decrease; decrease

13. The most important developments that have reduced banks' cost advantages in the past thirty years include:

    a.  the elimination of Regulation Q ceilings.
    b.  the competition from money market mutual funds.
    c.  the competition from junk bonds.
    d.  all of the above.
    e.  only (a) and (b) of the above.

14. The most important developments that have reduced banks' income advantages in the past thirty years include:

    a.  the growth of the junk bond market.
    b.  the competition from money market mutual funds.
    c.  the growth of securitization.
    d.  only (a) and (b) of the above.
    e.  only (a) and (c) of the above.

15. International banking facilities within the United States

    a.  accept time deposits from foreigners but are not subject to either reserve requirements or any restrictions on interest payments.
    b.  make loans to foreigners but not to domestic residents.
    c.  have grown rapidly with the encouragement of American governments.
    d.  all of the above.

# Chapter 11

## *Economic Analysis of Banking Regulation*

### CHAPTER SYNOPSIS/COMPLETIONS

This chapter develops an economic analysis of how banking regulation affects the behavior of banking institutions. This analysis explains why banking is among the most heavily regulated sectors of the economy, why the banking crisis occurred in the 1980s, and whether recent banking legislation or other proposed reforms are likely to ensure that future financial crises can be avoided.

In the United States, most depositors hold their funds in accounts insured by the FDIC. Federal deposit insurance has been a politically popular program since the Great Depression. Unfortunately, deposit insurance makes it necessary that bank and thrift regulators be particularly diligent. Because deposits up to $100,000 are completely insured, depositors' lose their incentives to (1)_____ their funds when they suspect that the bank is taking on too much risk. The attenuation of depositors' incentives exacerbates adverse selection and (2)_____ _____ problems, encouraging bank and thrift managers to take on excessive risk.

Because deposit insurance gives financial institutions greater incentives to take on additional risk, regulators must devise methods to discipline managers of banks and thrifts to reduce excessive risk taking. For example, chartering regulations reduce (3)_____ _____ problems by preventing undesirable people (e.g., crooks) from gaining control of financial institutions. Restrictions that prevent banks from holding risky assets such as common stocks and junk bonds, and requirements that banks hold minimum levels of capital reduce (4)_____ _____ by increasing the cost to owners of bank failures. Regular bank (5)_____ help to ensure that banks and thrifts comply with these requirements.

In the early-1990s, the FDIC came under increasing criticism for its "too-big-to-fail" policy. Under this policy, the FDIC uses the *purchase and assumption method* to resolve the failure of a big bank, in effect guaranteeing all deposits. The rationale for this policy is that the failure of a large bank increases the likelihood that a major (6)_____ disruption will occur. This policy, however, reduces the incentives of depositors at big banks to monitor the riskiness of bank assets, thereby encouraging moral hazard. Moreover, critics complain that the FDIC's policy discriminates against small banks as they find it more difficult to attract large depositors.

In today's world, financial innovation has made it easier for banks and their employees to make huge bets easily and quickly (as demonstrated by the failure of Barrings in 1995). This change in the financial environment has fostered new approaches to bank supervision. Bank examiners now place greater emphasis on evaluating risk management systems. Indeed, bank examiners now give a separate risk management rating as part of the CAMELS system.

Other requirements that regulators impose on banks include: adherence to standard accounting principles, mandates to protect consumer borrowers through "truth in lending" and anti-discrimination requirements, restrictions on assets holdings, and limits on off-balance-sheet activities.

The banking crisis in the 1980s – that saw banks fail at rates higher than at any time since the Great Depression – has sparked renewed interest in devising effective bank regulations. The crisis started as banks began to experience increasing competition for funds from money market mutual funds, and a loss of lending business to the commercial paper market and securitization. As earnings from these traditional activities declined, banks and thrifts sought other, but riskier, business to raise profits. Innovation produced new financial instruments – brokered deposits, for example – that widened the scope for risk taking. Moreover, legislation that deregulated banks and thrifts expanded their ability to engage in risky activities, further increasing moral hazard.

It is not a coincidence that the banking crisis followed the passage of legislation that gave bank and thrift managers greater opportunities to take on risk, which many did with adverse consequences. Factors contributing to rising moral hazard and adverse selection problems included: raising deposit insurance coverage from $40,000 to $100,000 per account, phasing out (7)_____ _____ ceilings, provisions that allowed federally chartered savings and loans and mutual savings banks to invest up to ten percent of their assets in commercial loans, and the sharp rise in (8)_____ rates from 1979 until 1981, and the severe recession in 1981-82.

The untimely combination of these factors had devastating consequences: by early 1982 as many as one-half of the S&Ls in the U.S. had a negative net worth and were thus insolvent. Instead of closing the insolvent thrifts and stemming the flow of red ink, regulators (9)_____ capital requirements to keep ailing S&Ls open for business. This strategy, called (10)_____ _____, backfired as industry conditions worsened.

In retrospect, regulators should have anticipated that *regulatory forbearance* would not have turned weak institutions into healthy ones. Regulatory forbearance increases (11)_____ _____ because an operating, but insolvent, thrift institution has nothing to lose by taking on greater risk. If the risky loans pay off, then the thrift's owners capture the benefits; if, however, the risky loans turn sour, it is the deposit insurance fund that bears the additional cost.

By 1989, conditions of the nation's savings and loans had deteriorated so dramatically that the government was forced to enact legislation to bail out the FSLIC, which had gone broke paying off the depositors of failed S&Ls. Under the legislation – the Financial Institutions Reform, Recovery and Enforcement Act (FIRREA) – the Federal Home Loan Bank Board and the FSLIC were abolished. Thrift regulation was transferred to the Office of (12)_____ _____, a bureau within the U.S. Treasury Department, and the FDIC became the sole administrator of the federal deposit insurance system.

Although an unfortunate set of economic factors combined to rock the thrift industry in the 1980s, fundamentally, the S&L crisis had its origins in a political structure that gave those individuals, who were responsible for monitoring industry affairs, incentives to pretend that thrifts were not in serious trouble and to pass blame to others. The thrift crisis is an example of the moral hazard problem in politics, also known as the principal-agent problem. Neither regulators nor politicians (i.e., taxpayers' agents) faithfully served the taxpayers, who are ultimately responsible for covering the cost of the S&L bailout.

Regulatory reforms that may make banking more sound include: limiting the level of deposits covered by insurance, coinsurance, risk-based insurance premiums, regulatory consolidation, and market-value accounting for capital requirements.

An examination of recent banking crises in other countries indicates that the economic and political forces are strikingly similar to those we experienced in the 1980s.

## EXERCISES

### Exercise 1: Problems of Deposit Insurance

Ironically, the existence of deposit insurance increases the likelihood that depositors will require deposit protection, because the threat of withdrawals no longer constrains the managers of banks and thrifts from taking on too much risk. List some of the problems that deposit insurance create or make worse.

1. _____

2. _____

3. _____

### Exercise 2: Bank Regulation – Reducing Adverse Selection and Moral Hazard

A. List the several ways that bank regulations reduce the adverse selection and moral hazard problems in banking.

1. _____

_____

2. _____

_____

3. _____

_____

4. _____

_____

B. Explain how regulations specifically designed to reduce moral hazard produce the additional benefit of reducing adverse selection.

_____

_____

_____

**Exercise 3: The "Too-Big-To-Fail" Policy**

A. Justification of the Policy

1. Describe the intended purpose of the "too-big-to-fail" policy.

_____

_____

B. Implications of the Policy

1. When Continental Illinois became insolvent in 1984, the FDIC guaranteed all deposits, even those exceeding $100,000. The Comptroller of the Currency defended this action, arguing that the largest eleven banks were too big to fail. In 1990, however, the FDIC argued that the Bank of New England was too-big-to-fail, though it was only the thirty-third largest bank in the United States. What are some of the implications of this regulatory policy?

_____

_____

_____

_____

2. Of the 169 banks that failed in 1990, 149 were resolved through "purchase and assumption" transactions, whereby all deposits – including those in excess of the $100,000 limit – were assumed by the healthy banks. How were the other 20 banks handled?

_____

_____

3. How are uninsured deposits handled in these type of transactions?

_____

_____

**Exercise 4: The 1980s – A Rocky Decade for Thrifts and Regulators**

A. In the thrift industry, moral hazard and adverse selection problems increased in prominence the 1980s. List the factors that contributed to worsening conditions in the thrift industry in the early 1980s.

1. _____

2. _____

3. _____

4. _____

B.  How did regulators respond to worsening thrift performance in the 1980s?

_____

_____

C.  Explain why regulators pursued this course of action.

1. _____

2. _____

3. _____

## Exercise 5: FIRREA of 1989

List the major provisions of the Financial Institutions Reform, Recovery and Enforcement Act of 1989.

1. _____

2. _____

3. _____

4. _____

5. _____

6. _____

## Exercise 6: The Political Economy of the S&L Crisis

That taxpayers were poorly served by thrift regulators in the 1980s is now quite clear.  An analysis of the political economy of the savings and loan crisis helps one to understand this poor performance, and explains why elected agents of the taxpayers failed to faithfully serve their constituents by directing regulators to do their job.  Explain why both politicians and thrift regulators shirked their responsibilities to the taxpayers in the 1980s.

_____

_____

_____

## Exercise 7: FDICIA of 1991

The central issue in preventing another saving and loan debacle is the reform of the bank regulatory system to reduce the adverse selection and moral hazard problems created by deposit insurance.  List the major provisions of the Federal Deposit Insurance Corporation Improvement Act of 1991 that are intended to prevent another savings and loan debacle.

1. _____

2. _____

3. _____

4. _____

5. _____

6. _____

## SELF-TEST

### Part A: True-False Questions

Circle whether the following statements are true (T) or false (F).

T  F  1. Actions taken by regulators to reduce moral hazard by preventing banks from taking on too much risk (such as regular bank examinations) also help to reduce adverse selection problems by discouraging risk-prone entrepreneurs from entering the banking industry.

T  F  2. The FDIC argues that the too-big-to-fail policy protects the soundness of the banking system, since the failure of a very large bank makes it more likely that a major financial disruption will occur.

T  F  3. Large banks are actually put at a competitive disadvantage relative to small banks as a result of the FDIC's too-big-to-fail policy.

T  F  4. A financial innovation that made it easier for high-rolling banks to raise funds was brokered deposits.

T  F  5. Part of the policy of regulatory forbearance pursued by thrift regulators in the 1980s included allowing S&Ls to include in their capital calculations a high value for tangible capital called "goodwill".

T  F  6. In the 1980s, regulators pursued a policy of regulatory forbearance in hopes that the problems of thrifts would go away.

T  F  7. The policy of regulatory forbearance was effective in reducing the risks that thrift institutions took on in the 1980s.

T  F    8. The agency established to manage and resolve insolvent thrifts placed in conservatorship or receivership, and has the responsibility for selling the assets owned by failed institutions, is the Resolution Trust Corporation.

T  F    9. In the 1980s, Congress provided inadequate appropriations to S&L regulators, hampering their ability to monitor thrifts properly.

T  F   10. The legislation eliminating the Federal Home Loan Bank Board and transferring its regulatory role to the Office of Thrift Supervision was the Financial Institutions Reform, Recovery and Enforcement Act of 1989.

## Part B: Multiple-Choice Questions

1. Moral hazard is an important feature of insurance arrangements because the existence of insurance

   a. reduces the incentives for risk taking.
   b. is a hinderance to efficient risk taking.
   c. causes the private cost of the insured activity to increase.
   d. does all of the above.
   e. does none of the above.

2. Deposit insurance

   a. attracts risk-prone entrepreneurs to the banking industry.
   b. encourages bank managers to take on greater risks than they otherwise would.
   c. increases the incentives of depositors to monitor the riskiness of their banks' asset portfolios.
   d. does all of the above.
   e. does only (a) and (b) of the above.

3. Regular bank examinations help to reduce the _____ problem, but also help to indirectly reduce the _____ problem because, given fewer opportunities to take on risk, risk-prone entrepreneurs will be discouraged from entering the banking industry.

   a. adverse selection; adverse selection
   b. adverse selection; moral hazard
   c. moral hazard; adverse selection
   d. moral hazard; moral hazard

4. If the FDIC decides that a bank is too big to fail, it will use the

   a. payoff method, effectively covering all deposits – even those that exceed the $100,000 ceiling.
   b. payoff method, covering only those deposits that do not exceed the $100,000 ceiling.
   c. purchase and assumption method, effectively covering all deposits – even those that exceed the $100,000 ceiling.
   d. purchase and assumption method, covering only those deposits that do not exceed the $100,000 ceiling.

5.  The too-big-to-fail policy

    a.  puts small banks at a competitive disadvantage relative to large banks in attracting large depositors.
    b.  treats large depositors of small banks inequitably when compared to depositors of large banks.
    c.  ameliorates moral hazard problems.
    d.  does all of the above.
    e.  does only (a) and (b) of the above.

6.  The policy of regulatory forbearance

    a.  meant delaying the closing of "zombie S&Ls" as their losses mounted during the 1980s.
    b.  had the advantage of benefiting healthy S&Ls at the expense of "zombie S&Ls", as insolvent institutions lost deposits to healthy institutions.
    c.  had the advantage of permitting many insolvent S&Ls the opportunity to return to profitability, saving the FSLIC billions of dollars.
    d.  meant all of the above.

7.  The major provisions of the Financial Institutions Reform, Recovery and Enforcement Act of 1989 include

    a.  transferring the regulatory role of the Office of Thrift Supervision to the Federal Home Loan Bank Board.
    b.  significantly reducing the responsibilities of the FDIC, which no longer administers the federal deposit insurance system.
    c.  the establishment of the Resolution Trust Corporation to manage and resolve insolvent thrifts placed in conservatorship or receivership.
    d.  all of the above.

8.  That taxpayers were poorly served by thrift regulators in the 1980s is now quite clear. This poor performance is explained by

    a.  regulators' desire to escape blame for poor performance, leading to a perverse strategy of "regulatory gambling".
    b.  regulators' incentives to accede to pressures imposed by politicians, who sought to keep regulators from imposing tough regulations on institutions that were major campaign contributors.
    c.  Congress's dogged determination to protect taxpayers from the unsound banking practices of managers at many of the nations savings and loans.
    d.  all of the above.
    e.  only (a) and (b) of the above.

9.  The bailout of the savings and loan industry was much delayed and, therefore, much more costly to taxpayers because

    a.  of regulators' initial attempts to downplay the seriousness of problems within the thrift industry.
    b.  politicians who received generous campaign contributions from the savings and loan industry, like regulators, hoped that the problems in the industry would ease over time.
    c.  Congress encouraged, and thrift regulators acceded to, a policy of regulatory forbearance.
    d.  of fraudulent practices in the S&L industry that went undetected because of weak monitoring efforts by thrift regulators.
    e.  of all of the above.

10. Eliminating deposit insurance has the disadvantage of

    a.  reducing the stability of the banking system due to an increase in the likelihood of bank runs.
    b.  not being a politically feasible strategy.
    c.  encouraging banks to engage in excessive risk taking.
    d.  all of the above.
    e.  only (a) and (b) of the above.

11. When a bank is well-capitalized, the bank has _____ to lose if it fails and is thus _____ likely to pursue risky activities.

    a.  more; more
    b.  more; less
    c.  less; more
    d.  less; less

12. One problem with the too-big-to-fail policy is that it _____ the incentives for _____ by big banks.

    a.  increases; moral hazard
    b.  decreases; moral hazard
    c.  increases; adverse selection
    d.  decreases; adverse selection

13. The Competitive Equality Banking Act of 1987

    a.  provided an additional $10.8 billion to the FSLIC.
    b.  directed the Federal Home Loan Bank Board to hasten the closing of insolvent S&Ls.
    c.  transferred regulatory responsibilities of the FSLIC to the FDIC.
    d.  did all of the above.

14. Banking crises in other countries indicates that

    a.  deposit insurance is to blame in each country.
    b.  a government safety net for depositors need not increase moral hazard.
    c.  expertise in screening borrowers cannot prevent loan losses.
    d.  deregulation combined with poor regulatory supervision raise moral hazard incentives.

15. Critics of the FDICIA of 1991 complain that the legislation does not

    a.  institute risk-based deposit insurance premiums.
    b.  institute market-value accounting for capital requirements.
    c.  limit the use of brokered deposits.
    d.  recapitalize the FDIC.

# Chapter 12

## *Nonbank Financial Institutions*

### CHAPTER SYNOPSIS/COMPLETIONS

This chapter introduces the student to a wide array of nonbank financial institutions. Not long ago this group of institutions was more appropriately studied in a course on financial institutions and of little importance to students of money and banking. Recent financial innovation, however, has erased many of the barriers that once separated banks and nonbank financial institutions, blurring the distinction between courses in financial institutions and money and banking. For this reason, a brief overview of the types and activities of these institutions provides the student with a better understanding of the functioning and structure of financial markets.

Financial institutions are all alike in one respect – they all facilitate the movement of funds from savers to (1)_____. The existence of these institutions provides strong evidence of just how highly (2)_____ _____ is valued. Yet each institution is unique, indicating that the diversity of services offered by nonbank financial institutions is the result of specialization in the market for financial services.

As in chapter 9, we see that adverse selection and moral hazard explain many of the management practices of nonbank financial institutions. For example, insurance companies try to screen good risks from poor ones, and charge risk-based premiums to limit adverse selection problems. Restrictive provisions, fraud investigations, threats to cancel insurance, deductibles, coinsurance, and coverage limits help insurance companies combat (3)_____ _____ problems.

Life insurance companies provide convenient savings plans and insure against the loss of life. Because life insurance companies are exempt from federal income tax, and since payouts can be predicted fairly accurately, they tend to invest in (4)_____-term securities such as corporate bonds.

Property and (5)_____ insurance companies protect against almost any type of event, such as medical malpractice, fire, automobile accidents, earthquakes, floods, and so on. Without the availability of this insurance, many activities would be too costly to undertake. For example, if physicians were forced to self-insure, many would either quit the profession or specialize in low-risk procedures, not wanting to risk the loss of everything they own due to a malpractice suit. Indeed, rising malpractice premiums for high-risk operations has led some doctors to change specialties or avoid high-risk cases.

Pension funds also act as financial intermediaries. By providing individuals with retirement (6)_____, these funds help reduce the uncertainty that individuals have adequately provided for their retirement. For some, pension funds are a very convenient savings plan because they may otherwise find it difficult to save or costly to make investment decisions. Recently, there has been more attention focused on the (7)_____ of pension funds, most notably Social Security.

Finance companies are financial intermediaries that specialize in the types of loans they issue. Sales finance and (8)_____ _____ companies provide small loans for consumer purchases. Often these companies make loans to people who cannot obtain credit from other sources, such as a commercial bank. Business finance companies specialize in (9)_____, that is, purchasing accounts receivable.

A type of financial intermediary that owes its existence primarily to financial regulations that prohibited interest payments on checking accounts is the (10)_____ _____ mutual fund. Money market mutual funds invest in short-term liquid securities. Other types of mutual funds invest in tax-exempt securities and stocks. These funds allow diversification to be purchased at a small price, especially if the fund is a (11)_____-_____ fund. In 1980, only 6% of households held mutual fund shares, while this number has risen to nearly 40% in recent years.

Hedge funds are a special type of mutual fund that have attracted more attention following the Long_term Capital debacle. Because hedge funds can and do take big risks, the federal government restricts the number of investors per fund to 99, each of whom must have steady annual incomes that exceed $200,000 or a net worth of $1 million, excluding their homes.

The government, not to be outdone, has established agencies that directly engage in financial intermediation. The Federal National Mortgage Association (FNMA, called "Fannie Mae"), the Government National Mortgage Association (GNMA, or "Ginnie Mae"), and the Federal Home Loan Mortgage Company (FHLMC, or "Freddie Mac") provide funds to the mortgage market by selling bonds and issuing the proceeds to buy mortgages.

Investment banks assist in the initial sale of securities in the primary market. Those that guarantee the corporation a price on its securities and then sells them to the public are (12)_____. Securities (13)_____ are pure middlemen who act as agents for investors wishing to purchase or sell securities. Securities dealers, on the other hand, hold inventories of securities and stand ready to buy or sell securities to complete a trade. Dealers make their money on the spread between the bid and ask prices. A specialist trades securities on the floor of organized exchanges. Because the specialist stands ready to buy stocks or sell them from his or her inventory when buy and sell orders do not match, he or she acts as both a broker and a dealer. Clearly, brokers, dealers, and specialists all facilitate exchange in the secondary financial markets.

## EXERCISES

### Exercise 1: Insurance Management

List the management tools used by insurance companies to reduce adverse selection and moral hazard.

1. _____

2. _____

3. _____

4. _____

5. _____

6. _____

7. _____

8. _____


## Exercise 2: Terminology

Match the following terms from the left column with the closely related term from the right. Place the letter of the term from right column in the blank provided next to the appropriate term on the left.

| | |
|---|---|
| ____ 1. Mutual companies | a. Property and casualty insurance |
| ____ 2. Term insurance | b. Regulator |
| ____ 3. Earthquake insurance | c. No cash value |
| ____ 4. ERISA | d. Owned by policyholders |
| ____ 5. Social Security | e. Underwriting |
| ____ 6. Investment banking | f. Underfunded |
| ____ 7. Mutual funds | g. "Penny Benny" |
| ____ 8. SEC | h. Load and no-load |
| ____ 9. Corporate takeovers | i. Specialist |
| ____ 10. Organized exchange | j. Junk bond financing |
| ____ 11. Hedge fund | k. Reinsurance |
| ____ 12. IPO | l. Moral hazard |
| ____ 13. Annuities | m. New securities |
| ____ 14. Lloyd's of London | n. Life insurance |
| ____ 15. Deductible | o. 99 investors |

**Exercise 3: Definitions and Terminology**

Match the following terms from the left column with the closely related term from the right.  Place the letter of the term from right column in the blank provided next to the appropriate term on the left.

_____

_____ 1.  Condition where those most likely to produce the adverse outcome insured against are the ones who purchase insurance.

a.  Coinsurance

_____ 2.  Occurs when the existence of insurance encourages insured parties to take increased risks.

b.  Deductible

_____ 3.  Premiums based on risk classifications.

c.  Moral hazard

_____ 4.  Insurance clause requiring the insured to do certain actions in order for the policy to be in effect.

d.  Adverse selection

_____ 5.  In the event of an accident the portion of loss that insured must pay before the insurance company pays anything.

e.  Risk-based premiums

_____ 6.  In the event of an accident the portion of loss that insured must pay once the deductible has been paid.

f.  Sallie Mae

_____ 7.  Purchases student loans granted by private financial institutions.

g.  Ginnie Mae

_____ 8.  Federal agency that buys mortgages.

h.  Restrictive provision

_____ 9.  Insurer allocates a portion of risk to another company for a portion of the premium.

i.  Hedge fund

_____10.  Prior stock issues that are currently selling on the market.

j.  Initial public offering

_____11.  Highly misleading name because fund is speculating when it pursues a "market neutral" strategy.

k.  Seasoned issues

_____12.  New stock issues by a firm that has not previously issued stock.

l.  Reinsurance

## SELF-TEST

### Part A: True-False Questions

Circle whether the following statements are true (T) or false (F).

T F 1. Insurance companies are unproductive middlemen, since they pay out less than they take in, proving that they produce a service that is valued less than the resources given up.

T F 2. Life insurance companies are able to invest their funds in long-term assets because their payouts to policyholders can be predicted fairly accurately.

T F 3. Property and casualty insurance companies are more likely to hold tax-exempt securities than are life insurance companies.

T F 4. The term *hedge fund* is an accurate description of this special type of mutual fund because they engage in what are called "market neutral" strategies to avoid losses based on wrong bets.

T F 5. The Social Security system is a public pension plan for which benefits are determined by the contributions into the plan and their earnings.

T F 6. Finance companies, unlike commercial banks, tend to make very large loans.

T F 7. Mutual funds specialize in the pooling of funds that are used to purchase a diversified portfolio of financial securities.

T F 8. Money market mutual funds allow shareholders to withdraw funds simply by writing a check.

T F 9. The chief executive officer of a large firm would likely seek the help of an investment banker if he or she wanted to issue more stock.

T F 10. When commercial and investment banking activities are combined under one firm, there is a potential for the risk inherent in investment banking to be transferred to the commercial bank.

### Part B: Multiple-Choice Questions

Circle the appropriate answer.

1. Which of the following are financial intermediaries?

   a. Commercial banks
   b. Insurance companies
   c. Pension funds
   d. Mutual funds
   e. all of the above

2. Life insurance policies typically contain a clause stating that the company will not be required to pay death benefits in the event that the insured commits suicide.  Life insurance companies include such clauses in insurance contracts to protect against the _____ problem.

   a.  moral hazard
   b.  adverse selection
   c.  restrictive covenant
   d.  defined contribution

3. Hedge funds

   a.  are limited to ninety-nine investors (limited partners).
   b.  require limited partners to have an annual income of $200,000 or net worth of $1 million, exclude their homes.
   c.  do not require investors to commit their money for long periods of time.
   d.  do all of the above.
   e.  do only (a) and (b) of the above.

4. General Motors Acceptance Corporation (GMAC) is an example of a

   a.  sales finance company.
   b.  consumer finance company.
   c.  business finance company.
   d.  public finance company.

5. Lisa wants to add a new room to her house.  What type of finance company will she deal with in getting the loan to finance the room addition?

   a.  Sales finance company
   b.  Consumer finance company
   c.  Business finance company
   d.  Public finance company

6. Mutual funds that charge a sales commission when shares are purchased are called

   a.  no-load funds.
   b.  loaded funds.
   c.  sinking funds.
   d.  sink-charge funds.

7. When an investment bank purchases a new issue of securities in the hopes of making a profit, it is said to _____ the issue.

   a.  pawn
   b.  backstock
   c.  underwrite
   d.  syndicate

8. The agency that helps ensure that potential security purchasers are well-informed is the

    a. FCC.
    b. FTC.
    c. NRC.
    d. SEC.

9. Brokers are distinguished from the dealers in that brokers do not

    a. hold inventories of securities.
    b. make profits.
    c. incur losses.
    d. deal directly with the public.

10. Lloyd's of London specializes in

    a. annuities.
    b. hedge funds.
    c. mutual funds,
    d. reinsurance.

11. Junk bond financing is controversial because the capital raised is sometimes used to

    a. finance corporate takeovers.
    b. reduce debt that limits moral hazard problem.
    c. reduce equity, raising moral hazard problems.
    d. finance companies that layoff workers.

12. Factoring refers to the

    a. syndication of underwriting large securities issues.
    b. selling of accounts receivable at a discount in return for cash.
    c. breaking up large mutual funds into smaller funds.
    d. syndication of insurance coverage among many insurance underwriters to spread risk.

13. They assume the risk of issuing new stock in the hope of earning a profit on its sale.

    a. stock brokers
    b. securities dealers
    c. underwriters
    d. stock speculators

14. To encourage higher enrollments at institutions of higher education, the government created the following agency to purchase student loans granted by financial institutions under the Guaranteed Student Loan Program.

    a. Fannie Mac
    b. Ginnie Mae
    c. Sallie Mae
    d. Freddie Mac

15. Charging insurance premiums on the basis of how much risk a policyholder poses for the insurance company is a time-honored principle of insurance management to reduce

   a.  moral hazard.
   b.  adverse selection.
   c.  free-riding.
   d.  principal-agent problems.

# Chapter 13

## *Financial Derivatives*

### CHAPTER SYNOPSIS/COMPLETIONS

Beginning in the 1970s and continuing into the 1980s and 1990s interest rates and foreign exchange rates became more volatile, increasing the risk to financial institutions. To combat this, managers of financial institutions have demanded financial instruments to better manage risk. These instruments called *financial derivatives* have become an important source of profits for financial institutions, particularly larger banks. In this chapter, we investigate the use of forward contracts, financial futures, options, and swaps to reduce risk.

*Interest-rate forward contracts* can be used to reduce interest-rate risk by forming a (1)_____. A hedge reduces risk because when the price of the underlying asset moves one way, the price of the forward contract will move by the same amount in the (2)_____ direction, effectively canceling any gains or losses due to unanticipated movements in interest rates. A forward contract is an agreement for the exchange of assets in the future. The price and date of the exchange are agreed upon up front. A long contract means the holder agrees to buy the asset in the future while the (3)_____ contract holder agrees to sell the asset.

Forward contracts have the advantage of being as flexible as the parties want them to be, but they have the disadvantages of lacking liquidity – finding a counterparty may be difficult – and being subject to default (4)_____, if one or the other party chooses not to complete their end of the bargain.

A *financial futures contract* is similar to an interest-rate forward contract, but differs in ways that overcome liquidity and default problems of forward contracts. For example, the quantities delivered and the delivery dates of financial futures are (5)_____ so that it is easier to find a counterparty. Moreover, financial futures contracts can be traded again at any time until the delivery date, and, in the case of a Treasury bond futures contract, any Treasury bond that neither matures nor is callable for 15 years can be deliverable on the delivery date. These three features increase the liquidity of financial futures.

A clearinghouse for the exchange requires that both buyers and sellers must make a *margin requirement* into a margin account at their brokerage firm. This feature of financial futures contracts (6)_____ the risk of default. Additionally, to protect the exchange from loss, they are *marked to market* everyday. This means that at the end of every trading day, the change in the value of the futures contract is added or subtracted from a margin account. If the margin account falls too low, the investor must replenish it.

A final advantage that futures have over forward contracts is that most futures contracts do not result in delivery of the underlying asset on the expiration date, (7)_____ transaction costs compared to forward contracts that do require delivery. A trader who sells short a futures contract can avoid making delivery on the expiration date by making an offsetting purchase of a long futures contract. A micro hedge occurs when a futures contract is purchased or sold to hedge one particular security.  Macro hedges occur when futures contracts are purchased or sold to offset an entire portfolio.

Alternatives to using forward and futures contracts to hedge risk are options and swaps.  Options are contracts that give the purchaser the option, or (8)_____, to buy or sell the underlying financial instrument at the (9)_____ (exercise) price.  Although the seller of an option is obligated to buy or sell, the owner (buyer) need not exercise the option.  Because the right to buy a financial instrument at a specified price has value, one must pay a *premium* to buy an option.  American options can exercised at any time up to the expiration date; (10)_____ options can be exercised only on the expiration date.

Options on individual stocks are called stock options.  Options on financial futures, commonly called futures options, were developed in 1982 and have become the most widely traded option contracts.  A call option is a contract that gives the owner the right to buy a financial instrument at the exercise price.  A put option gives the owner the right to (11)_____ a financial instrument at the strike price.

Interest-rate swaps are an important tool for controlling interest-rate risk.  In a simple swap, called the *plain vanilla swap*, one firm agrees to pay a fixed rate of interest on a stated sum and another firm agrees to pay a floating interest rate on the same sum.  The advantage of this arrangement is that it effectively converts fixed rate assets into floating rate assets and vice versa.  A bank that finds that it has more interest rate sensitive liabilities than assets can protect itself (hedge) from an increase in interest rates by agreeing to pay a fixed rate on a swap in exchange for receiving floating rate payments.  What this does is convert fixed rate assets into floating rate assets.

The use of swaps to eliminate interest-rate risk can be cheaper than rearranging a bank's balance sheet.  Swaps have an advantage over futures because swaps can be written for (12)_____ periods of time.  The disadvantage of swaps is that they suffer from the liquidity and default risk that plague the forward market.  Intermediaries have set up markets in swaps that help alleviate these problems.  For example, Citicorp will match firms together and each firm will deal exclusively with the bank.

There are three concerns about the dangers of derivatives: they allow financial institutions to increase their leverage, they are too complex for some managers to understand, and they expose financial institutions to large credit risks because the huge notional amounts of derivative contracts greatly exceed the capital of these institutions.  Of these dangers, most regard the first to be the most worrisome.

## EXERCISES

### Exercise 1: Forward Contracts and Financial Futures Contracts

List four features that distinguish futures contracts from forward contracts.

1. _____

2. _____

3. _____

4. _____

## Exercise 2: Definitions and Terminology

Match the following terms in the column on the right with the definition or description in the column on the left. Place the letter of the term in the blank provided next to the appropriate definition. Terms may be used once, more than once, or not at all.

_____ 1. A security that is derived from another security.

a. Micro hedge

_____ 2. A non-standardized agreement where one party agrees to sell an asset and another party agrees to buy the asset in the future

b. Lack of liquidity

_____ 3. A standardized agreement where one party agrees to sell an asset and another party agrees to buy the asset in the future.

c. Hedge

_____ 4. A method of reducing risk where the change in contract value just offsets the change in asset value.

d Derivative

_____ 5. The contract holder agrees to buy the asset in the future.

e. Macro hedge

_____ 6. The contract holder agrees to sell the asset in the future.

f. Futures contract

_____ 7. The change in the value of the futures contract is added or subtracted from a margin account.

g. Long contract

_____ 8. A futures contract designed to hedge one particular asset.

h. Forward contract

_____ 9. A futures contract designed to hedge an entire portfolio.

i. Short contract

_____ 10. A disadvantage of interest-rate forward contract is that it may be difficult to make or that it will have to be made at a disadvantageous price.

j. Marked to market

## Exercise 3: More Definitions and Terminology

Match the following terms in the column on the right with the definition or description in the column on the left.  Place the letter of the term in the blank provided next to the appropriate definition.  Terms may be used once, more than once, or not at all.

_____

_____ 1.  An option that gives the holder the right to sell an asset in the future.

a. Option

_____ 2.  An option that gives the holder the right to buy an asset in the future.

b. Premium

_____ 3.  The price an option permits the holder to buy or sell an asset.

c. European option

_____ 4.  The price of an option.

d. Call option

_____ 5.  An arrangement where one party pays a fixed interest rate and another pays a floating interest rate.

e. Notional principal

_____ 6.  An option that can be exercised any time up to maturity.

f. Strike price

_____ 7.  An option that can be exercised only at maturity.

g. Arbitrage

_____ 8.  The amount of funds on which the interest is being paid.

h. Swap

_____ 9.  A contract that gives the purchaser the right to buy or sell an underlying security.

i. American option

_____ 10.  The elimination of riskless profit opportunities in the futures market.

j. Put option

## Exercise 4: Forwards and Futures

Fill in the Blank

1.  A firm with a portfolio of U.S. Treasury notes may hedge by _____ futures contracts.

2.  A _____ contract is where the investor agrees to sell an asset at some time in the future at an agreed upon price.

3.  Forward contracts are subject to _____ risk since the counter party could go bankrupt.

4. The elimination of riskless profit opportunities in the futures markets is referred to as _____, and it guarantees that the price of the futures contract at expiration equals the price of the underlying asset to be delivered.

5. Because futures contracts are _____ it is easier for an investor to find a counterparty.

6. Each day futures contracts are marked to market, helping to _____ the chance of losses to the exchange.

## Exercise 5: Options and Swaps

Fill in the Blank

1. A contract that gives the purchaser the right to buy or sell an asset is a(n)_____.

2. A _____ option gives the holder the right to buy an underlying asset.

3. A _____ option gives the holder the right to sell an underlying asset.

4. The price that the holder of a call option can demand from exercising the option is the _____ price.

5. An option that cannot be exercised until maturity is call an_____ option.

6. An option that can be exercised any time up until maturity is called an _____ option.

7. A _____ can be used to reduce interest rate risk without requiring the firm to restructure its balance sheet.

## SELF-TEST

### Part A: True-False Questions

Circle whether the following statements are true (T) or false (F).

T  F  1.  Interest rate futures can be used to reduce the risk of selling goods overseas.

T  F  2.  Forward contracts are more flexible than futures contracts because they are not standardized.

T  F  3.  To hedge against interest rate increases, a bank with a portfolio of Treasury securities could sell futures contracts.

T  F  4.  A serious problem for the market in financial futures contracts is that it may be difficult to make the financial transaction or that it will have to be made at a disadvantageous price; in the parlance of financial economists, this market suffers from a lack of liquidity.

T  F  5.  To corner a market means that someone has purchased the bulk of a particular asset so that high prices can be charged when contracts are settled.

T  F   6.   Open interest refers to the number of futures contracts that have not been settled.

T  F   7.   Option premiums are generally higher the greater the exercise price.

T  F   8.   Option premiums are higher the greater the volatility of the underlying asset.

T  F   9.   A call option gives the holder the right to buy the underlying asset.

T  F  10.   A swap is a financial contract that obligates one party to exchange a set of payments it owns for another set of payments owned by another party.

## Part B: Multiple-Choice Questions

Circle the appropriate answer.

1.   An investor who chooses to hedge in the futures market

   a.   gives up the opportunity for gains.
   b.   reduces the opportunity for losses.
   c.   increases her earnings potential.
   d.   does both (a) and (b) of the above.

2.   A portfolio manager with $ 100 million in Treasury securities could reduce interest rate risk by

   a.   selling financial futures.
   b.   going long on financial futures.
   c.   buying financial futures.
   d.   both (b) and (c) are true.

3.   A bank sold a futures contract that perfectly hedges its portfolio of Treasury securities; if interest rates fall,

   a.   the bank suffers a loss.
   b.   the bank has a gain.
   c.   the bank income is unchanged.
   d.   none of the above.

4.   When an investor agrees to buy an asset at some time in the future he is said to have gone

   a.   long.
   b.   short.
   c.   ahead.
   d.   back.

5.  The main advantage of a forward contract is that it

    a.  is standardized, therby reducing the cost of finding a counter party.
    b.  is default risk free since the contract is between the exchange and the investor.
    c.  is flexible because it can be written any way the parties desire.
    d.  both (a) and (b) are true.

6.  At the expiration date of a futures contract, the price of the contract is

    a.  equal to the price of the underlying asset to be delivered.
    b.  equal to the price of the counterparty.
    c.  equal to the hedge position.
    d.  equal to the value of the hedged asset.

7.  Futures markets have been successful and have grown rapidly because

    a.  of standardization of the futures contract.
    b.  of the ability to buy or sell the contract up to the maturity.
    c.  of the reduced risk of default in the futures market.
    d.  all of the above.

8.  When compared to forward contracts, financial futures have the advantage that

    a.  thcy arc standardizcd, making it more likely that different parties can be matched, thereby increasing liquidity in the market.
    b.  they specifiy that more than one bond is eligible for delivery, to reduce the possibility that someone might corner the market and "squeeze" traders who have sold contracts.
    c.  they cannot be traded at any time before the delivery date, thereby increasing liquidity in the market.
    d.  all of the above are true.
    e.  only (a) and (b) of the above are true.

9.  Option premiums are increased when

    a.  time to maturity increases.
    b.  volatility is lower on the underlying asset.
    c.  strike price is lower.
    d.  both (b) and (c) are true.

10. An option that lets the holder buy an asset in the future is a

    a.  put option.
    b.  call option.
    c.  swap.
    d.  premium.

11. An option that lets the holder sell an asset in the future is a

    a.   put option.
    b.   call option.
    c.   swap.
    d.   premium.

12. The holder of an option

    a.   limits his gains.
    b.   limits his losses.
    c.   limits both his gains and his losses.
    d.   has no limits on his gains and losses.

13. An important tool for managing interest-rate risk that requires the exchange of payment streams on assets is a

    a.   futures contract.
    b.   forward contract.
    c.   swap.
    d.   micro hedge.

14. Which of the following is a disadvantage of the swap as a method for controlling interest rate risk?

    a.   Swaps, unlike forward contracts, are not subject to default risk.
    b.   Swaps are more expensive than simply restructuring the balance sheet.
    c.   Swaps, like forward contracts, lack liquidity.
    d.   All of the above are disadvantages of swaps.
    e.   Only (a) and (b) of the above are disadvantages of swaps.

15. Which of the following is an advantage of interest rate swaps?

    a.   Swaps lower interest-rate risk more cheaply than simply restructuring the balance sheet.
    b.   Swaps, unlike forward contracts, are quite liquid.
    c.   Swaps, unlike forward contracts, are not subject to default risk.
    d.   All of the above are advantages of swaps.
    e.   Only (a) and (b) of the above are advantages of swaps.

# Chapter 14

# *Structure of Central Banks and the Federal Reserve System*

## CHAPTER SYNOPSIS/COMPLETIONS

Until the creation of the European Central Bank, one could say that the Federal Reserve System had the most unusual structure of any central bank. Chapter 14 describes the unique structure of the Federal Reserve System and its evolution since 1913. Although the Federal Reserve has been granted a high degree of independence, a clearer understanding of its decisions requires that one acknowledge the political and bureaucratic forces influencing its behavior.

The formal structure of the Federal Reserve System reflects Americans' distrust of the concentration of power in banking. Although many feared the creation of a central bank, the (1)_____ of 1907 convinced many others that a banking system without a lender of (2)_____ _____ could be prone to failures, panics, and payment problems. Thus, the formal structure of the Federal Reserve reflects a compromise among these concerns.

Although responsibility is formally shared across separate, cooperating entities, the Federal Reserve is fundamentally a hierarchical organization. At the top is the (3)_____ _____ _____ – a group of seven members appointed to lengthy terms by the president of the United States and confirmed by the Senate. One member is chosen as chairman – currently, Alan Greenspan – who serves a four-year term and may be reappointed. First appointed by Ronald Reagan in 1987, Mr. Greenspan has been re-apponted by George Bush and re-appointed twice by Bill Clinton, most recently in early 2000. The chairman of the Board of Governors wields great power in Washington, D.C., as evidenced by his frequent trips to Capitol Hill to testify on economic policy matters.

Monetary policy decisions are determined by a majority vote of the twelve-member Federal Open Market Committee or FOMC. The voting members of the committee consists of the seven members of the Board of Governors, the president of the Federal Reserve Bank of (4)_____ _____, and four presidents from other Federal Reserve banks. The chairman of the Board of Governors also serves as the chairman of the FOMC. Presidents from the other seven Federal Reserve banks also attend FOMC meetings, and their input is important although they have no formal vote. It is, however, the Board of Governors that dictates the future course of monetary policy (though the FOMC goes to some lengths to achieve consensus).

If we are to understand the decisions of the FOMC, we need to understand the factors that motivate its behavior. Identification of these factors can help economists predict the future course of economic activity and suggest modification in the Fed's structure to improve policy performance. Of particular interest to economists are the bureaucratic and political forces that limit the Fed's (5)_____ and shape its decisions.

On the surface, the Federal Reserve is a highly independent government agency. Indeed, perhaps no other federal government institution enjoys greater formal independence. Federal Reserve independence is afforded primarily through three channels. First, the Fed is not directly dependent on congressional (6)_____ to finance its operations. The bulk of the Fed's budget is financed through the interest it earns on its massive holdings of United States' (7)_____ _____. These earnings are so significant that after expenses the Fed returns about $20 billion over to the Treasury every year. Thus the Fed has a degree of discretionary budgetary authority not granted to other agencies.

Second, the seven members of the Board of Governors of the Federal Reserve System are appointed to (8)_____ -year terms on a staggered biannual basis. Therefore, when appointees serve their entire terms, any individual president can at most appoint four members to the board in an eight-year period. Under this constraint, even a reelected president would be unable to appoint a majority of the board until the last year of his second term in office. The 14-year term affords greater autonomy to board members than is found almost anywhere else in government.

Third, the chairman of the Board of Governors presently serves a four-year term that is not necessarily concurrent with the presidential term. For example, Bill Clinton did not have the opportunity to appoint a Fed chairman until 1996, three years into his first term. Stuck with another's appointee for the first 3 years of his term, an incoming president is likely to feel strong pressure from the financial and banking community to retain the present chairman. The present chairman is a known quantity, and financial market participants often favor the known quantity to someone who may substantially change existing arrangements. Interestingly, some observers suggest that President Clinton succumbed to this pressure when in 1996 he re-appointed Alan Greenspan, a Republican.

While the Fed retains a relatively high degree of independence, it is not free from political pressure. Politicians need favorable economic conditions to help them win reelection, while lenders and the housing industry want low (9)_____ rates, and still other groups – such as those who have retired on fixed incomes – want low inflation. Given these pressures, the theory of (10)_____ behavior suggests that the Federal Reserve will do best for itself by avoiding conflict with these groups.

A short survey of the structure and independence of the central banks in Canada, England, Japan, and the new European Central Bank indicates that we have been seeing a remarkable trend toward greater (11)_____. Both theory and evidence suggest that more independent central banks produce better monetary policy, thus providing an impetus for this trend.

Good arguments have been made both for retaining the Fed's independence and for restricting it. The strongest argument to be made for an independent Federal Reserve rests on the belief that subjecting the Fed to more political pressure would impart an (12)_____ bias to monetary policy. However, critics of an independent central bank contend that it is (13)_____ to have monetary policy controlled by a group that is not directly responsive to the electorate. The jury is still out on how best to improve monetary policy (see chapter 20 on recent research), but recognition that the Fed is subject to political and bureaucratic forces helps one to better understand current and past monetary policy and helps one to predict how the Fed will respond to future events.

## EXERCISES

### Exercise 1: Structure of the Federal Reserve System

The authors of the Federal Reserve Act of 1913 designed a decentralized central banking system that reflected their fears of centralized financial power. Today, this decentralization is still evident in the allocation of responsibilities and duties among the various Federal Reserve entities. Match the Federal Reserve entity to its responsibilities and duties given on the left by placing the appropriate letter in the space provided.

| Responsibilities and Duties | Federal Reserve Entity |
|---|---|
| _____ 1. Clears checks | a. Board of Governors |
| _____ 2. "Establishes" discount rate | |
| _____ 3. Reviews discount rate | |
| _____ 4. Appointed by the president of the United States | |
| _____ 5. Serve 14-year terms | b. Federal Open Market Committee |
| _____ 6. Decides discount rate | |
| _____ 7. Decides monetary policy | |
| _____ 8. Evaluates bank merger applications | |
| _____ 9. Determines margin requirements | c. District Federal Reserve Banks |
| _____ 10. Sets discount rate in practice | |

### Exercise 2: What Motivates the Fed?

The Board of Governors had the power to set Regulation Q interest-rate ceilings until 1986. In 1966, the Fed may have feared losing control over interest-rate ceilings when some members of Congress discussed passing a bill lowering the ceiling below the rate set by the Board of Governors. In response to the threatened action by Congress, the Fed lowered Regulation Q ceilings in 1966, despite a recognition among some of the board members that such action would create undesirable side effects.[1] Explain why the Fed wanted to act to lower Regulation Q ceilings before Congress did, despite its recognition of undesirable side effects.

## Exercise 3: The Independence of The Federal Reserve

The Senate, on July 27, 1983, confirmed the nomination of Paul A. Volcker to a second four-year term as chairman of the Federal Reserve.  The 84 to 16 vote was generally regarded as a strong vote of confidence in Volcker's efforts to bring inflation under control.  Volcker, however, was not without his detractors.  For example, Senator DeConcini (D-Ariz.) complained that the Fed chairman had "almost single-handedly caused one of the worst economic crises" in U.S. history by not checking the rise in interest rates.  "We should be telling Mr. Volcker that in a democracy, we do not combat inflation by placing 12 million citizens on the rolls of the unemployed," DeConcini added.

Although congressional criticism of Fed policies, such as the remarks made by Senator DeConcini, is often intended for the representative's constituents, it does not go unnoticed at the Federal Reserve.  After all, the independence of the Federal Reserve was created by congressional legislation, not Constitutional guarantee.  Members of Congress have, at times, shown their displeasure of Fed policies by introducing bills threatening the removal of independence.  Observers complain that members of the Federal Open Market Committee are so mindful of these threats that political pressures affect monetary policy decisions by constricting the set of feasible policy options considered by the FOMC.

A.  How do statements such as those made by Senator DeConcini constrain Federal Reserve policymaking?

_____

_____

B.  Many proposals for reforming the Fed have been motivated by concerns that it has not been independent enough and has accommodated too much inflation.  Defenders of Federal Reserve independence note that inflation in Germany, Switzerland, and the United States was lower than that in France, Italy, and Great Britain over the period 1960-1984.  Speculate as to which countries had the relatively more independent central banks during this period.[2]

_____

_____

## Exercise 4: Should the Fed be Independent?

A.  List three arguments made by those who support a Federal Reserve that is  independent of direct control from either the executive or legislative branches of government.

   1. _____

   2. _____

   3. _____

_____

[2] See King Banaian et al., Central Bank Independence: An International Comparison, Federal Reserve Bank of Dallas *Economic Review*, March 1983, 1-13.

B.  List four arguments that favor a Federal Reserve that is brought under the control of Congress or the president.

1. _____

2. _____

3. _____

4. _____


## SELF-TEST

## Part A: True-False Questions

Circle whether the following statements are true (T) or false (F).

T  F  1. The Federal Reserve Act, which created a central banking system with regional banks, reflected a compromise between traditional distrust of monied interests and a concern for eliminating bank panics.

T  F  2. In practice, each of the 12 Federal Reserve banks sets the discount rate.

T  F  3. Membership in the Federal Reserve has continued to rise since a low in 1947.

T  F  4. It would be accurate to say that the European Central Bank was modeled after the Federal Reserve System.

T  F  5. District Federal Reserve Banks essentially have no input regarding monetary policy decisions, since the Board of Governors has sole responsibility for monetary policy.

T  F  6. Open-market operations, believe it or not, were not envisioned as a monetary policy tool when the Federal Reserve was created.

T  F  7. The theory of bureaucratic behavior may help explain why the Fed seems to be so preoccupied with the level of short-term interest rates.

T  F  8. Although all 12 Federal Reserve Bank presidents attend the FOMC meetings, only those five presidents who have a vote actively participate in the deliberations.

T  F  9. Placing the Fed under the control of the executive branch may lead to a monetary policy that is more responsive to political pressures.

T  F  10. Supporters of placing the Fed under control of the executive branch believe that the electorate should have more control over monetary policy.

**Part B: Multiple-Choice Questions**

Circle the appropriate answer.

1.  The primary motivation behind the creation of the Federal Reserve System was the desire to

    a.  lessen the occurrence of bank panics.
    b.  stabilize short-term interest rates.
    c.  eliminate state regulated banks.
    d.  finance World War I.

2.  The theory of bureaucratic behavior indicates that

    a.  government agencies attempt to increase their power and prestige.
    b.  government agencies attempt to avoid conflicts with the legislative and executive branches of government.
    c.  both (a) and (b) of the above are true.
    d.  neither (a) nor (b) of the above are true.

3.  The regional Federal Reserve banks

    a.  "establish" the discount rate.
    b.  ration discount loans to banks.
    c.  clear checks.
    d.  do all of the above.

4.  While the regional Federal Reserve banks "establish" the discount rate, in truth, the discount rate is determined by

    a.  Congress.
    b.  the president of the United States.
    c.  the Board of Governors.
    d.  the Federal Reserve Advisory Council.

5.  A majority of the Federal Open Market Committee is comprised of

    a.  the 12 Federal Reserve bank presidents.
    b.  the five voting Federal Reserve bank presidents.
    c.  the seven members of the Board of Governors.
    d.  none of the above.

6.  Monetary policy is determined by

    a.  the Board of Governors.
    b.  the Federal Reserve banks from each district.
    c.  the Federal Open Market Committee.
    d.  the Federal Reserve Advisory Council.

7. Power within the Federal Reserve is essentially located in

    a. New York.
    b. Washington, D.C.
    c. Boston.
    d. San Francisco.

8. While the Fed enjoys a relatively high degree of independence for a government agency, it feels political pressure from the president and Congress because

    a. Fed members desire reappointment every 3 years.
    b. the Fed must go to Congress each year for operating revenues.
    c. Congress could limit Fed power through legislation.
    d. of all of the above.
    e. of only (b) and (c) of the above.

9. The theory of bureaucratic behavior may help explain why the Fed

    a. remains concerned about short-term interest rates.
    b. lobbied for legislation that expanded jurisdiction of the Fed's reserve requirements to all banks, not just the member commercial banks.
    c. had delayed releasing FOMC directives to Congress or the public.
    d. did all of the above.

10. Supporters of keeping the Federal Reserve independent from both the executive and legislative branches of government believe that a less independent Fed would

    a. pursue overly expansionary monetary policies.
    b. be more likely to pursue policies consistent with the political business cycle.
    c. ignore short-run problems in favor of longer-run concerns.
    d. do only (a) and (b) of the above.

11. Professor Mishkin contends that

    a. the Fed is more independent than the European Central Bank.
    b. the Fed is less independent than the European Central Bank.
    c. the trend in industrialized countries has been to reduce the independence of their central banks.
    d. none of the above are true.

12. Although the Bank of Japan has new powers and greater autonomy under 1998 legislation, critics

    a. contend that the central bank's independence is limited because the Ministry of Finance has veto power over a portion of the bank's budget.
    b. contend that the central bank's independence is too great because the central bank need not pursue a policy of price stability even if that is the popular will of the people.
    c. contend that the central bank's independence is too great because the central bank can now ignore concerns of the Ministry of Finance since it no longer has veto power over the bank's budget.
    d. contend that the central bank's independence is limited because the Ministry of Finance retained the power to dismiss senior bank officials.

# Chapter 15

## *Multiple Deposit Creation and the Money Supply Process*

### CHAPTER SYNOPSIS/COMPLETIONS

Movements in the money supply influence us all by affecting the health of the economy; thus it is important to understand how the money supply is determined. Since deposits at banks (and other depository institutions) comprise the largest component of the money supply, understanding how these deposits are created is the first step in understanding the money supply process. In this and the next chapter we discover how the actions of the four players in the money supply process – the (1) _____ bank (2) _____, depositors, and borrowers from banks – cause changes in the money supply. Of the four players, the (3) _____ _____ _____, the central bank of the United States, is the most important and therefore receives the most attention.

Examination of the Fed's balance sheet provides us with a framework for understanding the money supply process. An increase in the Fed's monetary liabilities – currency in circulation and (4) _____ – leads to an increase in the money supply. The sum of Treasury currency in circulation (primarily coins) and Fed liabilities is called the (5) _____ _____, or high-powered money.

The primary method used by the Fed for changing the monetary base is through an (6) _____ _____ operation, the purchase or sale of a government bond. Open market purchases or sales may involve banks or the nonbank public. Open-market purchases from banks increase reserves and the monetary base by the amount of the purchase. If the open market purchase is from a member of the nonbank public who deposits the check, the purchase has an effect on reserves and the monetary base that is (7) _____ to the open market purchase from a bank. Thus the distinction between reserves and the monetary base is not important for these two transactions.

It is when a member of the nonbank public cashes the Fed's check (causing currency in circulation to increase) that a distinction between the effect on the monetary base and reserves needs to be made. The effect of an open-market purchase on the monetary base, however, is always the same, whether the proceeds are held as deposits or as (8) _____.

An open market sale will have a predictable impact on the monetary base. The decline in reserves will equal the decline in the monetary base if the sale is to the bank or if a check is drawn to pay for the security. If the security is purchased with currency, reserves remain unchanged, but the monetary base (9) _____. Thus the Fed is more certain about the effect of open-market operations on the monetary base than on reserves.

There is an additional reason why the Fed has greater control over the monetary base than over reserves. Shifts from (10) _____ to currency affect the volume of reserves in the banking system, but such shifts have no impact on the level of the monetary base, making it a more stable variable.

Although the preceding discussion indicates that the Fed has far better control over the monetary base than it does over reserves, factors other than Fed actions seemingly could thwart the Fed's ability to control the monetary base. As the Fed's balance sheet indicates, factors other than Fed actions – for example, float and Treasury deposits – can and do affect the monetary base. Nevertheless, even these substantial *short-run* fluctuations do not prevent the Fed from accurately controlling the monetary base, as changes in Treasury deposits and float are often predictable and easily offset.

While an individual bank can lend and create deposits of an amount equal to its excess reserves, the banking system can generate a (11)_____ expansion of deposits when reserves in the system increase. When the Fed provides additional reserves to the banking system, checkable deposits and, therefore, the money supply increase by an amount that exceeds the initial change in reserves. This expansion occurs whether a bank chooses to use its excess reserves to purchase securities or make loans. The expression describing the multiple increase in deposits generated from an increase in reserves is called the (12)_____ _____ _____ and is equal to the reciprocal of the required reserve ratio. A decline in reserves will cause a multiple contraction of deposits.

The simple deposit expansion model indicates that the Fed is able to exercise complete control over the level of deposits by setting the required reserve ratio and the level of reserves, but a realistic approach recognizes that the behavior of banks and depositors influences the level of deposits and hence the money supply. If depositors choose to hold more currency as deposits increase, or if banks choose to hold (13)_____ reserves, then the actual deposit expansion multiplier will be (14)_____ than the simple deposit expansion multiplier.

The next chapter presents a more accurate picture of the deposit-expansion process; still, the main findings of this chapter are retained: The Fed changes the money supply through its influence on the level of reserves, and a change in reserves leads to either a multiple expansion or contraction in deposits.

## EXERCISES

### Exercise 1: Open Market Operations, Reserves, and the Monetary Base

A. How will a Federal Reserve sale of $100 of government bonds to banks affect the monetary base and reserves? Fill in the following T-accounts in arriving at your answers:

Banking System

| Assets | Liabilities |
|---|---|
|  |  |

The Fed

| Assets | Liabilities |
|---|---|
|  |  |

Change in the monetary base = _____

Change in reserves = _____

B.  How will a Federal Reserve sale of $100 of government bonds to the nonbank public affect the monetary base and reserves if the nonbank public pays for the bonds with checks?  Fill in the following T-accounts in arriving at your answers:

### Nonbank Public

| Assets | Liabilities |
|--------|-------------|
|        |             |

### Banking System

| Assets | Liabilities |
|--------|-------------|
|        |             |

### The Fed

| Assets | Liabilities |
|--------|-------------|
|        |             |

Change in the monetary base = _____

Change in reserves = _____

C.  How will a Federal Reserve sale of $100 of government bonds to the nonbank  public affect the monetary base and reserves if the nonbank public pay for the  bonds with currency?  Fill in the following T-accounts in arriving at your answer:

### Nonbank Public

| Assets | Liabilities |
|--------|-------------|
|        |             |

The Fed

| Assets | Liabilities |
|---|---|
|  |  |

Change in the monetary base = _____

Change in reserves = _____

How do these answers differ from those in parts A and B? _____

_____

**Exercise 2: How the Fed Provides Reserves to the Banking System**

A.  Fill in the entries in the following T-accounts when the Fed sells $100,000 of T-bills to the First National Bank.

| First National Bank | | The Fed | |
|---|---|---|---|
| Assets | Liabilities | Assets | Liabilities |
|  |  |  |  |

What has happened to reserves in the banking system? _____

B.  If, instead, the First National Bank pays off a $100,000 discount loan what will be the entries in the T-accounts below?

| First National Bank | | The Fed | |
|---|---|---|---|
| Assets | Liabilities | Assets | Liabilities |
|  |  |  |  |

What has happened to reserves in the banking system? _____

**Exercise 3: Deposit Creation – The Single Bank**

Suppose that the balance sheet of Panther State Bank is currently as follows:

Panther State Bank

| Assets | | Liabilities |
|---|---|---|
| Vault cash | $  100 | Checkable Deposits   $9,000 |
| On deposit with Federal Reserve | 900 | |
| Loans | 8,000 | |

A.  Calculate the level of excess reserves held by Panther State Bank if the required reserve ratio is 10%.

_____

B.  How much can Panther State Bank lend?  _____

C.  Complete the following T-account showing the changes in assets resulting when Panther State Bank lends the amount you answered to Part B, assuming the deposits created by the bank are deposited with another bank.

Panther State Bank

| Assets | Liabilities |
|---|---|
| | |

**Exercise 4: Deposit Creation – The Banking System**

A.  Assume that the required reserve ratio is 0.20 and that the Fed purchases $1000 in government bonds from the First State Bank of Bozeman, which, in turn, lends the $1000 of reserves it has just acquired to a customer for the purchase of a used car.  If the used car dealer deposits the proceeds from the sale in Bank A, how much in additional loans can Bank A make?  What is the change in the money supply after Bank A lends this amount?

_____

_____

B.  Assume a similar process occurs for Bank B, Bank C, and Bank D.  Complete the following table for these banks (see Table 3, p. 405 in the text for an example) and the totals for all banks.

| Bank | Change in Deposits | Change in Loans | Change in Reserves |
|------|--------------------|-----------------|--------------------|
| A | + $1000.00 | + $800.00 | + $200.00 |
| B | + 800.00 | + 640.00 | + 160.00 |
| C | _____ | _____ | _____ |
| D | _____ | _____ | _____ |
| • • • | • • • | • • • | • • • |
| Total All Banks | _____ | _____ | _____ |

## Exercise 5: The Simple Deposit Multiplier

1.  Write down the formula for the simple deposit multiplier.

2.  Assuming that the required reserve ratio is 0.20, what is the change in reserves when the Fed sells $10 billion of government bonds and extends discount loans of $5 billion to commercial banks?

3.  Using the simple deposit multiplier formula, calculate the resulting change in checkable deposits.

## SELF-TEST

## Part A: True-False Questions

Circle whether the following statements are true (T) or false (F).

T   F   1.  The U.S. Treasury functions as the central bank of the United States.

T  F  2. Currency held by depository institutions (banks) is added to currency circulating in the hands of the public to get total currency in circulation.

T  F  3. The Fed's buying and selling of bonds in the open market is referred to as widening the market.

T  F  4. If the First Security Bank of Belfry has $50 in excess reserves, it will be able to lend more than an additional $50 as long as the required reserve ratio is below 100%.

T  F  5. Assuming that the required reserve ratio is 20%, and open market sale of $100 in government bonds by the Fed will cause the money supply to fall by $500 in the simple deposit expansion model.

T  F  6. When a bank chooses to purchase securities instead of making loans, deposit expansion is diminished.

T  F  7. In the simple model, deposits in the banking system contract by a multiple of the loss in reserves caused by a Federal Reserve sale of government bonds.

T  F  8. A rise in Treasury deposits at the Fed increases the monetary base.

T  F  9. The Federal Reserve can offset an increase in float by purchasing government securities.

T  F 10. Because many factors beyond the direct control of the Fed affect the monetary base, it is unreasonable to expect the Fed to have any meaningful control over the monetary base.

## Part B: Multiple-Choice Questions

Circle the appropriate answer.

1. The monetary base is comprised of

   a. currency in circulation and Federal Reserve notes.
   b. currency in circulation and government securities.
   c. currency in circulation and reserves.
   d. reserves and government securities.

2. The sum of vault cash and bank deposits with the Fed minus required reserves is called

   a. the monetary base.
   b. the money supply.
   c. excess reserves.
   d. total reserves.

3. When the Fed simultaneously purchases government bonds and extends discount loans to banks,

    a. the money supply unambiguously falls.
    b. the money supply unambiguously rises.
    c. the net effect on the money supply cannot be determined because the two Fed actions counteract each other.
    d. the Fed action has no effect on the money supply.

4. When the Fed simultaneously extends discount loans and sells government bonds,

    a. the money supply unambiguously increases.
    b. the money supply unambiguously falls.
    c. the net effect on the money supply cannot be determined without further information because the two Fed actions counteract each other.
    d. the Fed action has no effect on the money supply.

5. When the Fed wants to reduce reserves in the banking system, it will

    a. purchase government bonds.
    b. extend discount loans to banks.
    c. print more currency.
    d. sell government bonds.

6. The simple deposit multiplier is equal to 4 when the required reserve ratio is equal to

    a. 0.25.
    b. 0.40.
    c. 0.05.
    d. 0.15.

7. The First National Bank of Galata has $150 in excess reserves. If the required reserve ratio is 10%, how much extra can the First National Bank lend?

    a. $1500
    b. $750
    c. $150
    d. $0

8. If excess reserves in the banking system amount to $75 and the required reserve ratio is 0.20, checkable deposits could potentially expand by

    a. $75.
    b. $750.
    c. $37.50.
    d. $375.

9. A sale of government bonds by the Fed

   a. is called an open-market sale.
   b. reduces the nonborrowed base, all else the same.
   c. reduces the borrowed base, all else the same.
   d. does all of the above.
   e. does only (a) and (b) of the above.

10. If a member of the nonbank public purchases a government bond from the Federal Reserve with currency, then

    a. both the monetary base and reserves will fall.
    b. both the monetary base and reserves will rise.
    c. the monetary base will fall, but reserves will remain unchanged.
    d. the monetary base will fall, but currency in circulation will remain unchanged.
    e. none of the above will occur.

11. Which of the following are found on the asset side of the Federal Reserve's balance sheet?

    a. Treasury securities
    b. Treasury deposits
    c. Discount loans
    d. Both (a) and (b) of the above
    e. Only (a) and (c) of the above

12. Which of the following are found on the liability side of the Federal Reserve's balance sheet?

    a. Cash items in the process of collection
    b. Deferred availability cash items
    c. Gold
    d. All of the above
    e. only (b) and (c) of the above

13. When float increases,

    a. currency in circulation falls.
    b. the monetary base falls.
    c. the monetary base rises.
    d. the monetary supply falls.
    e. none of the above occurs.

14. A reduction in which of the following leads to an increase in the monetary base?

    a. U.S. Treasury deposits
    b. Float
    c. Discount loans
    d. All of the above

# Chapter 16

## *Determinants of the Money Supply*

### CHAPTER SYNOPSIS/COMPLETIONS

This chapter incorporates depositor and bank behavior into the monetary process, presenting a more realistic model of the money supply process. The analysis is separated into three steps. First, because the Fed's control of the monetary base is more precise than its control over reserves, the model links changes in the money supply to changes in the monetary base. Next, the money multiplier, a ratio that relates the change in the money supply to a given change in the monetary base, is derived. Third, factors determining the money multiplier are examined.

The sum of currency in circulation and total reserves is called the monetary base or high-powered money. Because Federal Reserve actions have a more predictable effect on the monetary base than on (1)_____, money supply models typically focus on the Fed's control over high-powered money.

In our model of multiple deposit creation in Chapter 15, we ignored the effects on deposit creation of changes in the public's holdings of (2)_____ and banks' holdings of excess reserves. We incorporate these changes into the deposit expansion model by assuming that the desired levels of currency and excess reserves grow proportionally with (3)_____ _____. That is, the currency and excess reserves ratios are constants.

The money multiplier is the key factor separating the Fed's control of the money supply from its ability to affect the (4)_____ _____. An important characteristic of the money multiplier is that it is less than the simple deposit multiplier found in chapter 15.

Inclusion of depositor behavior into the money supply model reveals that the money multiplier depends on depositor preferences for currency relative to checkable deposits. A numerical example that accounts for currency withdrawals reveals that the simple deposit multiplier greatly (5)_____ the expansion in deposits. The key to understanding this result is that although there is multiple expansion of deposits, there is no such expansion for currency. Since an (6)_____ in the monetary base will mean an increase in currency in circulation, only part of any increase in the monetary base will be available for deposit expansion. Because reserves leave the bank as currency in circulation, the money supply will not increase as much for a given change in the monetary base, meaning a smaller money multiplier.

When banks increase their holdings of excess reserves, their volume of loans contracts for a given level of the monetary base, thereby causing a (7)_____ in the money multiplier. The banking system's excess reserves ratio is negatively related to the market (8)_____ _____, but

(9)_____ related to expected deposit outflows.

Changes in the required reserve ratio, the currency ratio, and the excess reserve ratio alter the value of the money (10)_____. Increases in any of these ratios – because they reduce the reserves available for lending and deposit expansion – reduce the money multiplier.

Also, banks' decisions to borrow reserves from the Fed affect the money supply. If banks seek additional discount loans from the Fed, the money supply (11)_____, if the Fed does not act to offset the increase in reserves. Alternatively, if banks choose to reduce discount borrowing, the money supply contracts. The amount of discount loans demanded by banks is positively related to the market interest rate and (12)_____ related to the discount rate.

An examination of the 1980-1999 time period indicates that the behavior of players other than the Federal Reserve can lead to sharp changes in money supply growth in the short run. Importantly, the period indicates that the growth rate of the money supply is closely linked to the growth rate of the (13)_____ monetary base.

## EXERCISES

### Exercise 1: The Money Multiplier

A.  Write the formula for the money multiplier.

_____

B.  Calculate the currency ratio, the excess reserves ratio, and the money multiplier for the following numbers:

$$r_D = 0.10 \qquad C = \$280 \text{ billion}$$
$$D = \$800 \text{ billion} \qquad ER = \$40 \text{ billion}$$

{C/D} = _____

{ER/D} = _____

m = _____

C.  Calculate required reserves (RR), total reserves (R), and the monetary base (MB).

RR = \$_____

R = \$_____

MB = \$_____

D.  Calculate the new money multiplier and money supply assuming that the Fed lowers the required reserve ratio on checkable deposits to 0.08 and does nothing to change the monetary base. Assume that the deposit ratios remain unchanged.

m = _____

M = $_____

E.  Calculate the new level of deposits (D) and currency in circulation (C).

D = $_____

C = $_____

F.  Calculate the new level of required reserves (RR) and excess reserves (ER).

RR = $_____

ER = $_____

## Exercise 2: Adding Bank Behavior into the Money Supply Model

A.  Given the following values, calculate the money multiplier and the money supply:

$r_D = 0.10$                                 $\{C/D\} = 0.40$
$ER = DL = 0$                          $MB_n = \$400$ billion

m = _____

M = $_____

B.  Calculate the level of currency (C), the level of deposits (D), the level of required reserves (RR), and the level of total reserves (R) in the banking system.

C = $_____          RR = $_____

D = $_____          R = $_____

C.  Suppose that bankers suddenly decide to hold a cushion of excess reserves equal to six percent of their checkable deposits.  Calculate the new money multiplier, the new money supply, the level of deposits, currency in circulation, and the amount of excess reserves that banks will now hold.

m = _____

M = $_____

D = $_____

C = $_____

RR = $_____

ER = $_____

**Exercise 3: Factors that Affect the Money Supply**

Indicate how the money supply responds to the following changes by filling in the second column of the table below with either a ($\uparrow$) to indicate a rise in the money supply or a ($\downarrow$) to indicate a fall in the money supply.

| Player | Change in Variable | | Money Supply Response |
|---|---|---|---|
| Federal Reserve System | $r_D$ | $\downarrow$ | |
| | $MB_n$ | $\downarrow$ | |
| | $i_d$ | $\downarrow$ | |
| Depositors | {C/D} | $\downarrow$ | |
| Depositors & Banks | Expected Deposit Outflows | $\downarrow$ | |
| Borrowers & other Players | $i$ | $\downarrow$ | |

# SELF-TEST

## Part A: True-False Questions

Circle whether the following statements are true (T) or false (F).

T   F   1.  The ratio that relates the change in the money supply to a given change in the monetary base is called the money multiplier.

T   F   2.  Another name for the nonborrowed base is high-powered money.

T   F   3.  The banking system's excess reserves ratio is negatively related to the market interest rate.

T   F   4.  The excess reserves ratio is negatively related to expected deposit outflows.

T   F   5.  When individuals reduce their holdings of currency by depositing these funds in their bank accounts, the money multiplier increases.

T   F   6.  If the Fed purchases $10,000 in government securities from a bank and simultaneously extends $10,000 in discount loans to the same bank, then the Fed has kept the monetary base from changing.

T   F   7.  The Fed has better control over the nonborrowed base than the borrowed base.

T   F   8.  As the currency ratio falls, fewer reserves are available to support checkable deposits causing a decrease in the money supply.

T   F   9.   For a given level of the monetary base, if the Fed began to pay interest on deposits that banks maintain at the Federal Reserve, banks would have greater incentive to hold excess reserves, which would lead to a decline in the money supply, all else constant.

T   F   10.   The money multiplier from the money supply model that includes depositor and bank behavior is larger than the simple deposit multiplier.

## Part B: Multiple-Choice Questions

Circle the appropriate answer.

1.   When comparing the simple model of multiple deposit creation with the money supply model that accounts for depositor and bank behavior, the more complicated model indicates that

    a.   an increase in the monetary base that goes into currency is not multiplied.
    b.   the money multiplier is negatively related to the currency ratio.
    c.   the money multiplier is positively related to the excess reserves ratio.
    d.   all of the above occur.
    e.   only (a) and (b) of the above

2.   The money multiplier increases in value as the

    a.   currency ratio increases.
    b.   excess reserves ratio increases.
    c.   required reserve ratio decreases.
    d.   required reserve ratio increases.

3.   Depositors often withdraw more currency from their bank accounts during Christmastime. Therefore, one would predict that

    a.   the money multiplier will tend to fall during Christmastime.
    b.   the money multiplier will tend to rise during Christmastime.
    c.   discount borrowing will tend to fall during Christmastime.
    d.   none of the above will occur.

4.   The Fed lacks complete control over the monetary base because

    a.   it cannot set the required reserve ratio on checkable deposits.
    b.   it cannot perfectly predict the amount of discount borrowing by banks.
    c.   it cannot perfectly predict shifts from deposits to currency.
    d.   of each of the above.
    e.   of only (a) and (b) of the above.

5.  The money multiplier is smaller than the simple deposit multiplier when

    a.  the currency ratio is greater than zero.
    b.  the excess reserves ratio is greater than zero.
    c.  the required reserve ratio on checkable deposits is greater than zero.
    d.  all of the above occur.
    e.  both (a) and (b) of the above occur.

6.  The money multiplier is negatively related to

    a.  the excess reserves ratio.
    b.  the currency ratio.
    c.  the required reserve ratio on checkable deposits.
    d.  all of the above.
    e.  only (a) and (b) of the above.

7.  For a given level of the monetary base, a drop in the excess reserve ratio means

    a.  an increase in the money supply.
    b.  an increase in the monetary base.
    c.  an increase in the nonborrowed base.
    d.  all of the above.
    e.  only (b) and (c) of the above.

8.  For a given level of the monetary base, a drop in the currency ratio means

    a.  an increase in the nonborrowed base, but a decrease in the borrowed base of equal magnitude.
    b.  an increase in the borrowed base, but a decrease in the nonborrowed base of equal magnitude.
    c.  an increase in the money supply.
    d.  a decrease in the money supply.
    e.  none of the above.

9.  If banks reduce their holdings of excess reserves,

    a.  the monetary base will increase.
    b.  the money supply will increase.
    c.  both (a) and (b) of the above will occur.
    d.  neither (a) nor (b) of the above will occur.

10. An examination of the 1980-1999 period indicates that

    a.  the primary determinant of movements in the money supply is the nonborrowed base.
    b.  the shorter the time period, the better is the Fed's control over the money supply.
    c.  both (a) and (b) of the above are true.
    d   neither (a) nor (b) of the above are true.

11. The banking system's excess reserves ratio is

    a. negatively related to both the market interest rate and expected deposit outflows.
    b. positively related to both the market interest rate and expected deposit outflows.
    c. positively related to the market interest rate and negatively related to expected deposit outflows.
    d. negatively related to the market interest rate and positively related to expected deposit outflows.

12. The monetary base less discount loans is called

    a. reserves.
    b. high-powered money.
    c. the nonborrowed monetary base.
    d. the borrowed monetary base.

13. If the required reserve ratio is one-fourth, currency in circulation is $400 billion, excess reserves are not held, and checkable deposits are $1200 billion, then the money multiplier is approximately

    a. 2.3.
    b. 2.8.
    c. 2.0.
    d. 1.8.

The following questions cover the material in the appendix.

14. The M2 money multiplier is _____ than M1 multiplier because the required reserve ratio for a time deposit or a money market mutual fund share is _____ than the reserve requirement for checkable deposits.

    a. larger; lower
    b. larger; higher
    c. smaller; lower
    d. smaller; higher

15. The M2 money multiplier is positive related to

    a. high-powered money.
    b. the time deposit-checkable deposit ratio.
    c. the required reserve ratio.
    d. the excess reserves ratio.

# Chapter 17

## *Tools of Monetary Policy*

## CHAPTER SYNOPSIS/COMPLETIONS

Chapter 17 examines how the Federal Reserve uses its three policy tools – open market operations, changes in the (1)_____ _____, and changes in (2)_____ _____ – to manipulate the money supply and interest rates. The chapter begins with a supply and demand analysis of the market for reserves to explain how the Fed's settings for these three tools determine the federal funds interest rate.

By far the most important monetary policy tool at the Fed's disposal is its ability to buy and sell Treasury (3)_____. Open market operations is the Fed's most important monetary policy tool because it is the primary determinant of changes in reserves. When the Fed makes an open market purchase, the supply curve in the market for reserves shifts to the right, thereby lowering the federal funds interest rate.

The primary cost of borrowing discount loans from the Fed is the discount rate. For a given federal funds rate, banks borrow more from the Fed as the discount rate falls. A lower discount rate thus shifts the supply of reserves to the right, lowering the federal funds rate. When the Fed raises the required reserve ratio, banks raise the demand for reserves in the federal funds market, thereby raising the federal funds interest rate.

There are two types of open market operations. Open market operations designed to change the level of reserves in an effort to influence economic activity are called (4)_____ open market operations. Defensive open market operations are intended to offset movements in other factors that affect the monetary base, such as changes in Treasury deposits and float.

Open market operations are conducted at the Federal Reserve Bank of New York and are supervised by the head of domestic open market operations, currently Sandy Krieger. Sandy and her staff review the previous day's developments in the federal funds market and consider factors that are likely to affect the supply and demand for reserves. After collecting this information, Sandy and her staff decide how large a change in reserves is needed to obtain a desired level of the federal funds rate. Further consultation with major participants in the funds market, the Treasury, and members of the Monetary Affairs Division of the board is undertaken before plans are made to add or drain reserves.

Most of the time, the trading desk engages in repurchase agreements (repos) or reverse repurchase agreements (reverse repos). A repo is actually a temporary open market (5)_____ that will be reversed within a few days, and it is often argued to be an especially effective way of conducting defensive open market operations. Matched sale-purchase transactions or (6)_____

132

_____ are used when the Federal Reserve wants to temporarily drain reserves from the banking system.

Open market operations have several advantages over the other tools of the Federal Reserve that make them particularly desirable:

1. Open market operations occur at the initiative of the Fed. The Fed has complete control over the volume of open market operations, giving it control over the federal funds interest rate.

2. Open market operations can be varied in any degree. Thus open market operations are said to be (7)_____.

3. Open market operations are easily reversed.

4. Open market operations can be implemented quickly.

Discount loans to banks are of three types. Adjustment credit loans are intended to help banks with short-term (8)_____ problems. Seasonal credit is extended to meet the needs of banks in vacation and agricultural areas that experience seasonal demands for funds. (9)_____ credit is given to banks that are experiencing severe liquidity problems due to net deposit outflows – the $5 billion discount loan to Continental Illinois in 1984 provides a recent example.

Because the discount rate is usually kept below the federal funds interest rate, the Fed limits how often a bank can come to the discount window. At the time of its creation, the Fed's most important role was intended to be as a (10)_____ _____ _____ _____ so that the country might avoid financial panics as had occurred in 1893 and 1907. Unfortunately, the Fed failed in its role as lender of last resort during the Great Depression.

Some critics of the Federal Reserve now contend that discount borrowing ought to be eliminated. They argue that since the creation of the FDIC, the Fed's role of lender of last resort provides no useful purpose. Supporters counter that the Fed's role of lender of last resort complements the function of the FDIC and is not limited to the banking system, as when the Fed announced its intention to provide liquidity to the financial markets following the stock market crash in October 1987. Although discount rate changes can be used to change expectations that may reinforce the direction of monetary policy, the most important advantage of discount policy is that the Fed can use it to perform its role of lender of last resort.

While open market operations and discount policy influence the money supply by altering the monetary base, a change in reserve requirements changes the value of the (11)_____ _____. Because changes in reserve requirements are so powerful and costly to administer they are rarely used.

Two interesting reforms of reserve requirements have been proposed that proponents contend should improve monetary control. Some economists believe that reserve requirements should be eliminated because they act as a tax on banks. Abolishment of reserve requirements, however, could potentially make the money multiplier less stable, hampering monetary policy. Other economists suggest setting reserve requirements equal to (12)_____ of deposits. The desirability of this proposal rests on the assumption that financial institutions would develop no new liabilities to compete with checks. The discussion in another chapter suggests that 100 percent reserve banking – should it foster new financial innovations – might actually hamper the Fed's ability to control the money supply.

## EXERCISES

### Exercise 1: Supply and Demand in the Market for Reserves

**FIGURE 17A**

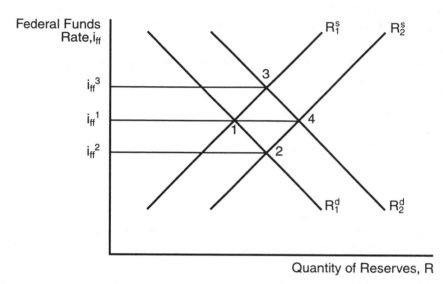

Refer to Figure 17A to complete the following statements regarding the Fed's use of its monetary policy tools to affect the federal funds interest rate.

1. Starting from point 1, if the Fed purchases U.S. Treasury securities, the _____ curve shifts to the _____, and the federal funds interest rate _____.

2. Starting from point 1, if the Fed lowers the discount rate, the _____ curve shifts to the _____,and the federal funds interest rate _____.

3. Starting from point 2, if the Fed raises the discount rate, as it did on May 16, 2000, the _____ curve shifts to the _____,and the federal funds interest rate _____.

4. Starting from point 4, if the Fed sells U.S. Treasury securities, the _____ curve shifts to the _____, and the federal funds interest rate _____.

5. Starting from point 3, if the Fed lowers reserve requirements, the _____ curve shifts to the _____,and the federal funds interest rate _____.

6. Starting from point 2, if the Fed raises reserve requirements, the _____ curve shifts to the _____,and the federal funds interest rate _____.

7. Starting from point 3, if the Fed purchases U.S. Treasury securities, the _____ curve shifts to the _____, and the federal funds interest rate _____.

## Exercise 2: Definitions and Terminology

Match the following terms on the right with the definition or description on the left. Place the letter of the term in the blank provided next to the appropriate definition.

_____ 1. Intended role of the Federal Reserve System at its inception

a. adjustment credit

_____ 2. Discount loan to meet short-term liquidity problems.

b. extended credit

_____ 3. Intended to offset temporary changes in factors affecting the monetary base.

c. dynamic open market operations

_____ 4. The FOMC directive is interpreted and implemented here.

d. defensive open market operations

_____ 5. Intended to affect economic activity by changing the monetary base.

e. matched sale purchase agreement (reverse repo)

_____ 6. Discount loan to meet the more serious problem of large deposit outflows.

f. repurchase agreement (repo)

_____ 7. Employed when the Fed wishes to temporarily absorb reserves.

g. lender of last resort

_____ 8. A change in this monetary policy tool causes the money multiplier to change.

h. Trading Desk

_____ 9. This monetary policy tool complements the Fed's role as lender of last resort.

i. reserve requirements

_____ 10. Employed when the Fed wishes to temporarily inject reserves into the system.

j. discount lending

## Exercise 3: Open Market Operations

A. Why is open market operations the most important monetary policy tool?

_____

_____

B. What are the two types of open market operations?

1. _____

2. _____

C. List the advantages of open market operations.

1. _____

2. _____

3. _____

4. _____

## Exercise 4: Discount Policy

A. List the three types of discount loans.

1. _____

2. _____

3. _____

B. Why might it be important to have a lender of last resort even with the existence of deposit insurance?

_____

_____

## Exercise 5: Reserve Requirements

A.  List two reasons why changes in reserve requirements are rarely used as a policy tool to conduct monetary policy.

1. _____

_____

2. _____

_____

B. Because of the disadvantages of using reserve requirements as a policy tool, some economists have suggested fixing reserve requirements at 100%. What is the main advantage of this proposal?

_____

_____

What is the main disadvantage of this proposal?

_____

_____

## SELF-TEST

### Part A: True-False Questions

Circle whether the following statements are true (T) or false (F).

T  F  1.  Open market operations are the most important monetary policy tool because they are the most important determinant of changes in the money multiplier, the main source of fluctuations in the money supply.

T  F  2.  Defensive open market operations are intended to change the level of reserves and the monetary base in an effort to influence economic activity.

T  F  3.  When the Fed purchases or sells a security in the open market, it is most likely trading in U.S. Treasury bills.

T  F  4.  The Fed has less than complete control over the volume of open market operations because banks can refuse to buy Treasury securities.

T  F  5.  Because banks in agricultural areas experience greater demands for funds in the spring, the Federal Reserve issues adjustment credit to these banks when they have deficient reserves.

T  F  6.  Evidence from the past twenty years suggests that Fed discount policy has approximated to some degree the variable discount rate proposal.

T  F  7.  The Fed's role of lender of last resort may still be useful even though deposit insurance has reduced the probability of bank panics.

T  F  8.  Changes in the discount rate may signal a change in monetary policy or may be an adjustment to a change in market interest rates, making it difficult to decipher the Fed's intentions regarding monetary policy.

T  F  9.  Abolishing discounting would reduce fluctuations in the borrowed base.

T   F   10.   Assume that the required reserve ratio set by the Fed exceeds that desired by banks, which tends to be volatile.  Then eliminating reserve requirements may tend to increase the instability in the money multiplier.

## Part B: Multiple-Choice Questions

Circle the appropriate answer.

1.   Open market operations are of two types:

    a.   defensive and offensive.
    b.   dynamic and reactionary.
    c.   actionary and passive.
    d.   dynamic and defensive.

2.   If the Federal Reserve wants to inject reserves into the banking system, it will usually

    a.   purchase government securities.
    b.   raise the discount rate.
    c.   sell government securities.
    d.   lower reserve requirements.
    e.   do either (a) or (b) of the above.

3.   To temporarily raise reserves in the banking system, the Fed engages in

    a.   a repurchase agreement.
    b.   a reverse repo.
    c.   a matched sale-purchase transaction.
    d.   none of the above.

4.   When float increases, causing a temporary increase in reserves in the banking system, the Fed can offset the effects of float by engaging in

    a.   a repurchase agreement.
    b.   an interest rate swap.
    c.   a matched sale-purchase transaction.
    d.   none of the above.

5.   The type of discount loan extended by the Fed in its role of lender of last resort is called

    a.   adjustment credit.
    b.   seasonal credit.
    c.   extended credit.
    d.   installment credit.

6. Which of the following proposed policies would tend to reduce instability in the monetary base?

    a. Penalty discount rate
    b. Discount rate that is tied to market interest rates
    c. Elimination of discounting
    d. All of the above
    e. Only (a) and (c) of the above

7. Changes in the reserve requirements are infrequently used for changing the money supply because

    a. reserve requirement changes tend to be powerful and are costly for banks to adjust to.
    b. reserve requirement changes tend to be ineffective.
    c. reserve requirement changes must be approved by the president.
    d. of only (a) and (c) of the above.
    e. of none of the above.

8. A reduction in reserve requirements causes the money supply to rise, since the change causes

    a. the money multiplier to fall.
    b. the money multiplier to rise.
    c. reserves to fall.
    d. reserves to rise.

9. Because the discount rate is frequently kept below the federal funds interest rate,

    a. the Fed must ration discount loans on a first-come, first-serve basis.
    b. the Fed limits how often a bank can come to the discount window.
    c. the Fed refuses to extend discount credit to banks that are not members of the Federal Reserve System.
    d. none of the above occurs.

10 Under 100% reserve banking, the money multiplier will be

    a. 0.
    b. 1.
    c. 10.
    d. 100.

11. Advantages of tying the discount rate to a market rate of interest include

    a. increasing the confusion concerning the Fed's intentions about future monetary policy because of the uncertainty about what a change in the discount rate is intended to signal.
    b. reducing the large fluctuations in the money multiplier from even small changes in the discount rate.
    c. simplifying the Fed's administration of the discount window.
    d. only (a) and (c) of the above.

12. When the Fed engages in a matched sale-purchase agreement, it _____ securities which the other party agrees to _____ sell back within a few days.

   a. buys; buy
   b. buys; sell
   c. sells; buy
   d. sells; sell

13. When the Fed wants to conduct a _____ open market _____, it engages in a _____.

   a. permanent; purchase; reverse repo
   b. permanent; purchase; repurchase agreement
   c. temporary; sale; reverse repo
   d. temporary; sale; repurchase agreement
   e. temporary; purchase; reverse repo

14. The Fed extends _____ credit to banks that are expecting chronic deposit outflows.

   a. adjustment
   b. seasonal
   c. extended
   d. emergency

15. If either Treasury deposits or foreign deposits at the Fed are predicted to _____, a _____ open market _____ would be needed to offset the expected decrease in the monetary base.

   a. rise; dynamic; purchase
   b. fall; dynamic; sale
   c. rise; defensive; purchase
   d. fall; defensive; purchase

16. When the Fed raises the discount rate, as it did on May 16, 2000, the _____ curve in the market for reserves shifts to the _____, thereby causing the federal funds interest rate to _____.

   a. supply; right; fall
   b. supply; right; rise
   c. supply; left; rise
   d. demand; right; fall
   e. demand; left; rise

# Chapter 18

## *Conduct of Monetary Policy: Goals and Targets*

### CHAPTER SYNOPSIS/COMPLETIONS

This first section of the chapter discusses the important goals that central banks attempt to achieve through their conduct of monetary policy and regulatory duties. The general operating strategy employed by central Banks to achieve these goals is presented in the second part of the chapter. The third section ties together the first two sections by examining the Fed's past policy procedures. This historical perspective provides important insights when it comes to assessing current and future monetary policy actions. The chapter concludes with a brief discussion of the Taylor rule as a guide for setting the federal funds rate.

The chapter presents six basic goals most often mentioned by personnel at the Federal Reserve and other central banks as objectives of monetary policy:

(1)_____

(2)_____

(3)_____

(4)_____

(5)_____

(6)_____

The Employment Act of 1946 and the Humphrey-Hawkins Act of 1978 commit the government to promoting high employment. By high employment, economists mean a level of unemployment consistent with labor market equilibrium. This level of unemployment is the (7)_____ _____ of unemployment.

Of these goals, price stability has received more attention in recent years. Many economists now believe that an inflationary environment distorts relative prices and makes planning for the future difficult, thereby slowing economic growth over time.

Because exchange rate fluctuations have a greater relative impact on the domestic economy now that international financial and goods markets have become more integrated, the Federal Reserve no longer treats the United States as a closed economy. Now, when deciding the course of monetary policy, the Fed pays careful attention to the expected change in the value of the dollar.

Although achieving all the above-mentioned goals would be highly desirable, conflicts arise between goals in the short run.  Higher employment or interest rate stability may mean (8)_____ inflation. Since expansionary monetary policies initially tend to stimulate aggregate output and employment and lower interest rates, such policies appear attractive at first.  But an expansionary monetary policy will lead to inflationary pressures if continued for long.  Thus the Federal Reserve faces difficult trade-offs and must weigh the benefits and costs of each action if it is to promote economic well-being.

Since the Fed's control over policy goals is imprecise, the Fed employs an intermediate targeting strategy to guide monetary policy.  The Fed judges its actions by observing the behavior of an intermediate target, such as an interest rate.  The intermediate target provides a readily available proxy (the Fed hopes that it does, anyway) for the Fed's goals which it manipulates through variations in its (9)_____ target.  In turn, the Fed changes its operating target, say, the federal funds interest rate, through use of its policy tools, primarily  (10)_____ operations.

In general, the Fed has a choice between targeting a monetary aggregate or an interest rate such as the federal funds interest rate.  Here again, the Federal Reserve faces a trade-off; if it targets a monetary aggregate, interest rate volatility is likely to increase, and if it targets the federal funds rate, it loses control over the (11)_____ supply.

The policy of intermediate targeting suggests three criteria for choosing between an interest rate and a monetary aggregate target.  The target must be measurable, as well as (12)_____ by the Fed, and it must have a predictable effect on the goal.

An examination of past Federal Reserve policy procedures indicates that Fed policy mistakes have led to severe contractions and rapid inflations.  Unfortunately, the Fed has often been extremely slow to alter procedures despite the warnings of economists.  History seems to indicate that nothing less than an economic crisis is necessary to convince the Fed of the inadequacy of its procedures.

Although the jury is still out, examination of Federal Reserve monetary policy from October of 1979 through October of 1982 suggests that Paul Volcker's statements regarding control of monetary aggregates provided a smokescreen that permitted the Fed to fight inflation.  The announced change in operating procedures allowed the Fed to increase interest rates sharply and slow economic activity to combat the rapidly rising price level.  This interpretation of events provides one explanation for the volatility in both interest rates and monetary aggregates during this period.

In late 1982 – inflation having declined to an acceptable level – the Fed returned to a policy of smoothing interest rates, shifting to borrowed reserves as an operating target.  In the early 1990s, the Fed changed its operating target, returning to a federal funds interest rate target.  This time, however, the Fed adopted a new policy procedure.  In February 1994, the Fed decided that it would henceforth announce changes in its federal funds target.  Taking one additional step, the Fed, in February 2000, began announcing the *bias*–the likely direction of future changes in the federal funds interest rate.

A controversial theory suggesting how the Fed should set the federal funds interest rate has been proposed by Stanford economist John Taylor.  The Taylor-rule setting for the federal funds rate is equal to the inflation rate plus the weighted average of two gaps: (1) an inflation gap, current inflation minus a target rate, and (2) an output gap, the percentage deviation of real GDP from an estimate of its full employment potential.

## EXERCISES

### Exercise 1: Intermediate and Operating Targets

Although there is some ambiguity as to whether a particular variable is better categorized as an intermediate target or an operating target, list below those variables generally thought to be in each category.

A.  Intermediate targets

1. _____

2. _____

3. _____

B.  Operating targets

1. _____

2. _____

### Exercise 2: Criteria for Choosing Intermediate Targets

Selecting an intermediate target requires careful thought by members of the Federal Open Market Committee.  The wrong choice can mean adverse consequences for the economy.  Debate has tended to center around the choice between targeting a monetary aggregate or an interest rate. List the three criteria for choosing one variable as an intermediate target over another.

1. _____

2. _____

3. _____

### Exercise 3: The Taylor Rule for the Federal Funds Rate

For the information given, use the Taylor rule to determine the approrpriate setting of the federal funds rate under the assumption that the central bank uses the Taylor rule to determine the appropriate federal funds interest rate.

| Inflation Rate | Equilibrium Federal Funds Rate | Inflation Target | Percentage Deviation of Real GDP from Potential GDP | Federal Funds Rate |
|---|---|---|---|---|
| 3% | 2% | 2% | 1% | _____ |
| 4% | 2% | 2% | 1% | _____ |
| 4% | 2% | 2% | 2% | _____ |
| 4% | 2% | 2% | −1% | _____ |
| 4% | 2% | 2% | −2% | _____ |
| 5% | 2% | 2% | 1% | _____ |
| 1% | 2% | 2% | −2% | _____ |
| 1% | 2% | 2% | 1% | _____ |

## SELF-TEST

### Part A: True-False Questions

Circle whether the following statements are true (T) or false (F).

T  F  1. The Federal Reserve desires interest rate stability because it reduces the uncertainty of future planning.

T  F  2. The Federal Reserve attempts to get the unemployment rate to zero, since any unemployment is wasteful and inefficient.

T  F  3. The discount rate is the Fed's preferred operating target.

T  F  4. If the Fed targets a monetary aggregate, it is likely to lose control over the interest rate because of fluctuations in the money demand function.

T  F  5. A monetary aggregate, such as M1, is often referred to as an operating target.

T  F  6. Open market operations did not play an important policy role in the Federal Reserve System until about the 1960s.

T  F  7. The passage of the Banking Act of 1935 limited the Fed's ability to alter reserve requirements by requiring it to secure presidential approval.

T  F  8. Treasury influence over the Fed was reduced when the Fed and Treasury came to an agreement known as the "Accord."

T  F  9. The difference between excess reserves and discount loans is known as free reserves.

T  F  10. While the Fed professed an interest in stabilizing interest rates, its actions during the 1960s and 1970s indicates that the Fed seemed to be preoccupied with stabilizing money growth.

### Part B: Multiple-Choice Questions

Circle the appropriate answer.

1. Even if the Fed could completely control the money supply, not everyone would be happy with monetary policy, since

   a. the Fed is asked to achieve many goals, some of which are incompatible with one another.
   b. the goals that are stressed by the Fed do not include high employment, making labor unions a vocal critic of Fed policies.
   c. the Fed places primary emphasis on exchange rate stability, often to the detriment of domestic conditions.
   d. its mandate requires it to keep Treasury security prices high.

2. Because timely information on the price level and economic growth is generally unavailable, the Fed has adopted a strategy of

   a. targeting the exchange rate, since the Fed has the ability to control this variable.
   b. targeting the price of gold, since it is closely related to economic activity.
   c. using an intermediate target such as an interest rate.
   d. stabilizing the consumer price index, since the Fed has a high degree of control over the CPI.

3. Which of the following are potential operating targets?

   a. Monetary base
   b. borrowed reserves
   c. Federal funds interest rate
   d. Nonborrowed monetary base
   e. All of the above

4. Fluctuations in money demand will cause the Fed to lose control over a monetary aggregate if the Fed emphasizes

   a. a monetary aggregate target.
   b. an interest-rate target.
   c. a nominal GNP target.
   d. all of the above.

5. While the Fed professed to target monetary aggregates in the 1970s, its behavior indicates that it actually targeted

   a. exchange rates.
   b. nominal GNP.
   c. nominal interest rates.
   d. the monetary base.

6. Many economists question the desirability of targeting real interest rates by pointing out that

   a. the Fed does not have direct control over real interest rates.
   b. changes in real interest rates have little effect on economic activity.
   c. real interest rates are extremely difficult to measure.
   d. all of the above are correct.
   e. only (a) and (c) of the above are correct.

7. The Fed's policy of keeping interest rates low to help the Treasury finance World War I by re-discounting eligible paper caused

   a. inflation to accelerate.
   b. aggregate output to decline sharply.
   c. the Fed to rethink the efficacy of the real bills doctrine.
   d. both (a) and (b) of the above.
   e. both (a) and (c) of the above.

8.  The Fed added to the problems it helped create in the early 1930s by

    a.  raising the discount rate in 1936-1937.
    b.  raising reserve requirements in 1936-1937.
    c.  contracting the monetary base in 1936-1937.
    d.  expanding the monetary base in 1936-1937.

9.  The March 1951 Accord gave the Fed greater freedom to let

    a.  interest rates rise.
    b.  unemployment rise.
    c.  interest rates fall.
    d.  inflation accelerate.

10. The Fed's policy of "leaning against the wind" through targeting free reserves and the federal funds interest rate actually proved to be

    a.  anticipated.
    b.  procyclical.
    c.  neutral.
    d.  stabilizing.

11. The real bills doctrine proved to be

    a.  inflationary during and after World War I.
    b.  inflationary during and after World War II.
    c.  deflationary during and after World War I.
    d.  deflationary during and after World War II.

12. The Fed's use of _____ as a guide to monetary policy in the 1960s proved a failure since it lead to _____ monetary growth.

    a.  commodity prices; procyclical
    b.  commodity prices; countercyclical
    c.  free reserves; procyclical
    d.  free reserves; countercyclical

13. In October 1982, the Fed changed to a policy of smoothing interest rates, thereby shifting to _____ as an operating target.

    a.  the monetary base
    b.  borrowed reserves
    c.  the federal funds interest rate
    d.  nonborrowed reserves

14. The strengthening dollar between 1980 and 1985

   a.   contributed to a deterioration in American competitiveness, putting pressure on the Fed to pursue a more contractionary monetary policy.
   b.   contributed to an improvement in American competitiveness, putting pressure on the Fed to pursue a more contractionary monetary policy.
   c.   contributed to a deterioration in American competitiveness, putting pressure on the Fed to pursue a more expansionary monetary policy.
   d.   contributed to an improvement in American competitiveness, putting pressure on the Fed to pursue a more expansionary monetary policy.

15. Federal reserve monetary policy in the 1990s was characterized by

   a.   a return to using the federal funds interest rate as an operating target.
   b.   a policy of preemptive strikes to head of any future inflationary pressures.
   c.   a return to using monetary aggregates as operating targets.
   d.   both (a) and (b) of the above.
   e.   both (b) and (c) of the above.

# Chapter 19

## *The International Financial System*

### CHAPTER SYNOPSIS/COMPLETIONS

The growing interdependence of the United States with other economies of the world means that our monetary policy is influenced by international financial transactions. Chapter 19 examines the international financial system and explores how it affects the way our monetary policy is conducted.

The current international environment in which exchange rates fluctuate from day to day is called a managed-float or a (1)_____ float regime. In a managed-float regime, central banks allow rates to fluctuate but intervene in the foreign exchange market in order to influence exchange rates. Interventions are of two types. An unsterilized central bank intervention in which the domestic currency is sold to purchase foreign assets leads to a gain in international reserves, an (2)_____ in the money supply, and a depreciation of the domestic currency. Sterilized central bank interventions have little effect on the exchange rate.

The balance of payments is a bookkeeping system for recording all payments that have a direct bearing on the movement of funds between countries. All payments from foreigners are entered as (3)_____ while all payments to foreigners are entered as debits. The current account shows international transactions that involve currently produced goods and services. The difference between merchandise exports and imports is called the (4)_____ _____. The capital account describes the flow of capital between the United States and other countries. The official reserves transaction balance is the sum of the current account balance plus the items in the capital account. It indicates the amount of international reserves that must move between countries to finance international transactions.

A change in a country's holdings of international reserves leads to an equal change in its monetary base, which, in turn, affects the money supply. A currency like the U.S. dollar, which is used by other countries to denominate the assets they hold as international reserves, is called a (5)_____ _____. A reserve currency country (the United States) has the advantage over other countries that balance of payments deficits or surpluses do not lead to changes in holdings of international reserves and the monetary base.

Before World War I, the world economy operated under a gold standard, under which the currencies of most countries were convertible directly into gold, thereby fixing exchange rates between countries. After World War II, the Bretton Woods system was established in order to promote a (6)_____ exchange rate system in which the U.S. dollar was convertible into gold. The Bretton Woods agreement created the International Monetary Fund (IMF), which was given the task of promoting the growth of world trade by setting rules for the maintenance of fixed exchange rates and by making loans to countries that were experiencing balance of payments difficulties. The Bretton Woods agreement also set up the World Bank in order to provide long-term loans to assist developing countries to build dams, roads, and other physical capital.

The Bretton Woods system – because it did not allow for smooth and gradual adjustments in exchange rates when they became necessary – was often characterized by destabilizing balance-of-payments crises. Because countries resisted revaluing their currencies, the Bretton Woods system was characterized by "fundamental disequilibrium." The Bretton Woods system finally collapsed in 1971. The European Monetary System, because it is a (7)_____ exchange rate system like the Bretton Woods system, suffers the potential weakness of exchange rate crises characterized by "speculative attacks" – that is, a massive sale of a weak currency (or purchases of a strong currency) that would hasten the change in exchange rates.

The international financial system has evolved into the current (8)_____ _____ regime, in which central banks intervene in the foreign exchange market, but exchange rates fluctuate from day to day.

Because capital flows were an important element in the currency crises in Mexico (1994) and East Asia (1997), politicians and some economists have advocated restricting capital mobility in emerging market countries. Controls on capital outflows could potentially prevent an emerging market country from being forced to (9)_____ its currency, which would otherwise exacerbate a financial crisis. Empirical evidence, however, indicates that controls are seldom effective during a crisis. Indeed, controls on capital outflows may be counterproductive because confidence in the government is weakened.

The case for controls on capital (10)_____ is stronger, as capital inflows can lead to a lending boom and excessive risk taking on the part of banks, which then helps trigger a financial crisis. Although the case for controls on capital inflows seems plausible, this regulation can lead to corruption and a serious misallocation of resources in the emerging market country.

Three international considerations affect the conduct of monetary policy: direct effects of the foreign exchange market on the money supply, balance of payments considerations, and (9)_____ _____ considerations. If a central bank intervenes in the foreign exchange market to keep its strong currency from appreciating, as did the German central bank in the early 1970s, it (10)_____ international reserves, and the monetary base and the money supply (11)_____. To prevent this, the central bank might engage in sterilization, which involves offsetting any increase in international reserves with equal open market sales of domestic securities in order to prevent the monetary base from rising. In order to prevent balance of payments deficits, a country's central bank might pursue (12)_____ monetary policy.

Monetary policy is also affected by exchange rate considerations. Because an appreciation of the currency causes domestic businesses to suffer from increased foreign competition, a central bank might (13)_____ the rate of money growth in order to lower the exchange rate. Similarly, because a (14)_____ of the currency hurts consumers and stimulates inflation, a central bank might slow the rate of money growth in order to prop up the exchange rate. Because the United States has been a reserve-currency country in the post-World War II period, U.S. monetary policy has been less affected by developments in the foreign exchange market than is true for other countries.

## EXERCISES

### Exercise 1: The Balance of Payments

Suppose that the U.S. economy in 2004 has generated the following data (in billions of dollars) for items in the balance of payments:

| | | | |
|---|---|---|---|
| Merchandise exports | 500 | Capital outflows | 50 |
| Merchandise imports | 600 | Capital inflows | 100 |
| Net investment income | -40 | Increase in U.S. official reserve assets | 5 |
| Net services | 20 | Increase in foreign official assets | 25 |
| Net unilateral transfers | -15 | | |

Fill in the figures for all the numbered items in the balance of payments table below. (Hint: The Statistical Discrepancy item is deduced from the fact that the balance of payments must balance.)

### U.S. Balance of Payments in 2004 (billions of dollars)

| | Receipts (+) | Payments (-) | Balance |
|---|---|---|---|
| **Current account:** | | | |
| 1. Merchandise exports | | | |
| 2. Merchandise imports | | | |
| 3. Trade balance | | | |
| 4. Net investment income | | | |
| 5. Net services | | | |
| 6. Net unilateral transfers | | | |
| 7. Current account balance | | | |

| | | | |
|---|---|---|---|
| **Capital account:** | | | |
| 8. Capital outflows | | | |
| 9. Capital inflows | | | |
| 10. Statistical discrepancy | | | |
| 11. Official reserves transactions balance | | | |

| | | | |
|---|---|---|---|
| **Method of financing:** | | | |
| 12. Increase in U.S. official reserve assets | | | |
| 13. Increase in foreign official assets | | | |
| 14. Total financing of surplus | | | |

## Exercise 2: Definitions and Terminology

Match the following terms on the right with the definition or description on the left.  Place the letter of the term in the blank provided next to the appropriate definition.  Terms may be used once, more than once, or not at all.

_____ 1.  A bookkeeping system for recording all payments that have a direct bearing on the movement of funds between a country and foreign countries.

a.  Speculative attack

_____ 2.  Account that shows international transactions that involve currently produced goods and services.

b.  Balance of payments

_____ 3.  Merchandise exports less imports.

c.  Gold standard

_____ 4.  Account that describes the flow of capital between the United States and other countries.

d.  Trade balance

_____ 5.  Massive sales of a weak currency or purchases of a strong currency that hasten a change in the exchange rate.

e.  Current account

_____ 6.  The current account balance plus items in the capital account.

f.  Reserve currency

_____ 7.  A situation in which the par value of a currency is reset at a lower level.

g.  Capital account

_____ 8.  A currency (like the U.S. dollar) that is used by other countries to denominate the assets they hold as international reserves.

h.  Bretton Woods

_____ 9.  A regime under which the currency of most countries is directly convertible into gold.

i.  Devalue

_____ 10.  The international monetary system in use from use from 1945 to 1971 in which exchange rates were fixed and the U.S. dollar was freely convertible into gold (by foreign governments and central banks only).

j.  Official Reserve Transactions Balance

**Exercise 3: Effects of Intervention in the Foreign Exchange Market and the Monetary Base**

Suppose that Americans are buying $1 billion more goods and assets from Mexicans than the Mexicans are buying from the United States.  If Americans pay for the Mexican goods and assets with dollars, the T-accounts for the American and Mexican public are as follows:

| American Public | | Mexican Public | |
|---|---|---|---|
| Assets | Liabilities | Assets | Liabilities |
| Mexican goods and assets<br>  + $ 1 billion<br>U.S. dollars<br>  - $1 billion | | Mexican goods and assets<br>  - $1 billion<br>U.S. dollars<br>  + $1 billion | |

Because Mexicans carry out their daily purchases with pesos, they will sell their dollars in the foreign exchange market to buy pesos.  If the Mexican central bank does not want the pesos to appreciate, they must buy the dollars the Mexican public is holding.

A.  After the Mexican central bank intervenes in the foreign exchange market, what is the effect on the balance sheet of the Mexican public and the Mexican central bank?  Answer this question by filling in the amounts in the balance sheets below.

| Mexican Central Bank | | Mexican Public | |
|---|---|---|---|
| Assets | Liabilities | Assets | Liabilities |
| U.S. dollars | Mexican pesos | Mexican goods and assets<br><br>U.S. dollars<br><br>Mexican pesos | |

What is the effect on the Mexican monetary base from the Mexican central bank's purchase of  the $1 billion of dollars?

_____

What is the effect on the Mexican central bank's holdings of international reserves?

_____

B.  If the U.S. dollar is a reserve currency so that the Mexican central bank uses its $1 billion  of dollars to buy U.S. securities from the American public, then what is the final outcome for the balance sheets of the American public and the Mexican central bank?  Answer this question by filling in the amounts in the balance sheets below.

| Mexican Central Bank | | American Public | |
|---|---|---|---|
| Assets | Liabilities | Assets | Liabilities |
| U.S. dollars | Mexican pesos | Mexican goods and assets | |
| U.S. securities | | U.S. dollars | |
| | | U.S. securities | |

What is the net effect on the U.S. monetary base from the Mexican central bank's intervention in the foreign exchange market?

_____

What effect is there on the foreign official assets entry in the U.S. balance of payments?

_____

## Exercise 4: How a Fixed Exchange Rate Regime Works

The most important feature of the Bretton Woods system was that it established a fixed exchange rate regime. Figure 19A describes a situation in which the domestic currency is initially overvalued: the expected return on the foreign deposits schedule ($RET^F_1$) intersects the expected return on domestic deposits schedule ($RET^D_1$) at an exchange rate that is below the fixed par rate, $E_{par}$.

FIGURE 19A

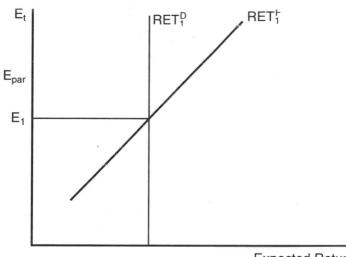

A.  Complete the following statements:

1.  In order to return the exchange rate to equilibrium at $E_{par}$, the central bank must intervene in the foreign exchange market to _____ the domestic currency by _____ foreign assets.

2.  The central bank's purchase of domestic currency has the effect of _____ the money supply, causes the interest rate on domestic deposits to _____, and shifts the expected return schedule on domestic deposits to the _____.

B.  Illustrate the effect of a central bank's purchase of domestic currency in Figure 19A by shifting the $RET^D$.

## Exercise 5: The IMF as a Lender of Last Resort

The IMF no longer attempts to encourage fixed exchange rates, but as is true of other agencies that have lost their missions, the IMF has discovered a new mission—it has taken on the role of an international lender of last resort.  List the advantages and disadvantages of this new role for the IMF.

A.  Advantages of the IMF as an International Lender of Last Resort.

1.  _____

_____

2.  _____

_____

B. Disadvantages of the IMF as an International Lender of Last Resort.

1.  _____

_____

2.  _____

_____

3.  _____

_____

4.  _____

_____

## SELF-TEST

### Part A: True-False Questions

Circle whether the following statements are true (T) or false (F).

T   F   1.   The capital account balance indicates whether the country is increasing or decreasing its claims on foreign wealth.

T   F   2.   The current account balance equals the difference between exports and imports.

T   F   3.   When the domestic currency is undervalued in a fixed exchange rate regime, the country's central bank must intervene in the foreign exchange market to purchase the domestic currency by selling foreign assets.

T   F   4.   The gold standard of the late nineteenth century always prevented inflation from developing.

T   F   5.   A particular problem with a fixed exchange rate system (or regime) is that it is periodically subject to speculative attacks on currencies.

T   F   6.   Special drawing rights (SDRs) are IMF loans to member countries.

T   F   7.   The World Bank makes loans to countries suffering balance of payments difficulties.

T   F   8.   The current international financial system is perhaps best described as a hybrid of fixed and flexible exchange rate systems.

T   F   9.   The IMF has, since the 1980s, been acting as an international lender of last resort.

T   F   10.   Monetary policy in a reserve currency country is less influenced by balance of payments deficits because they will be financed by other countries' interventions in the foreign exchange market.

### Part B: Multiple-Choice Questions

Circle the appropriate answer.

1.   Which of the following appear as debits in the U.S. balance of payments?

   a.   French purchases of American jeans
   b.   Purchases by Japanese tourists in the United States
   c.   American exports of Apple computers
   d.   Income earned by Coca-Cola from its factories abroad

2.  Which of the following appears in the current account part of the balance of payments?

    a.  An Italian's purchase of IBM stock
    b.  Income earned by Barclay's Bank of London, England, from subsidiaries in the United States
    c.  A loan by a Swiss bank to an American corporation
    d.  A purchase by the Federal Reserve System of an English Treasury bond
    e.  None of the above

3.  If Americans are buying $1 billion more English goods and assets than the English are willing to buy from the United States, and so the Bank of England therefore sells $1 billion worth of pounds in the foreign exchange market, then

    a.  England gains $1 billion of international reserves and its monetary base rises by $1 billion.
    b.  England loses $1 billion of international reserves and its monetary base falls by $1 billion.
    c.  England gains $1 billion of international reserves and its monetary base falls by $1 billion.
    d.  England loses $1 billion of international reserves and its monetary base rises by $1 billion.
    e.  England's level of international reserves and monetary base remains unchanged.

4.  An important advantage for a reserve currency country is that

    a.  its balance of payments deficits are financed by other countries' interventions in the foreign exchange market.
    b.  it has more control over its monetary policy than non-reserve currency countries.
    c.  it has more control over its exchange rate than non-reserve currency countries.
    d.  both (a) and (b) of the above are true.

5.  Under a gold standard in which one dollar could be turned into the U.S. Treasury and exchanged for 1/20th of an ounce of gold and one Swiss franc could be exchanged for 1/60th of an ounce of gold,

    a.  at an exchange rate of 4 francs per dollar, gold would flow from the United States to Switzerland and the Swiss monetary base would fall.
    b.  at an exchange rate of 4 francs per dollar, gold would flow from Switzerland to the United States and the Swiss monetary base would rise.
    c.  at an exchange rate of 2 francs per dollar, gold would flow from the United States to Switzerland and the U.S. monetary base would fall.
    d.  at an exchange rate of 2 francs per dollar, gold would flow from Switzerland to the United States and the U.S. monetary base would rise.

6.  In a speculative attack against a weak currency under a fixed exchange rate system, the central bank for this country must shift the expected return schedule for domestic deposits further to the _____ through the _____ of international reserves.

    a.  left; purchase
    b.  right; sale
    c.  left; sale
    d.  right; purchase

7. Countries with deficits in their balance of payments often do not want to see their currencies depreciate because

   a. this would hurt consumers in their country by making foreign goods more expensive.
   b. this would stimulate inflation.
   c. this would hurt domestic businesses by making foreign goods cheaper in their country.
   d. this would hurt domestic businesses by making their goods more expensive abroad.
   e. of both (a) and (b) of the above.

8. The International Monetary Fund is an international organization that

   a. promotes the growth of trade by setting rules for how tariffs and quotas are set by countries.
   b. makes loans to countries to finance projects such as dams and roads.
   c. since the 1980s, has been acting as an international lender of last resort.
   d. does each of the above.

9. When a central bank buys its currency in the foreign exchange market,

   a. they acquire international reserves.
   b. they lose international reserves.
   c. the money supply will increase.
   d. both (a) and (b) of the above occur.

10. A central bank's international reserves rise when

   a. it sells domestic currency to purchase foreign assets in the foreign exchange market.
   b. it sells foreign currency to purchase domestic assets in the foreign exchange market.
   c. it buys domestic currency with the sale of foreign assets in the foreign exchange market.
   d. it buys gold with the sale of foreign assets in the foreign exchange market.

11. Under the Bretton Woods system, the dollar was _____ if the _____ exchange rate (expressed as units of foreign currency per dollar) was _____ the _____ value of the exchange rate.

   a. overvalued; equilibrium; below; par
   b. overvalued; equilibrium; above; par
   c. undervalued; par; above; equilibrium
   d. undervalued; equilibrium; below; par

12. A central bank that wants to _____ strengthen its currency is likely to adopt a _____ monetary policy.

   a. strengthen; less contractionary
   b. strengthen; more contractionary
   c. weaken; less expansionary
   d. weaken; more contractionary

13. A central bank _____ of domestic currency and corresponding _____ of foreign assets in the foreign exchange market leads to an equal decline in its international _____ and the monetary base.

    a. sale; purchase; reserves
    b. sale; sale; liabilities
    c. purchase; sale; reserves
    d. purchase; purchase; liabilities

14. A higher domestic money supply leads to a higher domestic price level in the long run, resulting in an expected _____ of the domestic currency that shifts the _____ schedule to the _____.

    a. depreciation; $RET^F$; right
    b. appreciation; $RET^F$; right
    c. depreciation; $RET^D$; left
    d. appreciation; $RET^D$; left

15. If the central bank decreases the money supply, domestic interest rates rise causing $RET^D$ to shift _____, while causing $RET^F$ to shift _____ because of the expected appreciation of the dollar.

    a. out, in
    b. out, out
    c. in, in
    d. out, out

16. A case can be made for controls on capital inflows because capital inflows

    a. can lead to a lending boom and encourage excessive risk taking.
    b. never go to financing productive investments.
    c. never finance productive investments and can lead to a lending boom and encourage excessive risk taking.
    d. are more effective in preventing financial crises than are policies that regulate banking activities.

# Chapter 20

## *Monetary Policy Strategy: The International Experience*

### CHAPTER SYNOPSIS/COMPLETIONS

In this chapter, students discover that central banks in countries other than the United States have had remarkable success in conducting monetary policy, bringing inflation down to low levels and promoting stable financial environments that promote general economic health. A central feature of monetary policy strategies in these countries is the use of a (1)_____ _____ , a nominal variable such as the inflation rate, an exchange rate or the money supply that policymakers use to tie down the price level. The role of the nominal anchor is to guide a nation's monetary authority to conduct monetary policy to keep the nominal anchor variable—an exchange rate, the inflation rate, or the money supply—within a narrow range.

Adherence to the nominal anchor can limit the (2)_____-_____ _____ for monetary policymakers. The time-inconsistency problem arises because the effect that monetary policy has on the economy depends on people's expectations. If workers and firms expect the central bank to pursue a tight monetary policy to keep inflation low—because that is the announced policy of the central bank—then the central bank has an incentive to renege on this promise and adopt an (3)_____ policy to boost output and lower unemployment. Knowing that policymakers may on occasion renege on policy announcements—that is, be inconsistent over time—workers and firms will (4)_____ central bank announcements. Thus, to make its announcements credible, the central bank will want to commit to a nominal anchor that limits its discretion.

Targeting the (5)_____ _____ is a monetary policy strategy with a long history. Today, a number of countries fix the value of their domestic currencies to that of a large, low-inflation country like the United States or Germany. Exchange-rate targeting is popular because (a) it keeps the inflation rate of internationally traded goods to that found in the anchor country; (b) it is simple and clearly understood by the public; © it provides an automatic rule that moderates the time-inconsistency problem. If the currency starts to depreciate (appreciate), then the central bank must tighten (loosen) monetary policy.

Although France, the United Kingdom, and Mexico have all used exchange-rate targeting to lower inflation, exchange-rate targeting has two disadvantages. First, the targeting country can no longer pursue its own independent monetary policy. This means that the targeting country cannot respond to (6)_____ that are independent of those hitting the anchor country. Moreover, shocks that hit the anchor country get transmitted to the targeting country. Second, the targeting country is open to (7)_____ attack on its currency when speculators begin to question the targeting country's commitment to the exchange-rate target, especially if unemployment in the targeting country continues to rise.

Two variants of exchange-rate targeting are the currency board and dollarization. Both variants are stronger commitments to the fixed exchange rate. The (8)_____ _____ stands ready, at any time, to exchange the anchor country's currency out of reserves for the domestic currency at the fixed rate. Currency boards have the advantage of making the commitment to low inflation transparent and credible, reducing the likelihood of a speculative attack. Disadvantages of a currency board include the following: loss of control over an independent monetary policy, transmission of shocks from the anchor country, and loss of the central bank as a lender of (9)_____ _____. Dollarization, the adoption of a sound currency, like the U.S. dollar, as a country's money, eliminates the possibility of a speculative attack, but at the cost losing the central bank as a lender of last resort.

Monetary targeting was adopted by a number of industrialized countries in the 1970s to bring down inflation. Of these countries, both Germany and Switzerland were the most persistent in sticking to this strategy. It is because of their success in keeping inflation under control that monetary targeting still has strong advocates. Germany and Switzerland have shown that monetary targeting can restrain inflation in the long run even when monetary targets are missed by wide margins. Despite frequent misses of announced targets, both countries have openly communicated to the public their intention of keeping inflation under control.

The main advantage of monetary targeting is the flexibility it provides the central bank for dealing with (10)_____ considerations. The principal problem with monetary targeting occurs when the relationship between the monetary target and the goal variable proves to be too weak to guarantee that the goal can be achieved.

It is because of this breakdown between monetary aggregates and goal variables that many countries have recently adopted (11)_____ _____ as their monetary policy regime. New Zealand, Canada, and the United Kingdom were the first to adopt explicit inflation-targeting regimes in the early 1990s. Inflation targeting requires a commitment to price stability as the primary, long-run goal of monetary policy; public announcement of numerical inflation targets, including the plans and objectives of monetary policymakers; and increased accountability of the central bank for attaining its inflation objectives. Consider this last requirement. The governor of the Reserve Bank in (12)_____ _____ can be dismissed if the publicly announced goals are not satisfied. All three countries have succeeded in bringing inflation down, albeit at the cost initially of higher unemployment.

Inflation targeting is readily understood by the public and is thus highly (13)_____, permits monetary policymakers to respond to shocks to the domestic economy, and does not depend on a stable relationship between money and inflation. Because an explicit numerical inflation target increases the (14)_____ of the central bank, inflation targeting reduces the likelihood that the monetary authority will fall into the time-inconsistency trap. Indeed, the success of the Bank of England's inflation-targeting regime proved to be instrumental in the government's decision to grant the Bank its operational independence. An inflation-targeting regime makes it more palatable to have an independent central bank that focuses on long-run objectives but is consistent with a democratic society because it is accountable.

Critics of inflation targeting contend that long lags in the effects of monetary policy make it too difficult for markets to determine the stance of monetary policy. Also, they claim that inflation targeting limits the discretion of central bankers to respond to domestic shocks, creates the potential for increased fluctuation in aggregate (15)_____, and lowers the economic growth of output and employment. Although the available empirical evidence does not lend much support to these criticisms, some economists claim that targeting nominal GDP would guard against a slow-down in economic activity. A variant of inflation targeting, a nominal GDP targeting regime would suffer the problem of announcing a long-term target for GDP growth, which would be difficult to forecast and politically risky. Moreover, since GDP is not a statistic that is reported monthly, it would make targeting GDP difficult in practice. When all is said and done, inflation targeting has almost all the benefits of nominal GDP targeting, but without the problems.

In recent years the Fed has pursued a policy of targeting an (16)_____ nominal anchor in the form of an overriding concern to control inflation in the long run. The Fed's "just do it" approach has many of the advantages of an explicit inflation targeting regime, but suffers the disadvantage that the Fed's policy is much less transparent. In addition, some question whether the Fed's approach is consistent with democratic principles, given the lack of transparency to the Fed's implicit anchor. Perhaps the most serious problem with the "just do it" approach is the strong dependence on the preferences, skills, and trustworthiness of the individuals in charge of the central bank. For these reasons, the "just do it" approach may give way to an explicit inflation-targeting regime.

## EXERCISES

### Exercise 1: Definitions and Terminology

Match the following terms on the right with the definition or description on the left. Place the letter of the term in the blank provided next to the appropriate definition.

_____ 1. Nominal variable that central bank uses to tie down the price level such as the inflation rate, an exchange rate, or the money supply.

        a. Exchange-rate targeting

_____ 2. Policymakers follow different policies than what had been previously announced.

        b. Nominal anchor

_____ 3. Stands ready to exchange domestic currency for foreign currency at a fixed rate whenever the public demands it.

        c. Time-inconsistency problem

_____ 4. The adoption of a sound currency, like the U.S. dollar, as a country's money.

        d. Inflation targeting

_____ 5. The revenue that the government receives by issuing money.

        e. Seignorage

_____ 6. Fixing the value of the domestic currency to that of a large, low-inflation country called the anchor country.

        f. Currency board

_____ 7. Monetary policy that uses a monetary aggregate as an intermediate target.

        g. Dollarization

_____ 8. Central bank publicly announces medium-term numerical targets for inflation.

        h. Monetary Targeting

## Exercise 2: Advantages and Disadvantages of Exchange-Rate Targeting

A.  List the advantages of exchange-rate targeting.

1.  _____

    _____

2.  _____

    _____

3.  _____

    _____

B.  List the disadvantages of exchange-rate targeting.

1.  _____

    _____

2.  _____

    _____

3.  _____

    _____

## Exercise 3: Advantages and Disadvantages of Inflation Targeting

A.  List the advantages of inflation targeting.

1.  _____

2.  _____

3.  _____

4.  _____

5.  _____

B.  List the disadvantages of inflation targeting.

1.  _____

2.  _____

3.  _____

## Exercise 4: Advantages and Disadvantages of Inflation Targeting

A.  List the advantages of monetary targeting.

1.  _____

2.  _____

B. List the one disadvantage of monetary targeting.

1. _____

## Exercise 5: Advantages and Disadvantages of Fed's Implicit-Targeting Regime

A. List the advantages of the Fed's "just do it" monetary policy strategy.

1. _____

2. _____

3. _____

B. List the disadvantages of the Fed's "just do it" monetary policy strategy.

1. _____

2. _____

3. _____

## SELF-TEST

### Part A: True-False Questions

Circle whether the following statements are true (T) or false (F).

T  F  1.  A key fact about monetary targeting regimes in Germany and Switzerland is that the targeting regimes were not like a Friedman-type monetary targeting rule in which a monetary aggregate is kept on a constant-growth-rate path and is the primary focus of monetary policy.

T  F  2.  The European Central Bank has adopted a hybrid monetary policy strategy that has much in common with the monetary targeting strategy previously used by the Bundesbank but also has some elements of inflation targeting.

T  F  3.  A key reason why monetary targeting has been reasonably successful in both Germany and Switzerland, despite frequent target misses, is that the objectives of monetary policy are clearly stated and both central banks actively engaged in communicating the strategy of monetary policy to the public, thereby enhancing the transparency of monetary policy and the accountability of the central banks.

T  F  4.  A crawling exchange-rate targeting strategy is on in which a currency is allowed to appreciate at a steady rate so that inflation in the pegging country can be higher than in the anchor country.

T  F  5.  An exchange-rate targeting strategy provides an automatic rule for the conduct of monetary policy. When there is a tendency for the domestic currency to depreciate, the central bank must pursue an expansionary policy; when there is a tendency for the domestic currency to appreciate, the central bank must pursue a contractionary policy;

T  F  6.  In industrialized countries, the biggest cost to exchange-rate targeting is the loss of an independent monetary policy to deal with domestic considerations.

T  F  7.  A disadvantage of inflation targeting is that it relies on a stable relationship between money and the price level.

T  F  8.  Two problems with the Fed's "just do it" approach to monetary policy are the lack of transparency and the low degree of accountability since the Fed does not announce its long-run goals for policy.

T  F  9.  Governments of countries that have their own currencies have an incentive to over-expand the money supply to gain the revenue called seignorage. This explains why dollarization may be an effective monetary strategy to convince the public that the monetary authority is serious about reducing inflation.

T  F  10.  A major advantage of exchange-rate targeting over monetary targeting is that it permits a central bank to adjust its monetary policy to cope with domestic considerations.

## Part B: Multiple-Choice Questions

Circle the appropriate answer.

1.  Disadvantages of exchange-rate targeting in emerging market countries include:

   a.  Weakening the accountability of policymakers since the exchange rate loses its ability to signal central bank policy actions.
   b.  Opening the country to speculative attacks on its currency, which can have far more serious consequences for their economies than for the economies of industrialized countries.
   c.  Lack of transparency, as the public in emerging market countries do not understand how to determine whether the targeting strategy is working.
   d.  All of the above.
   e.  Only (a) and (b) of the above.

2.  Disadvantages of exchange-rate targeting include:

   a.  Losing the ability to pursue monetary policy that is independent of the anchor country.
   b.  Opening the country to speculative attacks on its currency, especially if unemployment starts to rise in the target country.
   c.  Transmitting shocks that hit the anchor country to the domestic economy.
   d.  All of the above.
   e.  Only (a) and (b) of the above.

3.  A currency board has the advantages of an exchange-rate targeting regime, but reduces the likelihood that the targeting country experiences

    a.  a transmission of shocks from the anchor country to the domestic economy.
    b.  speculative attacks on its currency.
    c.  below normal economic growth when the anchor country experiences a recession.
    d.  all of the above.
    e.  only (a) and (b) of the above.

4.  A breakdown in the relationship between money growth and inflation is

    a.  a disadvantage for countries that use a monetary-targeting regime.
    b.  not a disadvantage for countries that use an exchange-rate targeting regime.
    c.  not a disadvantage for countries that use an inflation-targeting regime.
    d.  all of the above.

5.  Critics of inflation targeting complain that it

    a.  the signal between monetary policy actions and evidence of success is too long delayed.
    b.  imposes a rule on monetary policymakers that is too rigid, taking away their ability to respond to shocks to the economy.
    c.  has the potential for making output fluctuations more pronounced.
    d.  does all of the above.
    e.  does only (a) and (b) of the above.

6.  Some economists question the desirability of the Fed's implicit targeting strategy by pointing out that

    a.  the lack of transparency in the Fed's policy creates uncertainty that leads to unnecessary volatility in financial markets.
    b.  the opacity of its policymaking makes it hard to hold the Fed accountable to Congress and the public.
    c.  the policy has not been very successful, as inflation and unemployment have been too high in the 1990s.
    d.  all of the above.
    e.  only (a) and (b) of the above.

7.  (I) A disadvantage of an exchange-rate targeting approach is that it leaves targeting countries open to speculative attacks on their currencies.  (II) An advantage of an exchange-rate targeting approach is that it reduces the discretion of the central bank, reducing the likelihood of the time-inconsistent monetary policy actions.

    a.  Both are true.
    b.  Both are false.
    c.  I is true, II is false.
    d.  I is false, II is true.

8.  (I) In industrialized countries, the biggest cost to exchange-rate targeting is the loss of an independent monetary policy to deal with domestic considerations. (II) The Italians were the most favorable of all those in Europe to the European Monetary Union, because the past record of Italian monetary policy was not good.

    a.  Both are true.
    b.  Both are false.
    c.  I is true, II is false.
    d.  I is false, II is true.

9.  (I) If the relationship between the monetary aggregate and the goal variable is weak, monetary aggregate targeting will not work. (II) Canada was the first country to formally adopt inflation targeting in 1990.

    a.  Both are true.
    b.  Both are false.
    c.  I is true, II is false.
    d.  I is false, II is true.

10. Disadvantages of nominal GDP targeting include:

    a.  the lack of timely information on nominal GDP since it is reported quarterly, not monthly.
    b.  the potential confusion that might arise with the public between nominal and real GDP.
    c.  the difficulty that policymakers would encounter in trying to calculate long-run potential GDP growth.
    d.  all of the above.
    e.  only (a) and (b) of the above.

# Chapter 21

## *The Demand for Money*

### CHAPTER SYNOPSIS/COMPLETIONS

Chapter 21 discusses in chronological order the major developments in the theory of the demand for money. These developments have attempted to explain the reasons people hold money and to what extent the quantity of money demanded is affected by changes in interest rates.

The earliest treatment of the demand for money was offered by the classical economists. The classical economists – most notably Irving Fisher – argued that the demand for money was a function of nominal aggregate income. This followed from their assumptions regarding (1)_____ (the average number of times per year that a dollar is spent on final goods and services produced in the economy) and the equation of exchange.

The classical economists argued that the speed with which money is spent is a function of the institutional features of the economy. Although these features certainly change over time (due to improvements in technology, for example), velocity could be regarded as fixed in the short run.

Nothing more than an identity, the equation of (2)_____ states that the quantity of money times velocity must equal nominal income. But when combined with Irving Fisher's assumption regarding the fixity of velocity, the equation of exchange is transformed into the quantity theory of (3)_____. Given the assumption of constant velocity, the quantity theory of money implies that changes in nominal income are determined solely by changes in the quantity of money. The classical economists also assumed that prices and wages were completely (4)_____, meaning that the economy would always remain at full employment. This last assumption meant that changes in the money supply had no effect on aggregate output and could therefore affect only the (5)_____ _____.

Dividing both sides of the equation of exchange by the constant velocity makes clear that the quantity of money people hold is a constant fraction of nominal income. Thus, the classical economists regarded the demand for money as a demand for a medium of exchange.

The Cambridge economists criticized the quantity theory of money as too mechanistic. Instead, they focused on the factors influencing how much money individuals would want to hold. Like Fisher, they regarded the level of income as the most significant factor influencing people's holdings of money. But they also believed that changes in (6)_____ _____ could affect individuals' decisions about using money as a store of wealth.

John Maynard Keynes believed that a decline in velocity helped to explain the Great Depression, and his efforts to explain this decline in velocity led to his theory of money demand, which he called (7)_____ _____ theory. Keynes contended that there were three separate and distinct motives for holding money: the transactions motive, the precautionary motive, and the (8)_____ motive.

It was the speculative motive that distinguished Keynes's theory from the other theories. Keynes argued that interest rates played an important role in determining the amount of wealth people desire to hold in the form of money. Though bonds pay interest, a rise in interest rates causes bond values to (9)_____, subjecting their holders to capital losses and even negative returns if bond values fall significantly. Thus at low rates of interest, people reduce their holdings of bonds and hold more money as they expect interest rates to rise, returning to their normal levels. Therefore, Keynes concluded that the demand for money was (10)_____ related to the level of interest rates.

Since Keynes's early attempt, economists have improved on his analysis providing a better rationale for the (11)_____ relationship between interest rates and velocity. The works of Baumol and Tobin indicate that the transaction component (and, by extension, the precautionary component) of the demand for money is negatively related to the level of interest rates.

Milton Friedman has offered an alternative explanation for the (12)_____ behavior of velocity. Rather than rely on the procyclical behavior of interest rates, Friedman argues that since changes in actual income exceed changes in permanent income, velocity will tend to move procyclically.

Friedman – noting that the interest rate paid on checking deposits tends to move with market rates so that the differential between market interest rates and the interest rate paid on money remains relatively constant – believes that changes in interest rates will have little effect on the demand for money. This result does not require the absence of deposit rate ceilings, as banks pay implicit interest on deposits by providing "free" services such as branch offices, more tellers, or "free" checking. Friedman's modern quantity theory of money is consistent with the procyclical behavior of velocity, as are the other modern money demand stories. We see in a later chapter that the anticipated effectiveness of fiscal policy depends upon one's view of money demand.

Research on the demand for money indicates that while the demand for money is sensitive to interest rates, there is little evidence that the liquidity trap has ever existed. Also, because of the rapid pace of financial innovation, since 1973, the demand for money has been quite unstable. It is because of this instability that setting rigid money supply targets in order to control aggregate spending in the economy may not be an effective way to conduct monetary policy.

## EXERCISES

### Exercise 1: The Keynesian Approach to Money Demand

A.  What are the three motives behind the demand for money postulated by Keynes?

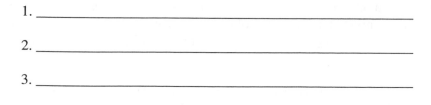

1. _____

2. _____

3. _____

B. What motive did Keynes believe was a function of the interest rate?

1. _____

C. Tobin's model of the speculative demand for money shows that people hold money as a store of wealth as a way of reducing

_____

## Exercise 2: Velocity and the Quantity Theory of Money

Complete the following table.

|     | M   | V   | P   | Y    |
| --- | --- | --- | --- | ---- |
|     | 200 | 5   | 1   | 1000 |
| 1.  | 200 | 6   | 2   | ____ |
| 2.  | 300 | 5   | 1.5 | ____ |
| 3.  | 400 | 6   | ____ | 1200 |
| 4.  | 400 | ____ | 1   | 1600 |
| 5.  | ____ | 5   | 2   | 2000 |

## Exercise 3: The Demand for Money

Indicate whether the following statements are associated with Fisher's quantity theory of money (Q), the Cambridge approach to money demand (C), Keynes's liquidity preference theory (K), or with Friedman's modern quantity theory of money (F).  Place the appropriate letter in the blank to the left of the statement.

_____ 1. Interest rates have no effect on the demand for money.

_____ 2. Money has two properties explaining why people want to hold it: money functions as a medium of exchange and as a store of wealth.

_____ 3. The demand for money is proportional to income, but the effect of interest rates on the demand for money cannot be completely ignored.

_____ 4. There are three distinct motives for holding money: (a) a transactions motive, where money balances are held if there is imperfect synchronization between receipts and expenditures; (b) a precautionary motive, where money is held because of uncertainty of future expenditures; and ©  a speculative motive, where money is held if bonds are expected to fall in value.

_____ 5. Permanent income is the primary determinant of money demand, and changes in interest rates should have little effect on the demand for money.

_____ 6. The demand for money is insensitive to interest rates, not because the demand for money is insensitive to changes in the opportunity cost of holding money, but because changes in interest rates actually have little effect on the opportunity cost of holding money.

_____ 7. More recent developments in this approach suggest that interest rates are important to the transactions and precautionary components of money demand, as well as to the speculative component.

_____ 8. The transactions and precautionary components of the demand for money are proportional to income, while the speculative component is negatively related to the level of interest rates.

_____ 9. Movements in the price level result solely from changes in the quantity of money.

_____10. The demand for money is purely a function of income; interest rates have no effect on the demand for money.

_____11. Theory that offered an explanation for the decline in velocity during the Great Depression.

_____12. The demand for money is a function of both permanent income and the opportunity cost of holding money.

## SELF-TEST

### Part A: True-False Questions

Circle whether the following statements are true (T) or false (F).

T  F  1.  The equation of exchange states that the product of the quantity of money and the average number of times that a dollar is spent on final goods and services in a given period must equal nominal income.

T  F  2.  Irving Fisher argued that velocity would be relatively constant in the short run, since institutional features of the economy, such as the speed at which checks were cleared, were likely to change only slowly over time.

T  F  3.  The classical economists' contention that velocity could be regarded as a constant transformed the equation of exchange (an identity) into the quantity theory of money.

T  F  4.  The Cambridge economists argued that the demand for money was unaffected by changes in interest rates.

T  F  5.  At relatively low interest rates, people might be reluctant to hold money due to a concern about capital losses should interest rates rise.

T  F  6.  Keynes's liquidity preference theory offered an explanation for why velocity had fallen during the Great Depression.

T F 7. The demand for money approach developed by Keynes is consistent with the procyclical movements in velocity observed in the United States.

T F 8. Studies by economists in the 1950s found evidence that even the transactions motive for holding money was sensitive to the level of interest rates.

T F 9. James Tobin suggested that people might prefer to hold money to bonds as a store of wealth in an effort to reduce risk.

T F 10. The permanent income argument in Friedman's demand for money formulation suggests that velocity will fluctuate with business cycle movements.

## Part B: Multiple-Choice Questions

Circle the appropriate answer.

1. The quantity theory of money suggests that cutting the money supply by one- third will lead to

   a. a sharp decline in output by one-third in the short run and a decline in the price level by one-third in the long run.
   b. a decline in output by one-third.
   c. a decline in output by one-sixth and a decline in the price level by one-sixth.
   d. a decline in the price level by one-third.
   e. none of the above.

2. The classical economists believed that velocity could be regarded as constant in the short run, since

   a. institutional factors, such as the speed with which checks were cleared through the banking system, changed slowly over time.
   b. the opportunity cost of holding money was close to zero.
   c. financial innovation tended to offset changes in interest rates.
   d. none of the above are true.

3. Empirical evidence supports the contention that

   a. velocity tends to be procyclical; that is, velocity declines (increases) when economic activity contracts (expands).
   b. velocity tends to be countercyclical; that is, velocity declines (increases) when economic activity contracts (expands).
   c. velocity tends to be countercyclical; that is, velocity increases (declines) when economic activity contracts (expands).
   d. velocity is essentially a constant.

4. Keynes's liquidity preference theory explains why velocity can be expected to rise when

   a. income increases.
   b. wealth increases.
   c. brokerage commissions increase.
   d. interest rates increase.

5.   Keynes argued that people were more likely to increase their money holdings if they believed that

    a.   interest rates were about to fall.
    b.   bond prices were about to rise.
    c.   bond prices were about to fall.
    d.   none of the above was true.

6.   The Baumol-Tobin analysis suggests that

    a.   velocity is relatively constant.
    b.   the transactions component of money demand is negatively related to the level of interest rates.
    c.   the speculative motive for money is nonexistent.
    d.   both (a) and (c) of the above are true.
    e.   both (b) and (c) of the above are true.

7.   One possible implication of the elimination of deposit rate ceilings is that the implicit interest rate on money will more closely approach bond rates.  This suggests that changes in interest rates will

    a.   have a greater impact on money demand.
    b.   have less effect on the demand for money.
    c.   no longer affect the speculative demand for money.
    d.   cause velocity to become more volatile.

8.   Milton Friedman argues that the demand for money is relatively insensitive to interest rates because

    a.   the demand for money is insensitive to changes in the opportunity cost of holding money.
    b.   competition among banks keeps the opportunity cost of holding money relatively constant.
    c.   people base their investment decisions on expected profits not interest rates.
    d.   transactions are not subject to scale economics as wealth increases.

9.   Friedman's belief regarding the interest insensitivity of the demand for money implies that

    a.   the quantity of money is the primary determinant of aggregate spending.
    b.   velocity is countercyclical.
    c.   both (a) and (b) of the above are correct.
    d.   neither (a) nor (b) of the above are correct.

10.  In Friedman's view, because income tends to decline relative to permanent income during business cycle contractions, the demand for money with respect to actual income will increase, causing velocity to

    a.   rise.
    b.   decline.
    c.   remain unchanged, since velocity is only sensitive to changes in interest rates.
    d.   decline, provided that interest rates increase when the economy contracts.

# Chapter 22

## *The Keynesian Framework and the* ISLM *Model*

### CHAPTER SYNOPSIS/COMPLETIONS

This chapter presents the simple Keynesian model and introduces the ISLM model of simultaneous money and goods markets equilibrium. These models allow us to better understand the functioning of the economy and to better assess the effects of fiscal and monetary policy actions. In addition, the ISLM model is used to derive the aggregate demand curve that is used in aggregate demand and supply analysis.

The Keynesian model arose from John Maynard Keynes's concern with explaining the cause of the Great Depression. Keynes came to the conclusion that the dramatic decline in economic activity was the result of insufficient (1)_____ _____. Aggregate demand in an open economy is the sum of four components of spending: consumer expenditure, (2)_____ _____, government expenditure, and net exports. A decline in any one of these components causes output to decline, potentially leading to recession and rising unemployment.

The Keynesian model, though highly simplified, provides a framework that is very useful for understanding fluctuations in aggregate output. This is more easily accomplished by examining the individual spending components separately.

Keynes argued that consumer expenditure is primarily determined by the level of disposable (3)_____. As income increases, consumers will increase their expenditures. The change in consumer expenditures that results from an additional dollar of disposable income is referred to as the (4)_____ _____ to consume, or simply *mpc*. At low levels of income it is likely that individuals consume more than their disposable income. Thus some amount of consumer expenditure is (5)_____, that is, independent of disposable income. This description of consumption behavior is summarized by the consumption function, where autonomous consumption is represented by a constant term, *a*, and the positive slope of the function is given by the *mpc*.

Investment spending includes fixed investment – spending by business on equipment and structures, and by households on residential houses – and planned inventory investment. (6)_____ _____ is the spending by business on additional holdings of raw materials, parts, and finished goods.

Keynes believed that managers' expectations of future conditions, as well as interest rates, explained the level of planned investment. If actual investment (the sum of fixed investment and unplanned inventory investment) differs from desired investment (fixed investment plus (7)_____ inventory investment), then the actions of business firms will move the economy toward a new equilibrium. Consider a situation where business firms' inventories have risen above desired levels. Because firms find inventories costly to hold, they will cut production in an attempt to reduce their excess inventories. Aggregate output will fall and the desired level of inventories will eventually be restored.

After this equilibrium is achieved, business firms may become more optimistic about the future health of the economy. As business firms spend more, inventory levels will fall below desired levels, inducing a further expansion in aggregate output. Hence, the initial increase in investment spending is likely to cause a multifold increase in aggregate output. The ratio of the change in aggregate output to the change in investment spending is called the expenditure (8)_____.

An increase in investment spending causes aggregate output to expand by an amount greater than the initial change because consumer expenditure also increases. As firms expand output, they hire more factor inputs such as labor, raising households' disposable incomes. Consumers respond by spending more, leading to a further expansion in output and creating a multifold increase. Since this multifold increase is dependent on additional consumer expenditure, it is not surprising that the value of the *mpc* is used to determine the value of the multiplier.

Once government spending and taxes are added to the simple Keynesian model, policy decisions can be evaluated. Although the tax multiplier is smaller than the government expenditure multiplier, changes in either taxes or government spending can be effective in returning the economy to a full (9)_____ equilibrium.

The ISLM model allows one to determine the influence monetary policy has on the economy in the Keynesian framework. The (10)_____ curve illustrates that at lower interest rates, the level of investment spending and aggregate output is greater. Because the IS curve represents goods market equilibrium, the economy must be on the IS curve to be in general equilibrium. Goods market equilibrium is not, however, sufficient to guarantee general equilibrium; the economy must also be on the LM curve.

The LM curve slopes up, indicating that as income rises, a (11)_____ interest rate is required to maintain money market equilibrium. The increase in money demand due to an increase in (12)_____ must be exactly offset by the decrease in money demand due to the increase in the interest rate.

The ISLM model determines both the level of aggregate output and interest rates when the price level is fixed. Therefore, the ISLM model can be used to illustrate the effect on aggregate output and interest rates of monetary or fiscal policy actions, a topic extensively discussed in the next chapter.

## EXERCISES

### Exercise 1: Definitions and Terminology

Match the following terms on the right with definition or description on the left.  Place the letter of the term in the blank provided next to the appropriate definition.

_____ 1. Spending by business firms on equipment and structures, and planned spending on residential houses.

a. Planned investment spending

_____ 2. Spending by business firms on additional holdings of raw materials, parts, and finished goods, calculated as the change in holdings in a given time period.

b. Consumer expenditure

_____ 3. Used by economic forecasters, this model explains how interest rates and aggregate output are determined for a fixed price level.

c. "Animal spirits"

_____ 4. Total demand for consumer goods and services.

d. IS Curve

_____ 5. Planned spending by business firms on equipment, structures, raw materials, parts and finished goods, and planned spending on residential houses.

e. Expenditure multiplier

_____ 6. Total quantity demanded of output produced in the economy.

f. LM Curve

_____ 7. Aggregate income less taxes, or the total income available for spending.

g. Fixed investment

_____ 8. Consumer expenditure that is independent of disposable income.

h. Inventory investment

_____ 9. The change in consumer expenditure that results from an additional dollar of disposable income.

i. ISLM model

_____10 Government purchases of goods and services.

j. Disposable income

_____11. The relationship that describes the combinations of aggregate output and interest rates for which the goods market is in equilibrium.

k. Marginal propensity to consume

_____12. The relationship that describes the combination of interest rates and aggregate output for which the money market is in equilibrium.

l. Aggregate demand

_____13. Emotional waves of business optimism and
pessimism that Keynes believed dominated
fluctuations in planned investment spending.

m Government spending

_____14. The ratio of the change in aggregate output
to the change in planned investment spending.

n. Aggregate demand function

_____15. The relationship between aggregate output
and aggregate demand that shows the
quantity of aggregate output demanded for
each level of aggregate output.

o. Autonomous consumer
expenditure

## Exercise 2: The Consumption Function

This exercise examines the relationship between the level of disposable income and consumer expenditures
known as the consumption function.

A. Assume that the consumption function is given by $C = 50 + 0.75DI$. Complete the following table:

| Point | Disposable Income (DI) | Change in DI | Change in C | Autonomous Consumption | Total Consumption |
|-------|------------------------|--------------|-------------|------------------------|-------------------|
| A | 0 | _____ | _____ | 50 | _____ |
| B | 100 | _____ | _____ | _____ | _____ |
| C | 200 | _____ | _____ | _____ | _____ |
| D | 300 | _____ | _____ | _____ | _____ |
| E | 400 | _____ | _____ | _____ | _____ |
| F | 500 | _____ | _____ | _____ | _____ |

B. In Figure 22A, plot the points on the consumption function you derived in the table.

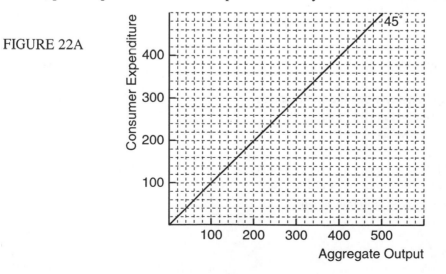

FIGURE 22A

**Exercise 3: Determination of Equilibrium Aggregate Output**

Suppose that for a particular economy, planned investment spending is 10, government spending is 10, taxes are zero, and consumer expenditure is given by the consumption function:

$C = 20 + 0.8DI$

which is plotted in Figure 22B.

A.  Plot the aggregate demand function and mark it as $Y^{ad}_1$ in Figure 22B.


B.  What is the equilibrium level of aggregate output?  $Y_1 =$


C.  If planned investment spending rises to 30, draw in the new aggregate demand function, $Y^{ad}_2$. What is the new equilibrium level of aggregate output?

$Y_2 =$ _____

D.  What is the value of the expenditure multiplier? _____

FIGURE 22B

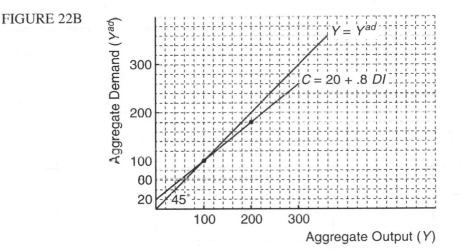

**Exercise 4: Unplanned Inventory Investment and the Determination of Aggregate Output**

Assume that planned investment spending is equal to 100, government spending is equal to 200, taxes are zero, and consumer expenditure is given by:

$C = 100 + 0.9DI$

A.  Write down the equation describing the aggregate demand function.

B. If current aggregate output is 3000, what is the level of unplanned inventory investment?

_____

C. What will happen to the level of aggregate output in the next time period?

_____

D. At what level of aggregate output will unplanned inventory disinvestment be zero?

_____

E. At what level will aggregate output eventually settle? _____

## Exercise 5: The Response of Aggregate Output

In the following matrix there is noted at the top of each column Autonomous Consumer Expenditure, Induced Consumer Expenditure, Planned Investment Spending, Government Spending, and Equilibrium Aggregate Income. At the beginning of each row there is a hypothetical change in some variable in the model. In each cell of the matrix indicate by a, +, -, or 0 whether the assumed change will increase, decrease, or cause no change in the variables in each column for the model in the text.

|  | Consumer Expenditure | | Planned Investment | Government | Equilibrium Aggregate |
|  | Autonomous | Induced | Spending | Spending | Income |
|---|---|---|---|---|---|
| Decrease in interest rate |  |  |  |  |  |
| Decrease in mpc |  |  |  |  |  |
| Decrease in tax rate |  |  |  |  |  |
| Increase in planned investment spending |  |  |  |  |  |
| Increase in autonomous consumer expenditure |  |  |  |  |  |
| Decrease in mps |  |  |  |  |  |
| Decrease in government spending |  |  |  |  |  |

## Exercise 6: The Expenditure Multiplier

Assume that the equilibrium level of income is 4000 and the mpc = 0.8.

A.  Calculate the value of the government expenditure multiplier. _____

B.  Calculate the value of the tax multiplier. _____

C.  Suppose that the government knows that the full-employment level of income is 4200.  Calculate the increase in government spending or the size of the tax cut necessary to raise equilibrium income to the full employment level.

Change in government spending = _____

Change in taxes = _____

## Exercise 7: Deriving the LM Curve

The LM curve is the relationship that describes combinations of interest rates and aggregate output for which the quantity of money demanded equals the quantity of money supplied.  Panel (a) of Figure 22C shows the equilibrium values of interest rates in the money market for aggregate income levels of $400 billion, $600 billion, and $800 billion.  Complete panel (b) by plotting the level of equilibrium output corresponding to each of the three interest rates.  Connect the three points with straight-line segments.

FIGURE 22C

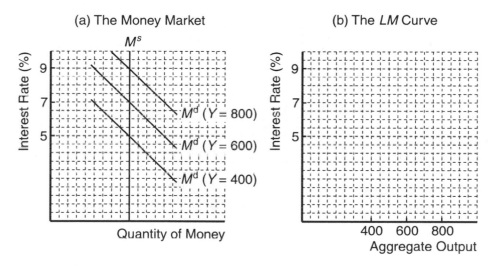

## Exercise 8: Deriving the IS Curve

The IS curve is the relationship that describes the combinations of aggregate output and interest rates for which the total quantity of goods produced equals the total quantity demanded.  The investment schedule in panel (a) of Figure 22D shows that as the interest rate rises from 5 to 7 to 9 percent, planned investment spending falls from $150 billion to $100 billion to $50 billion.  Panel (b) of Figure 22D indicates the levels of equilibrium output $400 billion, $600 billion, and $800 billion that correspond to those three levels of planned investment.  Complete panel (c) by plotting the level of equilibrium output corresponding to each of the three interest rates.  Then connect the points with straight-line segments.

FIGURE 22D

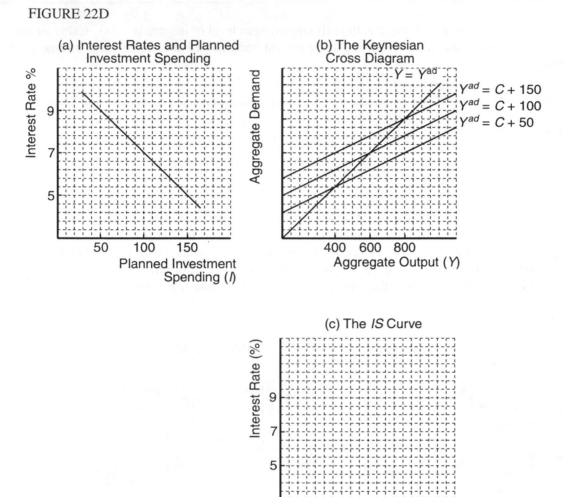

## SELF-TEST

### Part A: True-False Questions

Circle whether following statements are true (T) or false (F).

T  F  1.  The investment spending component of aggregate demand does not include unplanned inventory investment.

T  F  2.  Jean purchases 1000 shares of Exxon common stock through her broker. This transaction is included in the investment component of aggregate demand.

T  F  3.  The 45-degree line in the Keynesian cross diagram represents all possible or potential equilibrium points.

T  F  4.  If the level of aggregate output exceeds aggregate demand, income will rise, causing the level of output to expand.

T  F  5.  Unplanned inventory investment occurs when the level of aggregate demand exceeds aggregate output.

T  F  6.  Business firms are likely to cut production in the face of rising unplanned inventory levels.

T  F  7.  The simple Keynesian model suggests that an increase in planned investment will actually lead to an expansion in aggregate output that exceeds the initial change in investment spending. This is known as the multiplier effect.

T  F  8.  Keynes believed that business cycle fluctuations were dominated by changes in autonomous consumer expenditure.

T  F  9.  The slope of the IS curve reflects the fact that investment is negatively related to the interest rate.

T  F  10.  At any point along an IS curve the level of unplanned inventory investment is zero.

### Part B: Multiple-Choice Questions

Circle the appropriate answer.

1.  Which of the following describes the equilibrium condition in the simple Keynesian model?

    a.  Aggregate output equals aggregate demand.
    b.  Unplanned inventory investment is zero.
    c.  Actual investment equals planned investment.
    d.  All of the above.
    e.  Only (a) and (b) of the above.

2.  Keynes believed that the economy could achieve an equilibrium level of output

    a.  only at the full-employment level of output.
    b.  below the full-employment level of output.
    c.  only if the government took a "hands off" approach.
    d.  by doing none of the above.

3.  Inventory investment is distinguished from fixed investment in that

    a.  fixed investment is never unplanned.
    b.  inventory investment is never planned.
    c.  unplanned inventory investment is always zero.
    d.  there is no distinction.

4.  If one knows the value of the multiplier and the change in the level of autonomous investment, one can determine

    a.  the change in the interest rate.
    b.  the change in the money supply.
    c.  the change in the aggregate output.
    d.  all of the above.

5.  Keynes believed that fluctuations in aggregate output were largely the result of fluctuations in

    a.  the money supply.
    b.  autonomous investment spending.
    c.  autonomous consumer expenditure.
    d.  government spending.

6.  If the mpc is 0.75, the multiplier is

    a.  3.00
    b.  3.75.
    c.  0.25.
    d.  4.00

7.  Assume that an economy characterized by the simple Keynesian model is in equilibrium at full employment but the government budget is in deficit.  If the government raises taxes to balance the budget, then

    a.  the rate of unemployment will increase.
    b.  the level of aggregate output will increase.
    c.  the price level will increase.
    d.  all of the above will occur.

8. An increase in the interest rate will cause

    a. investment spending to fall.
    b. investment spending to rise.
    c. tax rates to rise.
    d. no change in aggregate spending.

9. Points to the left of the IS curve represent interest rate and output combinations characterized by reductions in

    a. unplanned inventory accumulations.
    b. unplanned inventory reductions.
    c. an excess demand for money.
    d. an excess supply of money.

10. The money market is in equilibrium

    a. at any point on the LM curve.
    b. at only one point on the IS curve.
    c. at any point on the IS curve.
    d. at only one point on the LM curve.
    e. when only (a) and (b) of the above occur.
    f. when only (c) and (d) of the above occur.

11. At points to the _____ of the LM curve there is an excess _____ of money which causes interest rates to fall.

    a. left; supply
    b. left; demand
    c. right; supply
    d. right; demand

12. If the economy is on the *IS* curve, but is to the _____ of the *LM* curve, then the _____ market is in equilibrium, but the interest rate is _____ the equilibrium level.

    a. left; goods; below
    b. left; goods; above
    c. right; money; below
    d. right; goods; above
    e. left; money; above

13. The multiplier effect means that a given change in _____ autonomous expenditures will change equilibrium _____ income by an amount _____ greater than the initial change in autonomous expenditures.

    a. autonomous; income; greater
    b. autonomous; income; less
    c. induced; income; greater
    d. induced; employment; greater
    e. autonomous; employment; less

14. If $I^u$ is positive, firms will _____ production and output will _____.

    a. cut; rise
    b. cut; fall
    c. increase; rise
    d. increase; fall

15. In the Keynesian framework, as long as output is _____ the equilibrium level, unplanned inventory investment will remain negative and firms will continue to _____ production.

    a. below; lower
    b. above; lower
    c. below; raise
    d. above; raise

# Chapter 23

## *Monetary and Fiscal Policy in the* ISLM *Model*

### CHAPTER SYNOPSIS/COMPLETIONS

In this chapter we explore the mechanics of the ISLM model, discovering how monetary policy – the control of the money supply and interest rates – and (1)_____ policy – the control of government spending and taxes – affect the level of aggregate output and interest rates. Since policymakers have these two tools at their disposal they will be interested in knowing the effects each policy can be expected to have on the economy. The ISLM model provides a convenient but powerful framework for comparing the relative effects of proposed monetary and fiscal actions. By comparing these predicted effects, policymakers can better decide which policy is most appropriate.

The ISLM model also provides a framework that allows one to compare the desirability of interest rate targeting against money supply targeting. In addition, the aggregate demand curve is derived using the ISLM model. It is for these three important reasons that we study the ISLM model in the money and banking course.

As is true of any economic model, we can better comprehend the workings of the ISLM model by first examining the behavior of the individual curves. Once this has been done, the effects that changes in fiscal and monetary variables will have on interest rates and aggregate output can be determined.

The (2)_____ curve shows the combinations of interest rates and aggregate output that ensure equilibrium in the goods market. Therefore, changes in autonomous consumer expenditures, autonomous (3)_____ spending, and government spending or taxes are all factors that shift the IS curve. For example, if Congress enacts legislation to spend $500 billion over the next ten years to repair the decaying infrastructure (roads, bridges, canals) of the economy, the added government spending shifts the IS curve to the (4)_____. An example of a leftward shift in the IS curve is provided by the precipitous drop in autonomous investment spending during the Great Depression. It is important to distinguish between autonomous changes in investment and changes in investment due to changes in interest rates. A change in investment that results from a change in interest rates is shown as a movement along a given IS curve, not as a shift in the IS curve.

Interest rate and aggregate output combinations that represent equilibrium in the money market define an (5)_____ curve. Therefore, changes in either money supply or money demand can cause the LM curve to shift.

Consider the effect an increase in money supply has on the LM curve. At the initial interest rate, an increase in the money supply creates an (6)_____ supply of money. Holding output constant, equilibrium is regained in the money market by a fall in the interest rates. Alternatively, the interest rate held constant, equilibrium is regained in the money market when the increase in aggregate (7)_____ is sufficient to raise money demand to a level that eliminates the excess supply of money.

Changes in money demand also shift the LM curve. If more people come to expect a surge in the stock market, they will try to conserve on their holdings of money, filling their portfolios with more stocks (recall the analysis of Chapter 5 on asset demand). The drop in money demand creates an excess supply of money at the initial interest rate. Therefore, interest rates will (8)_____, holding output constant, and the LM curve shifts to the (9)_____. Conversely, an increase in the demand for money shifts the LM curve left.

Putting the IS and LM curves together allows us to consider the effects of autonomous spending and policy changes on the equilibrium levels of the interest rate and aggregate output. For example, a tax cut aimed at reducing the budget surplus shifts the IS curve (10)_____ due to the increase in spending by consumers. The increase in output causes the demand for money to rise, which in turn creates an excess demand for money, putting upward pressure on interest rates. Although the rise in interest rates causes interest sensitive investment to decrease, the decrease is not enough to offset the expansionary effects of the tax cut. No wonder tax cuts are so popular among incumbent politicians: a tax cut may cause rising employment and a net gain of votes on election day.

Some economists contend that there is a tendency for the money supply to expand prior to elections. Since the ISLM model indicates that an increase in the money supply causes aggregate output to (11)_____ and interest rates to fall, and since both are likely to help the incumbent politician, such a contention has credibility.

The ISLM framework also has been used to analyze the appropriateness of Federal Reserve operating procedures. While interest rate targets can be shown to be more consistent with stable economic activity when the LM curve is unstable, a money supply target helps ensure greater stability when the (12)_____ curve is unstable. Since neither targeting procedure outperforms the other in every situation, it becomes an empirical question as to which curve is more stable and under which conditions. Thus it is not surprising that economists still debate over the appropriate targeting procedure the Fed should employ.

Another debate has centered around the slope of the LM curve. If the LM curve is very steep, approaching a vertical line, then an expansionary fiscal policy is likely to be an (13)_____ tool for expanding aggregate output since investment spending will be crowded out by the rising interest rates.

Finally, the ISLM model is useful in deriving the aggregate demand curve used in aggregate demand and supply analysis. Since aggregate demand and supply analysis is so powerful, this function of the ISLM model is especially important. A decline in the price level raises the real money supply, causing interest rates to fall and investment spending to rise. Simultaneous goods and money market equilibrium will correspond to higher levels of aggregate output as the price level falls, indicating that the aggregate demand curve slopes (14)_____ to the right.

The aggregate demand curve shifts in the same direction as a shift in the IS or LM curves. Increases in the money supply and government spending or decreases in taxes all cause the aggregate demand curve to shift to the (15)_____. We see in the next chapter that the aggregate demand and supply model provides a powerful framework for understanding recent economic events.

## EXERCISES

### Exercise 1: Factors that Cause the IS and LM Curves to Shift

This exercise provides a summary of the factors that cause the IS and LM curves to shift.

A. List the factors that cause the IS curve to shift to the right.

1. _____

2. _____

3. _____

4. _____

B. List the factors that cause the IS curve to shift to the left.

1. _____

2. _____

3. _____

4. _____

C. List the factors that cause the LM curve to shift to the right.

1. _____

2. _____

D. List the factors that cause the LM curve to shift to the left.

1. _____

2. _____

### Exercise 2: Response to a Change in Both Monetary and Fiscal Policy

The United States experienced its deepest post-World War II recession in the years 1981 and 1982 despite the fiscal stimulus provided by the Reagan tax cut. The recession was somewhat unusual in that interest rates rose throughout 1981 and the first half of 1982. In Figure 23A the stimulus provided by the tax cut is shown as the rightward shift of the IS curve from $IS_1$ to $IS_2$, moving the economy from point 1 to point 2. Draw in the new LM curve in Figure 23A consistent with the decline in aggregate output and rise in interest rates.

FIGURE 23A

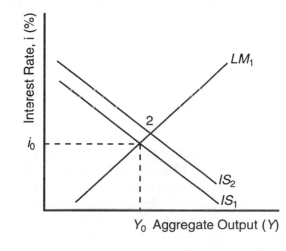

Explain why the LM curve might have shifted in the direction it did.

_____

_____


### Exercise 3: Expansionary Monetary and Fiscal Policy

When President Kennedy took office in 1961, he appointed Walter Heller as his chairman for the Council of Economic Advisors.  Heller was concerned with the high rate of unemployment and suggested that Kennedy adopt an expansionary fiscal policy.  Heller convinced Kennedy that a tax cut would lead to economic expansion, lowering unemployment and thereby fulfilling Kennedy's campaign promise to "get the economy moving again." As a consequence of these efforts, taxes were cut in 1964.  The results were favorable as unemployment fell from 5.7% in 1963 to 4.5% in 1965.  In addition, interest rates remained relatively stable over this period, suggesting that the Federal Reserve was pursuing an interest-rate targeting strategy, effectively accommodating the fiscal expansion.  The position of the economy just prior to the tax cut provides the initial conditions in Figure 23B at point 1.  Graph the position of the economy in 1965 in Figure 23B, showing the increase in aggregate output and stable interest rates.

FIGURE 23B

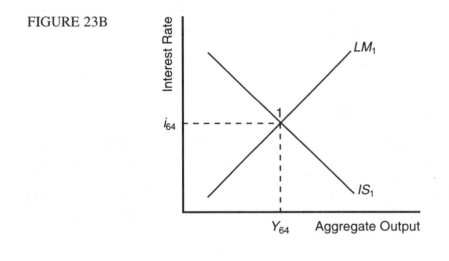

### Exercise 4: Contractionary Monetary and Fiscal Policies

The combination of the tax cut in 1964 and the increase in government spending due to involvement in the Vietnam war significantly reduced unemployment by 1968, but this reduction had come at the cost of higher inflation.  Response to the high inflation came on two fronts.  First, Congress enacted a measure in 1968 that imposed a 10% surtax on personal income taxes and on corporate incomes.  Then in 1969, Richard Nixon reduced federal spending growth.  Thus fiscal policy became contractionary in 1968- 1969.  Second, the Federal Reserve tightened monetary policy.  While both fiscal and monetary policy turned contractionary, it appears that fiscal policy proved less contractionary than monetary policy.  In Figure 23C, the condition of the economy in early 1968 is represented by the intersection of the IS curve (IS$_1$) and the LM curve (LM$_1$) at point 1. In Figure 23C, show the shifts in the IS and LM curves that took place in 1969.

FIGURE 23C

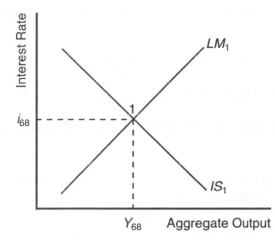

Predict what happened to interest rates and the unemployment rate by mid-1970.

_____

_____

## Exercise 5: Monetary and Fiscal Policy

Indicate whether the following statements are a description of monetary policy (M), fiscal policy (F), or both (B). Place the appropriate letter in the blank next to the statement.

_____ 1. Changes in money supply and interest rates.

_____ 2. Shown as a shift in the IS curve.

_____ 3. Changes in government spending and taxing.

_____ 4. Shown as a shift in the LM curve.

_____ 5. Policy made by the Federal Reserve.

_____ 6. Policy made by the president and Congress.

_____ 7. Shown as a shift in the aggregate demand curve.

## Exercise 6: Effectiveness of Monetary Versus Fiscal Policy

Policymakers often must choose between monetary and fiscal policies. Under some circumstances, fiscal policies will be preferred to monetary policies, while the converse may be true under alternative conditions. For the given hypothetical conditions, indicate whether the policymaker would have a preference for fiscal policy (F) or monetary policy (M).

_____ 1. Investment is relatively responsive to changes in interest rates.

_____ 2. The demand for money is unaffected by the interest rate.

_____ 3. Investment is relatively responsive to changes in the interest rate, and the demand for money is unaffected by the interest rate.

_____ 4. The demand for money is relatively responsive to changes in the interest rate, and investment is relatively unresponsive to changes in the interest rate.

_____ 5. Investment is completely crowded out when taxes are cut or government spending is increased.

## Exercise 7: Factors that Cause the Aggregate Demand Curve to Shift

In the following table, factors that cause the aggregate demand curve to shift are listed. For a decrease in the variable, indicate whether the aggregate demand shifts to the right ($\rightarrow$) or to the left ($\leftarrow$).

### Factors that Cause the Aggregate Demand Curve to Shift

| Change in Variable | | Direction of Aggregate Demand Curve Shift | |
|---|---|---|---|
| Taxes | $\downarrow$ | A. | _____ |
| Money Supply | $\downarrow$ | B. | _____ |
| Government spending | $\downarrow$ | C. | _____ |
| Autonomous consumption | $\downarrow$ | D. | _____ |
| Money demand | $\downarrow$ | E. | _____ |
| Business confidence | $\downarrow$ | F. | _____ |

## SELF-TEST

## Part A: True-False Questions

Circle whether the following statements are true (T) or false (F).

T   F   1.   An increase in the interest rate causes the IS curve to shift to the left, since investment spending will fall.

T  F  2.  If businesses should suddenly become "bearish" (pessimistic) about the future profitability of investment, aggregate output will fall, all else constant. This is shown as a leftward shift of the IS curve.

T  F  3.  Financial innovation – by increasing the liquidity of financial assets – has enabled some people to reduce their demand for money. The decline in the demand for money has the effect of shifting the LM curve to the left.

T  F  4.  An expansion of the money supply will lead to lower interest rates and an increase in investment spending as people attempt to rid themselves of excess money balances.

T  F  5.  The condition known as complete crowding out occurs when the demand for money is insensitive to the interest rate.

T  F  6.  The effect of an open market purchase is to shift the LM curve to the left.

T  F  7.  Assume that money demand is very unstable and the IS curve is stable. Such knowledge makes the case for monetary targeting stronger, since the IS curve will be stable relative to the LM curve.

T  F  8.  A decline in taxes, as occurred in 1964, causes the aggregate demand curve to shift to the left.

T  F  9.  Monetary policy changes have no effect on the aggregate demand curve, since it is only factors that shift the IS curve which affect aggregate demand.

T  F  10.  High unemployment leads the Federal Reserve to expand the money supply. Such a policy will shift both the LM and aggregate demand curves to the right.

## Part B: Multiple-Choice Questions

Circle the appropriate answer.

1.  Which of the following causes the IS curve to shift to the left?

    a.  Increase in taxes
    b.  Increase in government spending
    c.  Increase in the money supply
    d.  All of the above
    e.  Only (b) and (c) of the above

2.  An increase in government spending causes both interest rates and aggregate output to increase. In the ISLM framework, this is represented by a _____ shift of the _____ curve.

    a.  leftward; LM
    b.  rightward; LM
    c.  leftward; IS
    d.  rightward; IS

3.  In the early 1930s there was a significant contraction in the money supply.  In the ISLM framework, such a contraction is illustrated as a _____ shift of the _____ curve.

    a.  rightward; IS
    b.  rightward; LM
    c.  leftward; IS
    d.  leftward; LM

4.  In 1981, President Reagan was able to get through Congress a fiscal package containing a tax cut and increased federal expenditures.  Such a policy shifts the _____ curve to the _____.

    a.  LM; left
    b.  IS; right
    c.  LM; right
    d.  IS; left

5.  Assume that an economy suffers a recession in spite of an expansionary monetary policy.  The ISLM framework suggests that even if the LM curve shifts to the right, the level of aggregate output might fall if the

    a.  IS curve shifts to the right.
    b.  investment function shifts to the right.
    c.  IS curve shifts to the left.
    d.  taxes are cut.

6.  Suppose that the economy is suffering from both high interest rates and high unemployment.  Viewed from an ISLM framework, we can conclude that _____ policy has been too _____.

    a.  fiscal; expansionary
    b.  monetary; expansionary
    c.  monetary; contractionary
    d.  fiscal; contractionary

7.  Assume that econometric studies indicate that the demand for money is highly sensitive to interest rate changes.  Such evidence would tend to support the belief that

    a.  fiscal policy has no aggregate output effects.
    b.  fiscal policy is effective in increasing output.
    c.  monetary policy is effective in increasing output.
    d.  none of the above is true.

8.  Investment spending in the country Curtonia is highly unstable, making the IS curve very unstable relative to the LM curve.  Given the nature of the economy, the Central Bank of Curtonia will want to target the

    a.  money supply.
    b.  interest rate.
    c.  exchange rate.
    d.  discount rate.
    e.  monetary base.

9.  The aggregate demand curve slopes downward to the right, since

    a.  a decline in the price level raises the real money supply, lowering interest rates.
    b.  a decline in the price level raises the real money supply, causing output to fall.
    c.  an increase in the price level raises the real money supply, causing output to rise.
    d.  none of the above occurs.

10. A Federal Reserve purchase of government securities will shift the aggregate demand curve in which direction?

    a.  Right
    b.  Left
    c.  A Fed purchase of securities does not shift the aggregate demand curve.
    d.  All of the above are a possible result of an expansion in the money supply.

11. Assume that the Federal Reserve pursues a policy of pegging the interest rate.  If government policymakers _____ government spending, the Fed will be forced to _____ the money supply to keep interest rates from _____.

    a.  decrease; decrease; rising
    b.  decrease; increase; falling
    c.  increase; increase; rising
    d.  increase; decrease; rising

12. Within the ISLM framework an expansionary fiscal policy causes a(n) _____ in aggregate output and cause interest rates to _____.

    a.  increase; fall
    b.  increase; rise
    c.  decrease; fall
    d.  decrease; rise

13. Interest rates in the United States rose over the period 1965 through 1966.  Since this coincided with the Vietnam war buildup, we can assume that the _____ curve shifted to the _____.

    a.  LM; left
    b.  LM; right
    c.  IS; left
    d.  IS; right

14. The _____ responsive is money demand to the interest rate, the _____ effective is _____ policy.

    a.  more; more; fiscal
    b.  more; less; fiscal
    c.  less; more; fiscal
    d.  less; less; monetary

15. A _____ in the price level, ceteris paribus, will mean _____ interest rates and thus a _____ level of investment.

   a. rise; higher; higher
   b. rise; lower; higher
   c. decline; higher; lower
   d. decline; lower; higher

# Chapter 24

## *Aggregate Demand and Supply Analysis*

### CHAPTER SYNOPSIS/COMPLETIONS

This chapter develops the basic tool of aggregate demand and supply analysis in order to study the effects of money on aggregate output and the price level. The model is very powerful in gaining insight into the workings of the economy, yet it is relatively simple and, with a little work, relatively easy to master.

We construct the aggregate demand and aggregate supply model by first examining the individual curves. The aggregate demand curve describes the relationship between the (1)_____ level and the quantity of aggregate output demanded. The monetarists derive the aggregate demand curve from the quantity theory of money. Holding the money supply and velocity constant, an increase in the price level reduces the quantity of aggregate output demanded. A falling price level implies an increase in the quantity of aggregate output demanded. Keynesians argue that a falling price level – because it causes the real (2)_____ _____ to increase which in turn lowers interest rates – causes both investment spending and the quantity of aggregate output demanded to (3)_____. Both explanations are consistent with a downward sloping aggregate demand curve.

Though both monetarists and Keynesians agree that the aggregate demand curve is downward sloping, they hold different views about the factors that cause the aggregate demand curve to shift. Monetarists contend that changes in the (4)_____ supply are the primary source of changes in aggregate demand. An increase in the money supply shifts the aggregate demand curve to the (5)_____, while a decrease in the money supply shifts it to the left.

Keynesians do not dispute that a change in the money supply shifts aggregate demand, but they regard changes in fiscal policy and autonomous expenditure as additional factors that shift the aggregate demand curve. For example, Keynesians believe that increased government expenditures or a cut in taxes will shift the aggregate demand curve to the (6)_____, while a decrease in government expenditures or a tax increase shifts the aggregate demand curve to the left.

The aggregate supply curve is upward sloping, illustrating that an increase in the price level will lead to an increase in the quantity of output supplied, all else constant. Explaining why the aggregate supply curve slopes upward is fairly straightforward. Since the costs of many inputs (factors of production) tend to be (7)_____ in the short run, an increase in the price of the output will mean greater profits, encouraging firms to (8)_____ production, increasing the quantity of aggregate output supplied.

Note, however, that this increase in output cannot last. Eventually workers will demand higher wages, and resource suppliers will demand higher prices. As factor prices (9)_____, the aggregate supply curve shifts in, causing aggregate output supplied to fall back to its original level.

Combining the aggregate supply and the aggregate demand curves allows one to consider the effects on the price level and aggregate output when one of the factors affecting either aggregate demand or aggregate supply changes. For example, an increase in the money supply shifts the aggregate demand curve to the right. This implies that an increase in the money supply will cause both (10)_____

_____ and the price level to increase in the short run. In the long run, the (11)_____ _____ curve will shift in as workers demand higher nominal wages to compensate for the increase in prices. Since the aggregate supply curve will shift when unemployment and aggregate output differ from their natural rate levels, the long-run equilibrium will coincide with the natural rate level of output.

Therefore, changes in either monetary or fiscal policies can have only temporary effects on unemployment and aggregate output. In the long run, monetary and fiscal expansions can do nothing more than raise the (12)_____ _____. This concept is illustrated by the long run aggregate supply curve, a vertical line passing through the natural rate of aggregate output.

The aggregate supply curve will shift inward not only as workers come to expect higher inflation, but when negative supply (13)_____ hit the economy (as in the 1970s when OPEC dramatically increased the price of oil) or when workers push for higher real wages. Unfortunately, the economy experiences both rising prices and falling aggregate output in the short run, an outcome referred to as (14)_____. Eventually, the aggregate supply curve will shift outward returning the economy to the natural rate of output.

The aggregate demand and supply analysis indicates that aggregate output and unemployment can deviate from their natural-rate levels for two reasons: shifts in aggregate demand and shifts in aggregate supply. Whether these shifts cause aggregate output to rise or fall, the change will be temporary. Factor prices eventually adjust, moving the economy back to the vertical long-run aggregate supply curve. In the long run, shifts in aggregate demand merely change the price level, and shifts in short-run aggregate supply have no permanent effects.

## EXERCISES

### Exercise 1: Factors that Shift the Aggregate Demand Curve

A. List the factors that cause the aggregate demand curve to shift to the right.

1. _____

2. _____

3. _____

4. _____

5. _____

6. _____

B. List the factors that cause the aggregate demand curve to shift to the left.

1. _____

2. _____

3. _____

4. _____

5. _____

6. _____

### Exercise 2: The Monetarist View of Aggregate Demand

A. The equation of exchange tells us that aggregate spending will equal the product of the money supply and income velocity. Assume that the money supply is $600 billion and velocity is 6. Graph the aggregate demand function in Figure 24A.

FIGURE 24A

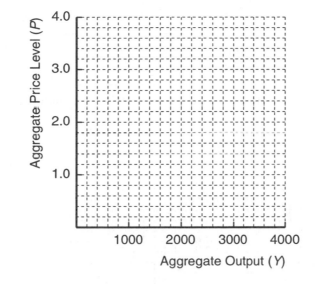

B. If the Fed lowers the money supply to $500 billion, what will happen to aggregate spending if velocity remains unchanged?

_____

C. Graph the new aggregate demand curve in Figure 24A representing the aggregate output price level combinations for the level of aggregate spending in part B.

### Exercise 3: Factors that Shift the Aggregate Supply Curve

In the following table, factors that cause the aggregate supply curve to shift are listed. For each factor indicate whether the aggregate supply curve shifts in ($\leftarrow$) or shifts out ($\rightarrow$).

Factors that Shift the Aggregate Supply Curve

| Factor | Shift in Aggregate Supply |
|---|---|
| 1. OPEC increases the price of oil | |
| 2. "Tightening" up of the labor market | |
| 3. A decline in the expected price level | |
| 4. Drought conditions in the Midwest | |
| 5. Citrus crops in Florida freeze | |
| 6. Improved productivity | |

## Exercise 4: Shifts in Aggregate Supply

A.  Using information provided in the following table and assuming that the aggregate demand curve remained at AD₁ in both periods, graph in Figure 24B the short-run aggregate supply curves for the two years.

| Year (1972$) | Real GNP (1972 = 100) | GNP Deflator | Unemployment Rate | Natural Unemployment Rate |
|---|---|---|---|---|
| 1974 | 1248.0 | 114.9 | 5.6 | 5.4 |
| 1975 | 1233.9 | 125.5 | 8.5 | 5.4 |

Source:  R. Gordon, *Macroeconomics*, 3d Ed. (Boston: Little, Brown, 1984), Appendix B.

FIGURE 24B

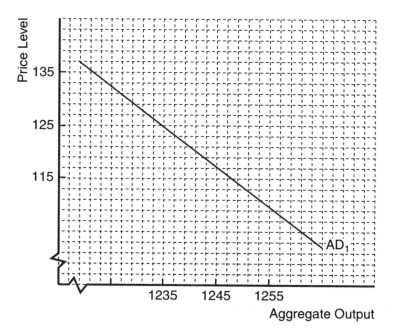

B. Is it likely that worker's expectations of higher wages were the force that shifted the aggregate supply curve in?

_____

_____

## Exercise 5: Shifts in Aggregate Demand

Using the information given in the following table, plot the price level and real output combinations for the years 1929 to 1936 in Figure 24C.  Also, in Figure 24C graph the decline in  aggregate demand from 1929 to 1933 (assume that the aggregate supply curve does not shift during this period). Then graph the aggregate demand and supply curves for 1936. Explain the behavior of the shifts.

| Year | GNP (1958$) | CPI (1958=100) | Money Supply | Expenditures (1958$) |
|------|-------------|----------------|--------------|----------------------|
| 1929 | 203.6 | 59.7 | ---- | 22.0 |
| 1930 | 183.3 | 58.2 | 25.8 | 24.3 |
| 1931 | 169.2 | 53.0 | 24.1 | 25.4 |
| 1932 | 144.1 | 47.6 | 21.1 | 24.2 |
| 1933 | 141.5 | 45.1 | 19.9 | 23.3 |
| 1934 | 154.3 | 46.6 | 21.9 | 26.6 |
| 1935 | 169.6 | 47.8 | 25.9 | 27.0 |
| 1936 | 193.0 | 48.3 | 29.9 | 31.8 |

Source: *Economic Report of the President*, 1966; and R. J. Gordon, *Macroeconomics*, 2d Ed. (Boston: Little, Brown, 1981), Appendix B.

FIGURE 24C

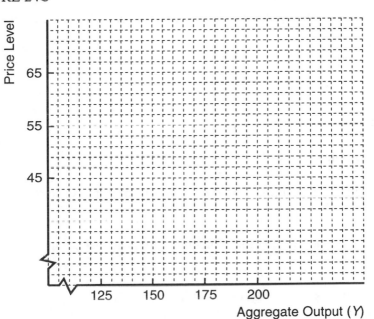

**Exercise 6: Differences Between Monetarist and Keynesian Analyses**

Indicate whether the following statements are consistent with monetarist aggregate demand and supply analysis (M), Keynesian aggregate demand and supply analysis (K), both (B), or neither (N).

_____ 1. The aggregate demand curve is downward sloping and shifts in response to changes in the money supply.

_____ 2. The short-run aggregate supply curve is vertical at the natural rate of output.

_____ 3. Movements in the price level and aggregate output are driven by changes in government spending and taxes in addition to changes in the money supply.

_____ 4. The economy will return to full employment in the face of shocks but active use of government intervention to stabilize the economy is to no avail.

_____ 5. An increase in government spending will not cause aggregate output to increase, since private spending will be "crowded out" by government spending.

_____ 6. Changes in consumer and business confidence, imports and exports, and government spending and taxes shift the aggregate demand curve.

_____ 7. Adjustments in wages and prices may be quite prolonged delaying the self-correction of the economy back to the natural-rate level.

_____ 8. Changes in aggregate spending are primarily determined by changes in the money supply.

_____ 9. The aggregate supply curve does not remain fixed over time.  Rather, it shifts whenever aggregate output is either above or below the natural-rate level.

_____10. A rise in the expected price level causes the aggregate supply curve to shift inward.


## SELF-TEST

### Part A: True-False Questions

Circle whether the following statements are true (T) or false (F).

T  F  1. Monetarists argue that a change in the money supply is the primary factor causing aggregate demand to shift.

T  F  2. Income velocity is defined as the value of nominal gross national product divided by the money supply.

T  F  3. Milton Friedman argues that changes in the money supply affect output almost immediately as if it were injected directly into the bloodstream of the economy.

T  F  4. Along a given aggregate supply curve, input prices are assumed fixed.

T  F  5. If workers come to expect higher inflation, the aggregate supply curve will shift out to reflect the expectation of lower real wages.

T  F  6. Persistently high unemployment is likely to force wage concessions by workers, resulting in an eventual outward shift in the aggregate supply curve.

T  F  7. Suppose that the economy is currently producing an aggregate output above the natural level of aggregate output.  We can expect price reductions in the future as firms lower prices to sell the excess output.

T   F   8. Aggregate demand and supply analysis indicates that if adverse weather causes major crop failures throughout the United States, aggregate output will fall and the price level will rise.

T   F   9. In 1970 both inflation and unemployment increased. Such a condition is called "stagflation."

T   F   10. Monetarists, unlike Keynesians, believe that wages and prices adjust very slowly over time.

## Part B. Multiple-Choice Questions

Circle the appropriate answer.

1.  Keynesians and monetarists have different views regarding the factors that cause the aggregate demand curve to shift. This difference is best explained by which of the following statements?

    a. Monetarists place greater emphasis on the importance of money yet believe that fiscal actions can shift the aggregate demand curve, while Keynesians contend that money has no effect on aggregate demand.
    b. Keynesians believe that only fiscal policy can affect aggregate demand, while monetarists believe that fiscal policy is ineffective in altering the level of aggregate demand.
    c. Keynesians contend that both fiscal and monetary policy actions influence the level of aggregate demand, while monetarists claim that monetary policy is far more important than fiscal policy in affecting the level of aggregate demand.
    d. Keynesians place more significance on monetary actions than on fiscal actions, while monetarists believe that neither monetary nor fiscal actions influence the level of aggregate demand.

2.  In Keynesian analysis, if investment is unresponsive to changes in the interest rate, the aggregate demand curve will be

    a. downward sloping.
    b. horizontal.
    c. downward sloping if consumer expenditures are sensitive to the interest rate.
    d. none of the above.

3.  The upward slope of the short-run aggregate supply curve reflects the belief that

    a. factor prices are more flexible than output prices.
    b. output prices are more flexible than factor prices.
    c. factor prices are fixed in the long run.
    d. factor prices are completely flexible even in the short run.

4.  Which of the following factors cause the aggregate supply curve to shift?

    a. Changes in the tightness of the labor market
    b. Changes in expectations of inflation
    c. Supply shocks such as commodity price changes
    d. Attempts by workers to push up their real wages
    e. All of the above

5. The aggregate demand and supply analysis suggests that the economy has a self-correcting mechanism which ensures that aggregate output and unemployment will move toward their natural-rate levels. However, Keynesians contend that this mechanism

   a.  is unacceptably slow due to the stickiness of wages.
   b.  cannot be improved on, even though the adjustment process is slow.
   c.  while slow, can be improved through activist policy.
   d.  does both (a) and (b) of the above.
   e.  does both (a) and (c) of the above.

6. If the economy experiences a period of both a rising price level and rising unemployment, one can reasonably infer

   a.  that the aggregate demand curve has shifted to the right.
   b.  that the aggregate demand curve has shifted to the left.
   c.  that the aggregate supply curve has shifted out.
   d.  that the aggregate supply curve has shifted in.

7. Which of the following statements accurately describes the difference between monetarists and Keynesians?

   a.  Monetarists believe that crowding out can be a major problem reducing the effectiveness of fiscal policy, while Keynesians contend that crowding out will not be complete.
   b.  Keynesians regard wage stickiness as a factor that prevents quick adjustment back to the natural rate of unemployment, while monetarists believe that wages are sufficiently flexible to ensure relatively quick adjustment.
   c.  Monetarists do not see a need for activist policies, while Keynesians argue that activist policies can prove highly beneficial.
   d.  All of the above.
   e.  Only (a) and (c) accurately represent differences between monetarists and Keynesians.

8. The long-run aggregate supply curve is a vertical line running through

   a.  the natural rate of output.
   b.  the natural-rate price level.
   c.  the natural rate of unemployment.
   d.  none of the above.

9. Which of the following statements is not one commonly associated with Keynesian analysis?

   a.  "The economy is inherently unstable, and failure to take corrective action now could mean prolonged unemployment."
   b.  "It would be foolish to tie the hands of government policymakers and prevent them from responding to a negative supply shock."
   c.  "Wages and prices, while not perfectly flexible, do respond quickly, and in the correct direction, to economic disturbances."
   d.  "Crowding out is unlikely to be a problem in the current economic recovery."

10. If policymakers accommodate supply shocks by increasing the money supply, unemployment will return to its natural level sooner, but

    a.  even Keynesians, in general, will oppose such a policy.
    b.  the price level will increase in the long run.
    c.  prices will take much longer in returning to their original level.
    d.  none of the above will occur.

11. Keynesians contend that at a _____ price level the real quantity of money _____, _____ higher spending.

    a.  lower; expands; encouraging
    b.  lower; expands; discouraging
    c.  lower; contracts; discouraging
    d.  higher; expands; encouraging
    e.  higher; expands; discouraging

12. OPEC oil price increases or citrus fruit crop freezes are referred to as _____ price shocks and cause the aggregate _____ curve to shift _____.

    a.  negative; demand; inward
    b.  negative; demand; outward
    c.  negative; supply; inward
    d.  positive; supply; inward
    e.  positive; supply; outward

13. The aggregate demand and supply framework indicates that in the long run the ultimate effect of a _____ in the money supply is an increase in _____.

    a.  fall; aggregate output
    b.  fall; the price level
    c.  rise; aggregate output
    d.  rise; the price level

14. _____ tend to question the effectiveness of _____ policy in shifting aggregate _____, since they believe that crowding out of investment will be nearly complete.

    a.  Keynesians; fiscal; demand
    b.  Keynesians; monetary; demand
    c.  Monetarists; monetary; demand
    d.  Monetarists; fiscal; demand
    e.  Keynesians; monetary; supply

15. The _____ supply shock from declining oil prices in 1986 did not produce the business cycle boom that some had predicted, in part, because a _____ in net exports that year caused a weakening in aggregate _____.

    a.  negative; decline; demand
    b.  negative; rise; supply
    c.  negative; decline; supply
    d.  positive; rise; supply
    e.  positive; decline; demand

# Chapter 25

## Transmission Mechanisms of Monetary Policy: The Evidence

### CHAPTER SYNOPSIS/COMPLETIONS

This chapter examines the connection between monetary policy and economic activity, focusing on the debate between the (1)_____ and the Keynesians over the years since the Great Depression, and illustrates how the accumulation of evidence has led to greater consensus regarding the importance of monetary policy on economic activity. Although views have converged, differences still exist, primarily because monetarists and Keynesians prefer different types of (2)_____.

Monetarists regard monetary policy's effect on economic activity as diverse and constantly changing; thus they prefer to model the impact of money supply changes directly. Evidence indicating a high correlation between changes in money growth and fluctuations in economic activity is referred to as (3)_____ _____ evidence. Reduced form evidence merely indicates the existence of a relationship; it does not describe how monetary policy affects economic activity.

Keynesians tend to be skeptical of reduced form evidence, preferring to model the channels by which monetary policy affects the economy. Keynesian models are constructed using a system of equations, each equation describing part of the monetary transmission mechanism. These models are called (4)_____ models because they attempt to describe the relationships among the various segments of the economy; that is, they attempt to describe how the pieces of the structure fit together.

The structural model approach has three major advantages over the reduced form approach:

1. Structural models allow us to evaluate each segment separately for its plausibility. This investigation improves our understanding of monetary policy's effect on economic activity.

2. Our improved understanding of the economy's workings may mean more accurate economic (5)_____.

3. Our ability to predict the consequences of institutional change may be improved from the knowledge of economic relationships provided by structural model evidence.

One disadvantage of the structural model approach is that it must be correctly (6)_____ or it will tend to give poor predictions. For example, suppose that a change in money growth causes stock prices to change, which in turn causes consumer expenditures to change. If this transmission mechanism is not part of the model, then the model will provide inaccurate results. In weighing the advantages and disadvantages monetarists conclude that reduced form models give more reliable results.

Although less sensitive to the correct specification, reduced form models can prove to be misleading. Since reduced form models focus on correlations, they may imply that movements in one variable cause the movements in another when causality actually runs in the other direction or is nonexistent. (7)_____ _____ refers to the condition where influence runs in the direction opposite that hypothesized. If two variables are highly correlated, it is possible that an independent (8)_____ factor influences the behavior of both variables in a way that gives the appearance that one influences the other.

Early Keynesian models were poorly specified, leading to results indicating that monetary policy had little effect on economic activity. Had the early Keynesians specified relationships in terms of (9)_____ interest rates, rather than nominal interest rates, they would have been less likely to conclude that monetary policy does not matter.

In the early 1960s, the monetarists presented evidence indicating that monetary policy had never been more contractionary than during the Great Depression. The implication was that monetary policy mattered a great deal in determining aggregate economic activity. Milton Friedman and other monetarists emphasized three types of evidence when making their case about the importance of monetary growth: timing evidence, (10)_____ evidence, and historical evidence. Of the three types of evidence, most economists find (11)_____ evidence to be the most supportive of monetarist theory.

The impact of the monetarist attack on early Keynesian models led to improvements in these models to account for more channels of monetary influence on aggregate economic activity. Initial efforts extended the traditional interest-rate channel to account for changes in *consumer durable expenditure*. An important feature of the interest-rate mechanism is its emphasis on *real* rather than the nominal interest rate as the rate that influences business and consumer decisions. Because it is the real interest rate that affects spending, monetary policy can stimulate spending even when the nominal interest rate drops to zero. An expansionary monetary policy will raise the expected (12)_____ _____ and hence expected inflation, thereby lowering the real interest rate.

In addition to the interest-rate transmission mechanism, monetary policy can affect spending through asset prices (primarily foreign exchange and equities) other than interest rates and through asymmetric information effects on credit markets (the so-called *credit view*). For example, an expansionary monetary policy, because it lowers the real interest rate, causes the domestic currency to depreciate, which stimulates net exports and gross domestic product. Tobin's *q* theory indicates that (13)_____ (or equity) prices can have an important effect on investment spending. Under this monetary channel, increasing stock prices stimulate investment as firms discover that the cost of replacement capital declines relative to the market value of business firms.

According to the credit view, an expansionary monetary policy increases bank reserves and deposits, increasing the volume of bank loans available to borrowers who do not have access to credit markets to finance their spending. In addition to this bank lending channel, monetary policy may influence spending through the balance sheet channel. An expansionary monetary policy raises the net (14)_____ of firms (improves their balance sheets), reducing adverse selection and moral hazard problems, increasing the willingness of banks to extend loans to these firms.

Other credit channels include: the cash flow channel, the unanticipated price level channel, and household liquidity effects. Expansionary monetary policy lowers nominal interest rates, reducing interest payments and thereby increasing (15)_____ _____. Because banks know that borrowers' improved liquidity reduces adverse selection and moral hazard problems, lending increases. Similarly, expansionary monetary policy raises the price level, lowering the real value of firms' liabilities. This improvement in firms' balance sheets reduces adverse selection and moral hazard problems, thereby increasing banks' willingness to lend. The view that unanticipated movements in the price level have important effects on aggregate demand is a key feature of the *debt-deflation* view of the Great Depression. Because households' interest payments, cash flow, liquidity, real value of assets and liabilities are affected by changes in interest rates and the price level, monetary policy influences consumer spending too.

These three monetary transmission mechanisms indicate that changes in monetary policy can have a significant effect on aggregate demand. Research findings from the Great Depression support the economic significance of these monetary channels. Declining stock prices, the decline in consumers' wealth, and the increase in real consumer debt (due to falling prices) depressed consumption, consumer durable expenditure (by over 50 percent from 1929 to 1933), and expenditure on housing (by 80 percent).

Although not all issues about monetary policy have been fully resolved, four lessons for monetary policy can be drawn from this chapter. First, changes in short-term nominal interest rates do not provide clear signals about monetary policy. Second, changes in prices of assets other than short-term debt instruments contain information about monetary policy. Third, fears about a liquidity trap are likely unfounded, as monetary policy can be effective in reviving a weak economy even when short-term interest rates are quite low. Fourth, price level stability is an important goal for monetary policy.

## EXERCISES

### Exercise 1: Two Types of Empirical Evidence

For each of the following statements, indicate whether reduced form evidence or structural model evidence is being presented by writing in the space provided an R for reduced form evidence and an S for structural model evidence.

_____ 1. Dutch researchers report that eating fish is associated with a lower risk of heart attack.

_____ 2. Eating fish appears to be effective in reducing heart attack risk. Fish oil reduces fat and cholesterol in the blood thereby preventing heart disease, the underlying cause of heart attacks.

_____ 3. Medical research has found that men who take one aspirin per day following a coronary attack significantly reduced the probability of a second coronary.

_____ 4. Drinking one ounce of alcohol per day seems to reduce cholesterol levels in the bloodstream, reducing the likelihood of coronary heart disease and heart attack.

_____ 5. Canadian researchers report that beer drinkers are less likely to report illness than nondrinkers, although they could not directly link the beverage itself to better health.

_____ 6. A reduction in the money supply causes the volume of loans to fall, which causes investment to fall as banks ration credit. This in turn causes aggregate output to fall.

_____ 7. An increase in the money supply causes interest rates to fall. Consumer durable expenditures rise in response, leading to an increase in aggregate output.

_____ 8. An increase in the money supply increases the demand for stocks. Rising stock prices cause Tobin's $q$ to increase, which induces firms to undertake more investment spending.

_____ 9. An increase in the money supply is followed by an increase in aggregate output.

**Exercise 2: Monetarists Versus the Keynesians**

Listed below are a number of statements. Indicate which of the following statements are associated with monetarists (M) and which are associated with Keynesians (K).

_____ 1. Structural model evidence is superior to reduced form evidence because it allows us to better understand how the economy works.

_____ 2. Reduced form evidence allows for the luxury of not having to know all the many ways in which money might affect economic activity.

_____ 3. The channels through which changes in the money supply affect output and employment are numerous and ever changing.

_____ 4. The problem with looking at simple correlations is that it may be extremely difficult to determine the direction of causation. How can one be sure that aggregate output does not affect money growth rather than the reverse?

_____ 5. Changes in the money supply are the most important determinants of economic fluctuations in output, employment, and prices.

_____ 6. The main advantage of employing a monetary rule is that it would greatly diminish the use of discretionary stabilization policies.

_____ 7. The economy tends to be very unstable, making the use of discretionary monetary and fiscal policy essential to the maintenance of full employment.

_____ 8. We agree with the belief that money matters, but the weight of empirical evidence suggests that money is not all that matters.

_____ 9. Money is extremely important, but fiscal policy as well as net exports and "animal spirits" also contribute to fluctuations in aggregate demand.

**Exercise 3: Interpreting Reduced Form Evidence**

Some economists contend that inflation is the result of cost-push pressures exerted on the economy by powerful labor unions and big businesses. To support their position, they produce empirical results which clearly indicate that rising costs tend to precede rising prices in many instances. Despite the existence of such evidence, many economists in the United States are highly skeptical of cost-push theories.

1. Could there be a problem of reverse causation in the data that makes it appear as though cost increases precede price increases?

_____

_____

2. How might the prevalence of three-year labor contracts help account for the perception that costs lead prices?

_____

_____

3. Many economists dismiss the cost-push theory of inflation by pointing to a third factor that is believed to drive both costs and prices. What do you suppose this third factor is?

_____

_____

## Exercise 4: Transmission Mechanisms of Monetary Policy

The traditional Keynesian view of the monetary transmission mechanism can be characterized as follows:

$$M \uparrow \to i_r \downarrow \to I \uparrow \to Y \uparrow$$

In response to monetarist challenges in the 1960s, many Keynesian economists began searching for new channels of monetary influence on economic activity. Match the names of transmission mechanisms on the right with their schematic depictions on the left.

_____

_____1.  $M \uparrow \to$ stock prices $\uparrow \to$ value of financial assets $\uparrow \to$ likelihood of financial distress $\downarrow$ $\to$ consumer durable expenditures $\uparrow$ and residential housing $\uparrow \to Y \uparrow$ 

a. Balance sheet channel

_____2.  $M \uparrow \to$ unanticipated $P \uparrow \to$ adverse selection $\downarrow$ moral hazard $\downarrow \to$ lending $\uparrow \to I \uparrow \cdot Y \uparrow$ 

b. Cash flow channel

_____3.  $M \uparrow \to$ bank deposits $\uparrow \to$ bank loans $\uparrow$ $I \uparrow \to Y \uparrow$ 

c. Exchange-rate effect

_____4.  $M \uparrow \to P_e \uparrow \to$ adverse selection $\downarrow$, moral hazard $\downarrow \to$ lending $\uparrow \to I \uparrow \to Y \uparrow$ 

d. Household liquidity effect

_____5.  $M \uparrow \to$ stock prices $\uparrow \cdot q \uparrow$ investment $\uparrow \to Y \uparrow$ 

e. Unanticipated price level channel

_____6.  $M \uparrow \to i \downarrow \to$ cash flow $\uparrow \to$ adverse selection $\downarrow$, moral hazard $\downarrow \to$ lending $\uparrow \to I \uparrow \to Y \uparrow$ 

f. Bank lending channel

_____7.  $M \uparrow \to i_r \downarrow \to$ exchange rate $\downarrow$ $\to$ exports $\uparrow \to Y \uparrow$ 

g. Tobin's $q$ theory

_____

**SELF-TEST**

**Part A: True-False Questions**

Circle whether the following statements are true (T) or false (F).

T  F  1.  Reduced-form evidence examines whether one variable has an effect on another by looking at a sequence of steps and describing the process at each step so that the channels of influence can be better understood.

T  F  2.  One advantage of the structural-model approach is that it can give us a better understanding of how money influences economic activity.

T  F  3.  Correlation does not necessarily imply causation.

T  F  4.  Though nominal interest rates fell during the Great Depression to extremely low levels, real interest rates rose.

T  F  5.  Historical evidence that has focused on the effects of exogenous changes in the money supply indicates that changes in aggregate output are related to changes in money growth.

T  F  6.  Keynesians argue that while banks may tend to ration credit in response to "tight" monetary policy, such credit rationing has no effect on economic activity.

T  F  7.  Many economists believe that the bank lending channel played an important role in the slow recovery in the U.S. from the 1990-91 recession.

T  F  8.  Though Tobin's q theory provides a good explanation for the economic recovery that started in late 1982, it is inconsistent with the events of the Great Depression.

T  F  9.  Assume that the stock market index falls by over 500 points in one week and remains at this level long enough that people adjust their expectations downward regarding the average level of the stock market index.  One should expect this event to affect the level of consumption.

T  F  10.  Economic theory suggests that the stock market crash of 1929 depressed consumer expenditures due to the loss of wealth and the increase in financial distress.

**Part B: Multiple-Choice Questions**

Circle the appropriate answer.

1.  Monetarists prefer reduced-form models because they believe that

    a.  reverse causation is never a problem.
    b.  structural models may understate money's effect on economic activity.
    c.  money supply changes are always exogenous.
    d.  each of the above is true.

2. Scientists tend to be skeptical of reduced-form evidence because

   a. the finding of a high correlation between two variables does not always imply that changes in one cause changes in the other.
   b. reduced-form evidence may not account for all the channels of influence.
   c. it fails to add insight to the process that leads movements in one variable to cause movements in another.
   d. if the model is poorly specified it can lead to poor predictions about the future behavior of the variable of interest.
   e. of both (a) and (c) of the above.

3. Monetarist evidence in which declines in money growth are followed by recessions provides the strongest support for their position that monetary policy matters.

   a. statistical
   b. historical
   c. timing
   d. structural

4. Early Keynesians tended to dismiss the importance of monetary policy due to their findings that

   a. indicated the absence of a link between movements in nominal interest rates and investment spending.
   b. interest rates had fallen during the Great Depression.
   c. surveys of businessmen revealed that market interest rates had no effect on their decisions of how much to invest in new physical capital.
   d. all of the above are true.

5. Monetarists contend that reduced-form evidence provides valid proof that monetary policy affects economic activity when it can be shown that the change in the money supply

   a. is an endogenous event.
   b. is an exogenous event.
   c. preceded the change in economic activity.
   d. was expected.

6. What were the monetarists' main conclusions from the early reduced-form evidence?

   a. One had to be careful to distinguish between real and nominal magnitudes.
   b. The early Keynesian models were incorrectly specified because they accounted for too few channels of monetary influence.
   c. Monetarists models showed that fiscal policies had little or no effect on economic activity.
   d. Both (a) and (b) are correct.
   e. Both (b) and (c) are correct.

7.  The availability hypothesis suggests that in periods characterized by "tight" money, banks may

    a.  stop making any loans.
    b.  continue to make loans, but only at much higher interest rates.
    c.  ration credit rather than significantly raise interest rates.
    d.  make available more loans to businesses with which they have had no previous dealings.

8.  Because of asymmetric information problems in credit markets, monetary policy may affect economic activity through the balance sheet channel, which holds that an increase in money supply

    a.  raises equity prices, which lowers the cost of new capital relative to the market value of firms, thereby increasing investment spending.
    b.  raises the net worth of firms, decreasing adverse selection and moral hazard problems, thereby increasing banks' willingness to lend to finance investment spending.
    c.  raises the level of bank reserves, deposits, and the quantity of bank loans available, which raises the spending by those individuals who do not have access to credit markets.
    d.  does none of the above.

9.  Assume that a contractionary monetary policy lowers the price level by more than anticipated, raising the real value of consumer debt. New Keynesian structural models suggest that a contractionary monetary policy is channeled into lower consumer expenditure through which of the following effect?

    a.  Bank lending channel
    b.  Tobin's $q$
    c.  Traditional interest-rate effect
    d   Household liquidity effect

10. The household liquidity effect suggests that higher stock prices lead to increased consumer expenditures because consumers

    a.  feel more secure about their financial position.
    b.  will want to sell their stocks and spend the proceeds before stock prices go back down.
    c.  believe that they will receive higher wages in the near future because companies are now more profitable.
    d.  believe none of the above.

11. _____ prefer to emphasize _____ model evidence because they believe that _____ models do not add insight into how monetary policy affects the economy.

    a.  Keynesians; structural; reduced form
    b.  Keynesians; reduced form; structural
    c.  Monetarists; structural; reduced form
    d.  Monetarists; reduced form; structural

12. Monetarists claim that simple _____ models, because they may ignore important transmission mechanisms, tend to _____ the importance of monetary policy's effect on the economy.

    a.  structural; overstate
    b.  reduced form; overstate
    c.  structural; understate
    d.  reduced form; understate

13. Because they believed that _____ policy was _____, early Keynesians stressed the importance of _____ policy.

    a.  fiscal; ineffective; monetary
    b.  monetary; ineffective; fiscal
    c.  monetary; potent; monetary
    d.  fiscal; too potent; monetary

14. Economic theory suggests that _____ interest rates are a _____ important determinant than _____ interest rates in explaining the behavior of investment spending.

    a.  nominal; more; real
    b.  real; less; nominal
    c.  real; more; nominal
    d.  market; more; real
    e.  real; less; market

15. Which of the following accurately describe the current state of the monetarist-Keynesian debate on monetary policy and economic activity?

    a.  Keynesians still insist that monetary policy is not an important source of business cycle fluctuations.
    b.  Although Keynesians now agree that monetary policy matters, they do not believe that it is all that matters.
    c.  There is now general agreement among Keynesians that fiscal policy is indeed an extremely important source of business cycle fluctuations.
    d.  Only (a) and (c) of the above.

# Chapter 26

## *Money and Inflation*

### CHAPTER SYNOPSIS/COMPLETIONS

In this chapter the aggregate demand and supply analysis introduced in Chapter 24 is used to examine the role of monetary policy in creating inflation. Economists are in general agreement that inflation is always and everywhere a (1)"_____ phenomenon." Evidence from both historical and recent inflationary episodes confirms the proposition that sustained inflation results from excessive monetary expansion.

The consensus must appear at first to be highly unusual, given that much of the two previous chapters has been devoted to the disagreements between monetarists and Keynesians. The apparent paradox is solved by the precise way in which economists define inflation. A one-shot (or one-time) increase in the price level is simply not defined as inflation by economists. Only when the price level is continually rising do economists consider such episodes to be inflationary.

Keynesians, unlike monetarists, believe that one-shot tax cuts or government-spending boosts are likely to raise aggregate demand, and thus the price level, but they contend that any effect on inflation will be merely (2)_____. In their view, fiscal actions are incapable of generating sustained price increases. Thus monetarists and Keynesians agree that rapid money growth is both a sufficient and necessary condition explaining inflation.

Regarding negative supply shocks, economists are again in general agreement that it is only through monetary (3)_____ that such shocks prove inflationary. In the absence of an increase in money growth, the price level would rise, but it would not continue to do so.

One must naturally wonder why, if it is well understood, inflation continues to plague so many countries to this day. Examination of the U.S. experience suggests that governments pursue many goals, some of which are not (4)_____ with price stability. Specifically, federal government efforts designed to reduce unemployment in the 1960s proved incompatible with the goal of general price stability. In the 1970s, a series of negative (5)_____ _____ compounded the problem by pressuring government policymakers toward accommodation in order to prevent high rates of unemployment.

Higher wage demands by workers can lead to inflation if policymakers fear that such demands will cause rising unemployment. Additionally, the government may set its (6)_____ target too low, causing overexpansion and inflation.

214

Large government budget deficits are another possible source of excessive money growth. Politicians are extremely reluctant to cut government expenditures and raise taxes because such actions are often politically unpopular. Thus the political process is likely to generate a bias toward large budget deficits and inflation.

Economists often find it difficult to distinguish between demand pull and (7)_____ _____ inflation. Both types of inflation result when money growth becomes excessive. At first glance, one distinguishes between the two by looking at the behavior of employment. Demand pull inflation is associated with high employment, and cost push inflation is associated with (8)_____ employment. Once inflation is underway, however, demand pull inflations may exhibit cost push tendencies as workers demand higher wages in expectation of higher inflation.

The German experience from 1921 to 1923 illustrates a classical scenario of (9)_____. The unwillingness of German government officials to raise taxes and their inability to borrow an amount sufficient to finance huge budget deficits left money creation as the only available means of financing government expenditures. This scenario has been repeated many times, for example, in Argentina and Brazil in the 1980s. In both instances, massive government budget deficits initiated rapid expansions in the money supply, which in turn led to rapidly accelerating rates of inflation.

While these episodes, along with others, confirm that sustained inflation can only occur if there is a continually increasing money supply, a variety of sources are actually responsible for the inflationary monetary policies of many countries. Budget deficits, concerns over unemployment, negative supply shocks, union wage pushes, and concerns over interest rates often lead to inflationary monetary expansions.

The government budget (10)_____ indicates that an increase in the government budget deficit must lead to an increase in the sum of the monetary base and outstanding government bonds held by the public. If the government pays for additional spending with higher taxes, the deficit does not increase and the monetary base does not change. Should the government run a deficit, the Treasury must issue bonds to pay for the additional spending. If individuals buy these newly issued bonds, there will be no change in the monetary base. When the public purchases the bonds, the Treasury spends the proceeds returning the funds to the public. Hence the Treasury sale of bonds to the public has no effect on the monetary base.

Deficit financing through central bank security purchases, however, leads to an increase in the monetary base. This method of deficit financing is often referred to as "printing money" because high-powered money is created in the process. The action is probably better referred to as *monetizing the debt* because the money supply increases as a result of the increase in government debt.

An examination of inflation in the United States from 1960 through 1980 dismisses the importance of budget deficits in explaining rapid money growth. It appears that the concern over unemployment led to over-expansionary policies which kept unemployment low over the period 1965 to 1973. In the latter half of the 1970s, inflation resembles the (11)_____ _____ variety as unemployment rose to a level that exceeded the natural rate level.

The debate over the appropriateness of activist stabilization policy has important implications for anti-inflationary policies. Monetarists argue against the use of activist policy to reduce unemployment. They believe the effort is fruitless because any reduction in unemployment will be merely temporary, and it may hinder anti-inflationary efforts. Monetarists hold that the economy is inherently (12)_____, as wages are sufficiently flexible so that deviations from the natural rate of output are quickly reversed. Further, monetarists contend that even in those instances where adjustment tends to be relatively slow, activist policies are not likely to improve circumstances. In their view, policy responses are ineffectual, or even harmful, due to the long (13)_____

_____ that plague government decision making. For this reason, monetarists tend to support monetary rules that limit the discretion of policymakers.

Keynesians are optimistic about the effectiveness of activist policies. They believe that available evidence indicates that wages and prices are sticky, implying prolonged deviations from the natural rate of output and unemployment. Therefore, they contend that government fiscal or monetary actions are required to restore the economy to full employment. Unlike the monetarists, Keynesians contend that fiscal policy actions will be effective and dismiss the possibility of complete (14)_____ _____.

The phenomenon of "stagflation" in the latter half of the 1970s focused greater attention on the importance of expectations. People had come to expect that macroeconomic policies would always be accommodating; thus, when policymakers announced intentions of fighting inflation, few people believed them. Following this experience, economists in greater numbers began to question the desirability of (15)_____ policy. Some economists argued that nonaccommodating policy would yield better inflation performance with no more unemployment. Although this conclusion is not universally accepted, the recognition of the importance expectations play in economics has led to a new field of macroeconomics which is presented in Chapters 27 and 28.


## EXERCISES

### Exercise 1: Forces of Inflationary Monetary Policy

Monetarists and Keynesians agree that inflation is a monetary phenomenon. In other words, inflation would not persist in the absence of excessive money growth. Of interest to many economists, therefore, is the source of inflationary monetary policy. Why at times does the Fed expand the money supply at a rapid rate? Two explanations have been offered, both of which give us an insight into the forces that affect Fed decision making. List below the two explanations presented in the text that help explain expansionary monetary policy. Provide a brief explanation for each factor listed.

1. _____

   _____

2. _____

   _____


### Exercise 2: High Employment Targets and Inflation

The Full Employment and Balanced Growth Act of 1976 would have required the federal government to adopt policies to reduce unemployment to a level of 3% by 1980 (corresponding to an output level of $Y_{3\%}$ in Figure 26A). A modified version of this bill known as the Humphrey-Hawkins Act was signed by Jimmy Carter in 1978, but it amounted to little more than wishful thinking since the Act included no specific enforcement measures.

Assume that the economy is initially at the natural-rate level of output, where the aggregate demand curve, $AD_1$, and aggregate supply curve, $AS_1$, intersect at point 1 in Figure 26A. If the original version of the

Humphrey-Hawkins bill had passed, show where the government would shift the aggregate demand curve in Figure 26A and mark it as AD$_2$.

FIGURE 26A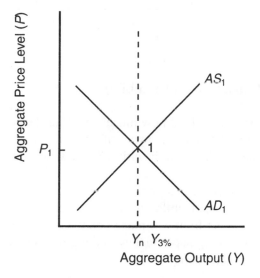

What would now happen to the aggregate supply curve? _____

Why? _____

Draw in the new aggregate supply curve as AS$_2$. Now what would the government do to aggregate demand?

_____

Draw in the new aggregate demand curve as AD$_3$. Where will the aggregate supply curve shift to now?

_____

Draw it in as AS$_3$  What is the outcome as the scenario discussed above repeats itself?

_____


## Exercise 3: Budget Deficits and Money Creation

When the U.S. government is running a budget deficit, does this necessarily cause the rate of money growth to increase?

_____

What two facts must be true in order for budget deficits to lead to higher money growth?

1. _____


2. _____

Do you think that both facts were true during the 1960-1980 period? _____

Why or why not? _____


### Exercise 4: Eliminating Inflation: The Importance of Credibility

The German hyperinflation provides a classic example of how mistaken policies can generate dire consequences. More importantly, the successful cure of the hyperinflation at a relatively low cost illustrates the importance of adopting an anti-inflationary policy that the citizenry views as credible.

The German government adopted several reforms at the time it announced its intention of controlling inflation. First, the government transferred the responsibility for monetary control to a new authority. Second, new currency was issued. Third, an upper limit was placed on the issue of this new currency. Fourth, the central bank was prohibited from issuing paper money to the government. Finally, the government took immediate steps to reduce budget deficits.

In the first half of the 1980s, Argentina was beset by hyperinflation. During this period, the Argentine government and central bank adopted numerous reforms, including some of the monetary reforms enacted by the German government of the 1920s. For example, Argentina has issued new currency, several times, and since 1955 there have been more than 30 different finance ministers, each of whom vowed to stop inflation. However, prior to June of 1985, Argentina made no effort to appreciably reduce its budget deficit in conjunction with its monetary reforms. Do you think that Argentina's monetary reforms were credible? Why or why not?

_____

_____

_____

Can the lack of credibility explain why the Argentine monetary reforms of the early 1980s proved unsuccessful in fighting inflation while the Germans were successful in the 1920s?

_____

_____

In June of 1985, Argentina instituted a set of policies to reduce its 1000% inflation rate. Argentina declared a one-week bank holiday, created a new currency in the interim, imposed wage and price controls, and implemented budget reforms that reduced the budget deficit from 8% to 4% of GDP. The strict anti-inflation plan proved successful in lowering the annual inflation rate to 50% by August of 1986. Disappointingly, however, the austerity plan only produced short-run benefits. By March of 1988, inflation was running at an annual rate of 207% – four times higher than predicted one year earlier by the economic team of President Raul Alfonsin. Recurrent price and wage freezes during 1987 and 1988 could not counteract the inflationary effects of budget deficits that had once again reached 8% of GDP by late 1987. Does the temporary success of the Argentine reforms suggest a key element to reducing inflation? Explain.

You may recall from chapter 20 that Argentina has had great success in reducing inflation since the adoption of a currency board in 1991.

_____

_____

_____

## Exercise 5: Credibility and the Prevention of Inflation

In October 1979, the Federal Reserve under the direction of its new chairman Paul Volcker made two dramatic announcements. First, it announced that it was changing the procedure it employed for conducting monetary policy. The Fed's new policy strategy would emphasize controlling monetary aggregates by targeting bank reserves. Prior to this announcement the Federal Reserve had focused on stabilizing the federal funds interest rate within a narrow range. Second, the Fed announced an increase in the discount rate. Significantly, the second announcement coincided with the Fed's move to get inflation – then running at double-digit rates – under control. Explain why the discount rate hike may have been important. After all, the discount rate plays only a minor role in monetary policy and the Fed could have reduced money growth simply by setting its federal funds rate target higher.

_____

_____

## Exercise 6: The Budget Deficit and the Monetary Base

A. List the three methods that can be used to finance government spending.

1. _____

2. _____

3. _____

B. Which of the three methods has an affect on the monetary base?

_____

C. When the government borrows from the Fed, the monetary base increases. This method of finance is referred to as

_____

D.  Does a large government deficit necessarily lead to a rapid growth in the monetary base?  Why or why not?

_____

_____

## SELF-TEST

### Part A: True-False Questions

Circle whether the following statements are true (T) or false (F).

T  F  1.  If inflation is defined as a continuous rise in the price level, then it is true that inflation can be eliminated by reducing the growth rate of the money supply to a low level.

T  F  2.  Keynesians disagree with the monetarists' proposition that inflation is a monetary phenomenon. That is, Keynesians believe that inflation can occur even when money growth has not been excessive.

T  F  3.  In the early 1980s, both Argentina and Israel experienced hyperinflation.  They differed, however, in that Israel had not overly expanded its money supply.

T  F  4.  The price level may rise in any one month due to factors unrelated to changes in the money supply.  Thus one can conclude that continual price-level increases need not be related to changes in the money supply.

T  F  5.  Keynesians argue that factors other than a continually increasing money supply may lead to sustained inflation.

T  F  6.  Sustained inflation occurs when unions successfully push up wages, even if the monetary authorities refuse to accommodate the higher wages by expanding the money supply.

T  F  7.  Inflation according to one view, is the side effect of government efforts to cure high unemployment.

T  F  8.  At first glance, one would expect falling unemployment to be associated with demand-pull inflation.

T  F  9.  Huge government budget deficits have been the initiating source of inflationary monetary policies in every instance of hyperinflation.

T  F  10. An examination of the period from 1960 through 1980 suggests that large government deficits are to blame for the inflationary monetary policies of this period.

**Part B: Multiple-Choice Questions**

Circle the appropriate answer.

1.  A continual increase in the money supply, according to Keynesian analysis, will cause

    a.  the price level to increase, but have no lasting effect on the inflation rate.
    b.  the price level to fall.
    c.  inflation.
    d.  output to increase and will have no effect on either the price level or inflation.
    e.  none of the above.

2.  Inflation occurs whenever

    a.  the price level rises.
    b.  the money supply increases.
    c.  the price level rises continuously over a period of time.
    d.  any of the above occur.

3.  In general, most economists believe that inflation can only occur if

    a.  government spending increases.
    b.  strong labor unions demand higher wages.
    c.  negative supply shocks continuously hit the economy.
    d.  the money supply is continually expanded.

4.  Monetarists emphasize the importance of a constant money growth rate rule more than the balanced-budget amendment or restrictions on union power because

    a.  they tend to regard excessive money growth as the cause of inflation.
    b.  while they do not believe that excessive money growth is the cause of inflation, they do believe that it is related to excessive government expenditures.
    c.  while they regard unions as the source of inflation, they know that they are too powerful politically to deal with.
    d.  of each of the above.

5.  Analysis of hyperinflationary episodes indicates that the rapid money growth leading to the inflation results when

    a.  governments finance massive budget deficits by printing money.
    b.  central banks attempt to peg interest rates.
    c.  government taxes become too excessive.
    d.  central banks lower reserve requirements too much.

6. A one-shot increase in government spending will have what effect on the inflation rate, according to the Keynesian analysis?

   a. Permanent increase
   b. Temporary increase
   c. Temporary decrease
   d. No effect

7. Assume workers know that government policymakers, because unemployment is politically unpopular, always accommodate wage increases by expanding the money supply. What type of inflation is likely to result if workers demand higher wages not fearing a rise in unemployment?

   a. Demand-pull inflation
   b. Hyperinflation
   c. Cost-push inflation
   d. Demand-shock inflation

8. If an economist were interested in testing whether federal budget deficits had been the source of excessive money growth for a particular country during the time period 1900-1930, she would be interested in the behavior of

   a. inflation
   b. the money supply-to-monetary-base ratio.
   c. interest rates.
   d. the government debt-to-GDP ratio.

9. When the government sets an unemployment target that is unrealistically low without realizing it, what is the likely result?

   a. Inflation
   b. An unemployment rate that may actually drop below the natural rate for a period of time
   c. Excessive money growth
   d. All of the above

10. Governments are likely to lose credibility in fighting inflation when

    a. government budget deficits remain high.
    b. government policymakers continue to accommodate wage demands and negative supply shocks.
    c. the commitment to high unemployment is viewed as government's number-one goal for political reasons.
    d. all of the above are true.

11. The German hyperinflation of the 1920s supports the proposition that excessive money growth leads to higher prices, and not the other way around, since the increase in money growth appears to have been

    a. unintentional.
    b. intentional.
    c. exogenous.
    d. endogenous.

12. A common element of hyperinflationary episodes discussed in the text is government unwillingness to

    a. finance expenditures by raising taxes.
    b. increase expenditures.
    c. finance expenditures by printing money.
    d. finance transfer payments by printing money.

13. Which of the following statements are true?

    a. The price level may rise in any one month due to factors unrelated to changes in the money supply. Thus one can conclude that continual price-level increases need not be related to changes in the money supply.
    b. Within the aggregate demand and supply framework, a continually increasing money supply has the effect of continually shifting the aggregate demand curve to the right.
    c. Keynesians argue that factors other than a continually increasing money supply may lead to sustained inflation.
    d. Sustained inflation occurs when unions successfully push up wages, even if the monetary authorities refuse to accommodate the higher wages by expanding the money supply.

14. Workers will have greater incentives to push for higher wages when government policymakers place greater concern on _____ than _____ and are thus _____ likely to adopt accommodative policies.

    a. inflation; unemployment; less
    b. inflation; unemployment; more
    c. unemployment; inflation; less
    d. unemployment; inflation; more

15. Which of the following statements are true?

    a. Cost-push inflation is not a monetary phenomenon.
    b. At first glance, one would expect rising unemployment to be associated with demand pull inflation.
    c. Huge government budget deficits have been the initiating source of inflationary monetary policies in every instance of hyperinflation.
    d. Large government deficits are to blame for the inflationary monetary policies of the 1970s in the United States.

16. Economists such as Robert Barro reject hold the view that deficits

    a. cause the monetary base to decrease.
    b. cause the monetary base to increase.
    c. have no effect on the monetary base.
    d. are inflationary even when financed by tax hikes.

# Chapter 27

## The Theory of Rational Expectations and Efficient Capital Markets

### CHAPTER SYNOPSIS/COMPLETIONS

Chapter 27 develops the theory of rational expectations and discusses the implications of this theory as applied to financial markets, where it is known as the theory of efficient capital markets. Recently, expectations theory has received great attention as economists have searched for more adequate explanations of the observed behavior of economic variables such as unemployment, interest rates, and asset prices.

Prior to the rational expectations revolution, economists tended to model expectations as if they were formed (1)_____, meaning that people adjusted slowly over time in response to changes in economic variables. Adaptive expectations imply that people look only at current and (2)_____ behavior of an economic variable in forming expectations of it, never adjusting to predicted changes in economic variables.

Beginning in the 1960s a number of economists began to question the desirability of adaptive expectations models, since they imply that people never learn from their past mistakes. They suggested an alternative to adaptive expectations known as (3)_____ _____. As the name implies, this theory assumes that people behave rationally when faced with new information, adjusting their expectations quickly. For example, if people believe that the Federal Reserve is about to embark on an expansionary monetary policy to reduce unemployment, people will revise their estimates of inflation upward. The possibility of this result is ignored in adaptive expectation models because people are assumed to respond only to past events; that is, people do not respond to predicted future actions.

Rational expectationists contend that individuals make (4)_____ (formulate expectations) about the future course of an economic variable based on its past behavior and on their assessment of future policies that affect the variable. These predictions – known as (5)_____ _____ – will be correct on average, although they will not always be perfectly accurate. Individuals make mistakes, but they will not be persistently wrong in any one direction. Alternatively, forecast errors of expectations will not be biased.

The theory of rational expectations contends that people have a strong incentive to form rational expectations since failing to do so is costly. This is especially true in financial markets.

The theory of (6)_____ _____ _____ is the application of rational expectations to the pricing of securities in financial markets. Efficient markets theory suggests that security (7)_____ reflect all available information at that time. If this were not the case, an unexploited profit opportunity would exist giving individuals with superior information an incentive to capture profits by either buying (they expect a higher price) or selling (they expect a lower price) the security.

Importantly, their actions quickly eliminate the profits. If, for example, the price of IBM common stock is expected to rise because a new invention makes IBM computers more valuable to own, then those individuals with this information will attempt to buy more shares of IBM common stock before its price rises. But their actions increase the demand for IBM stock, raising its price. The price of IBM common stock will continue to rise until the optimal forecast of the rate of return falls to the
(8)_____ return. At this price, all unexploited profit opportunities are eliminated. This result does not depend on everyone being well informed.

The evidence on efficient markets theory is mixed. Although evidence on the performance of investment advisors and mutual funds tends to support the random walk hypothesis for stock prices, in recent years anomalies to efficient markets indicates that the theory may not be correct. For example, the small-firm effect, the January effect, the *Value Line* survey, market overreaction, excessive volatility, and mean reversion indicates that efficient market theory may not be generalizable to all behavior in financial markets.

Efficient markets theory suggests that individuals ought to be skeptical of stock brokers' hot tips and the recommendations found in the published reports of (9)_____ _____.
By the time you acquire the information, others are likely to have already used it to their benefit. Thus acting on this information will not yield abnormally high returns on average because market prices already reflect this information. Many studies confirm the proposition that published recommendations cannot allow you to outperform the overall market. Even when economists select analysts who have done well in the past, the evidence indicates that financial analysts do not consistently outperform the overall market.

The (10)_____ _____ hypothesis contends that future changes in stock prices should for all practical purposes be unpredictable. This implication follows from efficient markets theory, since any new information that might create an unexploited profit opportunity will be quickly eliminated through the adjustment in the stock's price.

Interestingly, efficient markets theory also explains why a stock's price sometimes falls when good news about the stock is announced. This occurs when announced earnings fall short of those
(11)_____ by market participants. The lower earnings mean a lower rate of return at the current price. Consequently, the stock's price must fall to bring the rate of return into conformity with the rest of the market.

So how can one get rich by investing in the stock market? The efficient markets theory suggests that relying on the published reports of financial analysts and the hot tips given to you by your broker is probably an inferior strategy when compared to the "buy and (12)_____ strategy." The buy and hold strategy will on average give the investor the same return (exclusive of transactions costs), but her net profits will be higher because she pays fewer (13)_____ commissions. The only other alternative is to rely on (14)_____ _____. This, however, is a risky strategy since the government prosecutes traders using this information.

The stock market crash of 1987 has convinced many that the strong version of efficient markets theory – asset prices reflect the true fundamental value of securities – is not correct. Whether or not the stock market crash proves rational expectations theory is incorrect is of some dispute. To the extent that the crash could not have been predicted, rational expectations theory would seem to hold.

## EXERCISES

### Exercise 1: Definitions and Terminology

Match the following terms on the right with the definition or description on the left.  Place the letter of the term in the blank provided next to the appropriate definition.  Terms may be used more than once.

_____

_____ 1. Price of a security is such that optimal forecast of its return exceeds the equilibrium return.

a. Efficient markets theory

_____ 2. Expectations that are formed from past data on a single variable.

b. Random walk

_____ 3. Information not available to the public, but only to those who have close contact with a company.

c. Unexploited profit opportunity

_____ 4. Past movements of stock prices are of no use in predicting the future movement of stock prices.

_____ 5. A method for predicting future stock prices using past price data.

d. Insider information

_____ 6. Expectations that are formed using optimal predictions of future movements in relevant variables.

_____ 7. The best guess of the future using all available information.

e. Technical analysis

_____ 8. Theory that indicates that hot tips, financial analysts' published recommendations, and technical analysis cannot help the investor to outperform the market.

f. Adaptive expectations

_____ 9. The application of rational expectations to the pricing of securities in financial markets.

g. Rational expectations

_____ 10. A situation in which someone can earn a higher than normal return.

h. Optimal forecast

**Exercise 2: Interest Rates and Rational Expectations - Efficient Markets**

Three different outcomes for long-term interest rates are possible when the Federal Reserve slows the growth of the money supply. Describe the possible conditions leading to each of these outcomes listed below.

A. No change in long-term interest rates

_____

_____

_____

B. A decline in long-term interest rates

_____

_____

_____

C. A rise in long-term interest rates

_____

_____

_____

D. What does the example here suggest about the difficulty of conducting monetary policy when expectations are rational?

_____

_____

_____

## SELF-TEST

### Part A: True-False Questions

Circle whether the following statements are true (T) or false (F).

T  F  1.  The speed with which inflation expectations respond to accelerating money growth is an important factor determining whether interest rates rise or fall when money growth increases.

T  F   2.  Expectations that are formed solely on the basis of past information are known as rational expectations.

T  F   3.  The theory of rational expectations argues that optimal forecasts need not be perfectly accurate.

T  F   4.  An important implication of rational expectations theory is that when there is a change in the way a variable behaves, the way expectations of this variable are formed will change as well.

T  F   5.  If the optimal forecast of a return on a financial asset exceeds its equilibrium return, the situation is called an unexploited profit opportunity.

T  F   6.  In an efficient market, all unexploited profit opportunities will be eliminated.

T  F   7.  Everyone in a financial market must be well informed about a security if the market is to be considered efficient.

T  F   8.  The efficient markets theory suggests that published reports of financial analysts can guarantee that individuals who use this information will outperform the market.

T  F   9.  The overwhelming majority of statistical studies indicate that financial analysts do indeed pick financial portfolios that outperform the market average.

T  F  10.  According to the efficient markets hypothesis, picking stocks by throwing darts at the financial page is an inferior strategy compared to employing the advice of financial analysts.

## Part B: Multiple-Choice Questions

Circle the appropriate answer.

1.  Suppose you read a story in the financial section of the local newspaper that announces the proposed merger of Dell Computer and Gateway.  The announcement is expected to greatly increase the profitability of Gateway.  If you should now decide to invest in Gateway stock, you can expect to earn

   a.  above average returns since you will get to share in the higher profits.
   b.  above average returns since your stock will definitely appreciate as the profits are earned.
   c.  a normal return since stock prices adjust to reflect changed profit expectations almost immediately.
   d.  none of the above.

2.  Assume that you own a ranch and lease land from the Bureau of Land Management (BLM), which allows you to graze cattle on the government land at a price that is below the market equilibrium price.  If the government should raise the price for grazing cattle on BLM land, you can expect the value of the ranch to

   a.  fall since ranching is no longer as profitable.
   b.  be unaffected.  (The value of the ranch is not dependent on the price of grazing rights.)
   c.  rise since the value of the BLM land rises.
   d.  rise since the value of the BLM land falls.

3.  In countries experiencing rapid rates of inflation, announcements of money supply increases are often followed by immediate increases in interest rates. Such behavior is consistent with which of the following?

    a.  Rational expectations
    b.  Expectations of higher inflation in the near future
    c.  A tight current monetary policy
    d.  Both (a) and (b) of the above
    e.  Both (a) and (c) of the above

4.  Efficient markets theory suggests that purchasing the published reports of financial analysts

    a.  is likely to increase one's returns by an average of 10%.
    b   is likely to increase one's returns by an average of about 3 to 5%.
    c.  is not likely to be effective strategy for increasing financial returns.
    d.  is likely to increase one's returns by an average of about 2 to 3%.

5.  After the announcement of higher quarterly profits, the price of a stock falls. Such an occurrence is

    a.  clearly inconsistent with efficient markets theory.
    b.  possible if market participants expected lower profits.
    c.  consistent with efficient markets theory.
    d.  not possible.

6.  Since a change in regulations permitting their existence in the mid-1970s and the explosive growth in the number of people who surf the internet, discount brokers have grown rapidly. Efficient markets theory would seem to suggest that people who use discount brokers

    a.  will likely earn lower returns than those who use full-service brokers.
    b.  will likely earn about the same as those who use full-service brokers, but will net more after brokerage commissions.
    c.  are going against evidence that suggests that the financial analysis provided by full-service brokers can help one outperform the overall market.
    d.  are likely to be poor.

7.  Efficient markets theory suggests that stock prices tend to follow a "random walk." Thus the best strategy for investing stock is

    a.  a "churning strategy" of buying and selling often to catch the market swings.
    b.  turning over your stock portfolio each month, selecting stocks by throwing darts at the stock page.
    c.  a "buy and hold strategy" of holding onto stocks to avoid brokerage commissions.
    d.  to do none of the above.

8.  Rational expectations theory suggests that forecast errors of expectations

    a.  tend to be persistently high or low.
    b.  are unpredictable.
    c.  are more likely to be negative than positive.
    d.  are more likely to be positive than negative.

9. Unexploited opportunities are quickly eliminated in financial markets through

    a. changes in asset prices.
    b. changes in dividend payments.
    c. accounting conventions.
    d. exchange-rate translations.

10. Stockbrokers have at times paid newspaper reporters for information about articles to be published in future editions. This suggests that

    a. your stockbroker's hot tips will help you outperform the overall market.
    b. financial analysts' reports contain information that will help you earn a return that exceeds the market average.
    c. insider information may help ensure returns that exceed the market average.
    d. each of the above is true.

11. If expectations are formed rationally, forecast errors of expectations will on average be _____ and therefore _____ be predicted ahead of time.

    a. positive; can
    b. positive; cannot
    c. zero; cannot
    d. zero; can

12. That stock prices do not always rise when favorable earnings reports are released suggests that

    a. the stock market is not efficient.
    b. people trading in stocks sometimes incorrectly estimate companies' earnings.
    c. stock prices tend to be biased measures of future corporate earnings.
    d. all of the above are true.

13. According to the theory of efficient capital markets since all relevant, publicly available information is discounted in asset prices as soon as it becomes available,

    a. investors cannot construct systematically profitable trading rules based only on this information.
    b. investors have no incentive to buy stock based on favorable information, since the market will have already discounted it.
    c. investors have an incentive to buy stock based on favorable information, since the market takes time to discount it.
    d. both (a) and (b) of the above.

14. Mutual funds that outperform the market in one period are

    a. highly likely to consistently outperform the market in subsequent periods due to their superior investment strategies.
    b. likely to under-perform the market in subsequent periods to average the funds' returns.
    c. not likely to consistently outperform the market in subsequent periods.
    d. not likely to outperform the market in any subsequent periods.

15. According to the theory of efficient capital markets

    a.  incorrectly valued assets are quickly discovered and bought or sold until their prices are brought into line with their correct underlying value.
    b.  most investors will not earn excess returns from spending resources on technical market analysis.
    c.  the best strategy for most investors is to buy and hold a well-diversified portfolio of securities.
    d.  all of the above are true.

# Chapter 28

# *Rational Expectations: Implications for Policy*

## CHAPTER SYNOPSIS/COMPLETIONS

Chapter 28 discusses the implications of rational expectations theory for macroeconomic stabilization policies. Rational expectations theory arose in the 1970s as an attempt to explain "stagflation" and the failure of government policies to prevent this unhappy state. How can the apparent ineffectiveness of government stabilization policies be explained? This chapter introduces models that attempt to answer this question.

In his famous paper, "Econometric Policy Evaluation: A Critique," Robert Lucas argues that stabilization policies formulated on the basis of conventional econometric models will fail to stabilize the economy since (1)_____ about policy will alter the intended effects. Lucas argues that while conventional econometric models may be useful for forecasting economic activity, they cannot be used to evaluate the potential impact of particular policies on the economy. The short-run forecasting ability of these models provides no evidence of the accuracy to be expected from simulations of hypothetical policy alternatives.

To understand Lucas's argument, one needs to recognize that conventional econometric models contain equations that describe the relationships between hundreds of variables. These relationships (parameters), estimated using past data, are assumed to remain (2)_____. Lucas contends that such models will likely provide misleading results about the effects of a policy change (say, a monetary expansion); the actual effects are likely to be different than predicted because the change in policy will mean that the way expectations are formed will change, causing the real-world relationships (parameters) to change. Thus the effects of a particular policy depend heavily on the public's expectations about the policy.

Two schools of rational expectations economists have formed: the new classical and the new Keynesian schools. (3)_____ _____ rational expectationists contend that anticipated macroeconomic policies have no effect on aggregate output and employment. This conclusion rests on the assumption that all wages and prices are completely (4)_____ with respect to expected changes in the price level. For example, if policymakers are known to act in certain systematic ways, the public will come to anticipate policy changes, causing the aggregate (5)_____ curve to shift. People will respond to expected expansionary macropolicies by raising wages and factor prices. The aggregate demand curve shifts out, but the aggregate supply curve shifts in, neutralizing the impact on aggregate output. The (6)_____ _____ rises, but output remains unchanged at the natural-rate level.

Policymakers can affect the level of aggregate output and employment in the new classical rational expectations model only through policy surprises. Unanticipated policies will cause the aggregate demand curve to shift while leaving the aggregate supply curve unchanged, resulting in a change in the price level and aggregate output. Only unanticipated macropolicies can affect the level of output in the new classical model; anticipated policies cannot affect the level of output. This conclusion is referred to as the policy (7)_____ _____. The proposition depends critically on two assumptions: rational expectations and perfect wage and price flexibility.

Many economists find the assumption of wage and price flexibility unacceptable. They note that the prevalence of long-term labor and supply contracts create (8)_____ which prevent wages and prices from fully responding to expected changes in the price level.

New Keynesians argue that the existence of long-term labor contracts – both explicit and implicit – leads to wage and price stickiness. In contrast to the new classical school, the assumption of rational expectations does not imply that (9)_____ policies are ineffectual in altering the level of aggregate output. The public may understand the consequences of a newly announced macropolicy yet be unable to fully respond in the face of contracted fixities.

(10)_____ _____ agree that unanticipated policies are more effective than anticipated policies in changing the level of aggregate output. Anticipated policies are effective in altering the level of aggregate output, but unanticipated policies have a larger impact. The new Keynesians suggest that activist stabilization policies can be used to affect the level of output in the economy, but policymakers must be cognizant of the Lucas (11)_____ _____. In other words, since expectations affect the outcome of policies, making predictions about a proposed policy's effects is more difficult than is implied by the traditional model.

New classical economists are less optimistic. They contend that (12)_____ macropolicies can only be counterproductive. Activist policies are likely to be destabilizing and inflationary.

A significant implication of rational expectations is that anti-inflationary policies can achieve their goal at a lower cost if these policies are viewed as (13)_____ by the public. The traditional model suggests that fighting inflation will be quite costly in terms of lost output and higher unemployment. Arthur Okun's rule of thumb indicates that a reduction of one point in the inflation rate requires a nine percent loss in a year's GNP, a staggering cost for such a small gain. Recall that Okun's rule of thumb holds in a world where anti-inflation policies are not viewed as credible. To the extent that such policies foster credibility, fighting inflation will be less costly.

Evidence indicates that credible policies do reduce the adverse consequences of anti-inflationary policies. Actions designed to reduce government (14)_____ _____ appear to be particularly important in this regard. It appears that anti-inflationary policies that do not address budget-deficit problems may be viewed with little credibility and prove to be relatively costly. Some economists contend that recessions in Great Britain and the United States in the early 1980s were more severe because deficit issues went unresolved. Although this conclusion is controversial, it indicates the importance expectations play in economic theory.

## EXERCISES

### Exercise 1: The Effect of Anticipated Policy

Suppose the economy is initially at point 1 in Figure 28A, at the intersection of the $AD_1$ and $AS_1$ curves. If Congress decides to cut military spending in an attempt to ease world tensions, draw in Figure 28A the new aggregate demand curve AD₂.  If this spending cut were widely anticipated, draw in the new aggregate supply curve $AS_{NC}$ if the new classical model is the best description of the economy.

FIGURE 28A

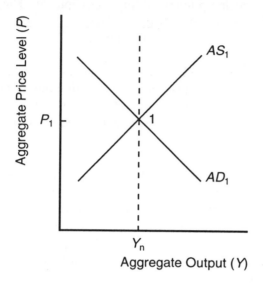

What is the effect on output and price level? _____

_____

If, instead, the new Keynesian model is the best description of the economy, draw in the new aggregate supply curve $AS_{NK}$ when the policy is anticipated.

What is the effect on output and price level? _____

_____

Would output rise by more or by less than your answers above if the traditional model best describes the economy?

_____

_____

_____

**Exercise 2: The Effects of Unanticipated Policy**

Suppose the economy is initially at point 1 in Figure 28B, at the intersection of the $AD_1$ and $AS_1$ curves. If Congress reduces military spending in an attempt to ease world tensions, but reduces it by less than expected (where the aggregate demand curve for the expected policy is $AD_e$), draw in the new aggregate demand curve $AD_2$ and the new aggregate supply curve $AS_{NC}$ if the new classical model is the best description of the economy.

FIGURE 28B

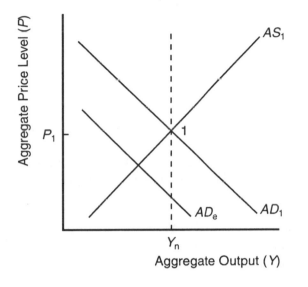

Does aggregate output fall as a result of the decline in government spending?

_____

_____

If, instead, the new Keynesian model is the best description of the economy, draw in the new aggregate supply curve $AS_{NK}$ when the spending reduction is less than anticipated. Will aggregate output fall in this case?

_____

_____

If, the traditional model best describes the economy, will aggregate output fall in response to the spending reduction?

_____

_____

## Exercise 3: The Lucas Critique and Monetary Policy

Suppose that the Fed follows a monetary rule designed to stabilize nominal interest rates.  If interest rates suddenly rise, what will most likely be the Fed's response?  If people come to expect this response, will the Fed's efforts be helped or hindered?  Explain.

_____

_____

_____

_____

## Exercise 4: A Comparison of the Schools of Thought

In the space provided next to each statement, indicate whether the statement reflects a view held by Keynesians (K), monetarists (M), new classical rational expectationists (NC), or new Keynesians (NK). Use more than one letter if appropriate.

_____ 1.  Any policy move that is widely expected will have no impact at the time it is taken, since it will have already been discounted by the public.

_____ 2.  No systematic economic policy can be devised that is capable of affecting anything other than the inflation rate.

_____ 3.  The private economy is inherently unstable; thus monetary and fiscal policy can be important in stabilizing the economy whether or not the policy is anticipated.

_____ 4.  There is no serious need to stabilize the economy, and even if there were a need, it could not be done, for stabilization policies would be more likely to increase than to decrease instability.

_____ 5.  Only policy moves that people do not expect will cause changes in aggregate output and employment.

_____ 6.  Traditional econometric models cannot be relied on to evaluate the potential impact of particular policies on the economy.  In other words, the short-run forecasting ability of these models provides no evidence of the accuracy to be expected from simulations of hypothetical policy rules.

_____ 7.  The existence of long-term labor contracts are one source of rigidity that prevents instantaneous price and wage adjustment.  Thus, even with rational expectations, anticipated monetary and fiscal policies may affect output in the short run.

_____ 8.  The policy ineffectiveness proposition does not hold in a world such as ours where both explicit and implicit long-term labor contracts impart a degree of wage and price rigidity in the economy.

## Exercise 5: A Comparison of Rational Expectations Models with the Traditional Model

Listed below are statements that reflect the beliefs of economists regarding stabilization policy. If the statement most accurately reflects views held by the new classical economists, write NC in the space provided. If the statement most closely reflects views held by new Keynesians, place an NK in the space provided. If the statement does not reflect views held by either school of rational expectationists, place a T in the space. You may use more than one letter if the statement reflects views held by more than one of the groups.

_____ 1.  An unanticipated expansion in the money supply will boost employment in the short run, but after a period of from 12 to 24 months, prices win begin to rise.

_____ 2.  Stabilization policy – what some might call an activist policy – can and should be employed in an effort to eliminate the high level of unemployment.

_____ 3.  An increase in government spending or a tax cut would be appropriate at this time because unemployment is too high and inflation is almost nonexistent. In addition, the announcement of such a plan would bode well for stock prices – this is the policy the market has been expecting to hear from Washington.

_____ 4.  Mr. President, since you have decided that an anti-inflation policy of slower money growth and higher taxes is appropriate at this time, I think it wise that you make the announcement at your televised press conference tonight. Remember, it is important for you to convince the public that you plan to stick with the contractionary strategy even if unemployment begins to rise.

_____ 5.  Fighting inflation is extremely costly – probably more costly than it's worth – and announcing an anti-inflationary policy in advance does nothing to lower that cost.

_____ 6.  An activist stabilization policy will have no predictable effect on output, and it cannot be relied on to stabilize economic activity.

## Exercise 6: The Effects of Announced Policy and Credibility

Assume for a moment that you are president of the United States and currently running for reelection. The unemployment rate is 5.8% and the inflation rate is 2.0%. In a private meeting with the chairman of the Federal Reserve Board you are given assurances that monetary policy will be expansionary in the next few months in an attempt to lower the unemployment rate. If the traditional model best describes the economy, does it matter if you publicly announce the chairman's assurances?

_____

_____

If the new classical model best describes the economy?

_____

_____

If the new Keynesian model best describes the economy?

_____

_____

If no one believes you when you make your announcement, how does it affect the answers above?

_____

_____

## SELF-TEST

### Part A: True-False Questions

Circle whether the following statements are true (T) or false (F).

T  F  1.  Robert Lucas in his famous critique argued that econometric model simulations provide no useful information with which to evaluate the effects of alternative economic policies.

T  F  2.  A monetary acceleration may have different effects in 1999 than in 2000 if the public's expectations about the policy are different in those two years.

T  F  3.  The new classical economists argue that neither anticipated nor unanticipated policies affect the level of unemployment.

T  F  4.  The new classical economists argue that only unanticipated increases in the money supply can affect the general level of prices.

T  F  5.  While an expansionary monetary policy can never lead to a decline in output in the traditional model, such a result is possible in the new classical model.

T  F  6.  Anticipated policies have no effect on aggregate output or the rate of unemployment in the New Keynesian model.

T  F  7.  The expansion of aggregate output will be smaller for an anticipated policy than for an unanticipated policy in the nonclassical rational expectations model.

T  F  8.  It is the existence of rigidities such as sticky wages and prices, not adaptive expectations, that explains why anticipated policies can affect output in the New Keynesian model.

T  F  9.  If expectations about policy are formed adaptively, then anticipated policies will actually have greater output effects than unanticipated policies.

T  F  10.  If expectations are formed rationally, and prices and wages are completely flexible, then the best anti-inflation policy is likely to consist of a gradual reduction in the money supply over a period of several years.

**Part B: Multiple-Choice Questions**

Circle the appropriate answer.

1.  Robert Lucas argues that using an econometric model that has been constructed on the basis of past data

    a.  may be appropriate for short-run forecasting, but is inappropriate for evaluating alternative policies.
    b.  may be appropriate for alternative policies, but is not appropriate for evaluating short-run forecasting.
    c.  is appropriate for both short-run forecasting and policy evaluation.
    d.  is not appropriate for either short-run forecasting or policy evaluation.

2.  An anticipated expansion in the money supply will have no effect on aggregate output in which model?

    a.  New Keynesian model
    b.  Traditional model
    c.  New classical rational expectations model
    d.  All of the above

3.  In which of the following models does an anticipated increase in money growth affect the price level?

    a.  Traditional model
    b.  New classical model
    c.  New Keynesian model
    d.  All of the above models

4.  The new Keynesian model indicates that anticipated policies affect aggregate output because of rigidities resulting from

    a.  long-term contracts.
    b.  adaptive expectations.
    c.  the reluctance of some firms to alter prices and wages frequently, creating what can be considered implicit contracts.
    d.  All of the above.
    e.  Only (a) and (c) of the above.

5.  The traditional model is distinguished from both the new classical and the new Keynesian model by the following:

    a.  The traditional model assumes that expectations are formed adaptively, that is, on past behavior of the relevant variable.
    b.  The traditional model does not distinguish between anticipated and unanticipated policies.
    c.  The traditional model assumes that the price level remains fixed.
    d.  Both (b) and (c) of the above.
    e.  Both (a) and (b) of the above.

6. Assume that the economy is characterized by sticky wages and prices, and rational expectations. If the Fed wishes to reduce unemployment by expanding the money supply, how win the preannouncement of such a policy influence the policy's effectiveness?

   a. The preannouncement eliminates the policy's effectiveness.
   b. The preannouncement diminishes the policy's effectiveness.
   c. The preannouncement has no effect on the policy's effectiveness.
   d. The preannouncement enhances the magnitude of the policy's effectiveness.

7. Kristin argues at a meeting of the Federal Open Market Committee that the committee should vote to quickly lower the federal funds interest rate in an attempt to return the economy to full employment. One can infer from her argument that Kristin is

   a. either a new classical or a traditional economist.
   b. either a new classical or a new Keynesian economist.
   c. definitely not a new classical economist.
   d. definitely not a new Keynesian economist.

8. If people form rational expectations, an anti-inflation policy win be more successful if it

   a. is credible.
   b. comes as a surprise.
   c. is unanticipated.
   d. does all of the above.

9. At a meeting of the central bank's policy-making committee, Meghan argues that any decision regarding a contractionary monetary policy should be postponed until the legisltive body votes on a deficit-reduction package currently before it. Meghan seems to be implying that

   a. an anti-inflationary policy would make more sense if people saw evidence of lower deficits.
   b. an anti-inflationary policy might be too costly in terms of lost output if such a policy was not believed to be credible.
   c. both (a) and (b) of the above are possible.
   d. neither (a) nor (b) of the above are a concern.

10. Assume that irrefutable evidence proves that while anticipated monetary expansions cause aggregate output to expand, unanticipated monetary expansions proved more potent than anticipated policies. What economic model would the evidence support?

   a. New classical model
   b. New Keynesian model
   c. Traditional model
   d. Uninformed median-voter model

11. _____ policies have no effect on aggregate output or the rate of unemployment in the _____ model.

   a. anticipated; new Keynesian
   b. unanticipated; new Keynesian
   c. anticipated; new Classical
   d. unanticipated; new Classical

12. The expansion of aggregate output will be _____ for an _____ policy than for an _____ policy in the _____ model.

    a. smaller; unanticipated; anticipated; new classical
    b. smaller; anticipated; unanticipated; new classical
    c. smaller; unanticipated; anticipated; new Keynesian
    d. smaller; anticipated; unanticipated; new Keynesian
    e. larger; anticipated; unanticipated; new Keynesian

13. It is the existence of rigidities such as sticky wages and prices, not adaptive expectations, that explains why _____ policies can affect output in the _____ model.

    a. unanticipated; new classical
    b. anticipated; new classical
    c. unanticipated; new Keynesian
    d. anticipated; new Keynesian

14. According to _____ economists, policymakers' attempts to stabilize the economy will be ineffective and may even make conditions worse.

    a. new classical
    b. new Keynesian
    c. Keynesian
    d. activist

15. If the government _____ budget deficits, an anti-inflationary policy is _____ likely to be regarded as credible.

    a. reduces; less
    b. reduces; more
    c. increases; more
    d. eliminates; less

# ANSWERS

## ANSWERS TO CHAPTER 1

### Chapter Synopsis/Completions

| | | | |
|---|---|---|---|
| 1. | financial | 2. | exchange rates |
| 3. | stock market | 4. | stronger |
| 5. | expensive | 6. | financial institutions |
| 7. | bank | 8. | spend |
| 9. | financial intermediation | 10. | business cycle |
| 11. | inflation | 12. | spending |
| 13. | saving | 14. | high |
| 15. | money | | |

### Exercise 1

| | | | |
|---|---|---|---|
| 1. | B | 2. | S |
| 3. | S | 4. | F |
| 5. | S | 6. | F |

### Exercise 2

A.  One would predict a fall in prices and economic output.  This is in fact what happened.  The worst depression of the nineteenth century lasted from 1839 to 1843.

B. He is referring to an upswing in the business cycle.

### Exercise 3

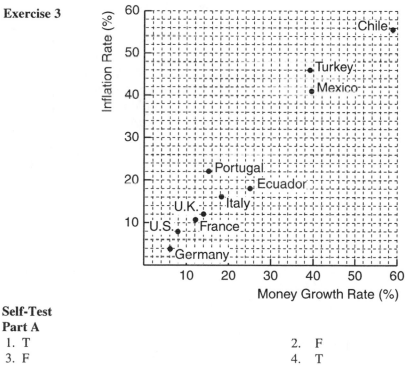

### Self-Test
### Part A

| | | | |
|---|---|---|---|
| 1. | T | 2. | F |
| 3. | F | 4. | T |
| 5. | F | 6. | T |
| 7. | T | 8. | T |
| 9. | F | 10. | T |

**Part B**

| | |
|---|---|
| 1. d | 2. c |
| 3. c | 4. a |
| 5. d | 6. c |
| 7. b | 8. a |
| 9. b | 10. b |
| 11. a | 12. c |
| 13. a | 14. e |
| 15. a | |

# ANSWERS TO CHAPTER 2

## Chapter Synopsis/Completions

| | |
|---|---|
| 1. direct | 2. financial intermediaries |
| 3. equity | 4. over-the-counter |
| 5. capital | 6. short |
| 7. equity | 8. exchanges |
| 9. money | 10. liabilities |
| 11. adverse selection | 12. depository |
| 13. one year | 14. soundness |
| 15. reserves | |

## Exercise 1

| | Money Market Instrument | Capital Market Instrument |
|---|---|---|
| Traded in an Organized Exchange | | Corporate bonds<br>Common stocks |
| Traded in an Over-the-counter Market | U.S. Treasury bills<br>Negotiable CDs<br>Federal Funds<br>Commercial paper | U.S. Treasury Bonds<br>Corporate Bonds<br>Common stocks |

## Exercise 2

| | |
|---|---|
| 1. I | 2. D |
| 3. D | 4. I |
| 5. D | 6. I |
| 7. I | 8. D |
| 9. I | 10. D |

## Exercise 3

**Part A**

| | | | |
|---|---|---|---|
| 1. a, b, d, f, h | 2. a | | |
| 3. a | 4. b | | |
| 5. a, e | 6. e, g | | |
| 7. e, f, h | 8. e, g | | |
| 9. c | 10. b, c | | |

**Part B**

| | |
|---|---|
| 1. a, c | 2. a, c |
| 3. a, c | 4. a, c |
| 5. b | 6. d |
| 7. b | 8. f |
| 9. f | 10. e, g, h |

**Exercise 4**

| | |
|---|---|
| 1. b | 2. e |
| 3. a, b, d, e, f | 4. a, b, d, e |
| 5. a, b, d, | 6. a |
| 7. c | 8. g |

**Self-Test**
**Part A**

| | |
|---|---|
| 1. T | 2. T |
| 3. T | 4. F |
| 5. T | 6. F |
| 7. T | 8. T |
| 9. F | 10. T |

**Part B**

| | |
|---|---|
| 1. c | 2. a |
| 3. e | 4. c |
| 5. d | 6. b |
| 7. d | 8. c |
| 9. d | 10. b |
| 11. e | 12. b |
| 13. b | 14. e |
| 15. b | |

# ANSWERS TO CHAPTER 3

**Chapter Synopsis/Completions**

| | |
|---|---|
| 1. money | 2. money supply |
| 3. flow | 4. specialization |
| 5. store of value | 6. barter |
| 7. time | 8. liquid |
| 9. paper currency | 10. electronic funds transfer system |
| 11. monetary aggregates | 12. initial |

**Exercise 1**

In this example the R.E.M. CD has actually served the function of money. It has served as a medium of exchange, since Barbi took an inferior position (trading for the R.E.M. CD) in hopes of getting something she valued more than she gave up. This is exactly what you do when you accept money in exchange for your labor efforts. It really is not money that you want, but the things that money can be exchanged for.

| Individual | Initial CD | Intermediate CD | Final CD |
|---|---|---|---|
| A | R | S | S |
| B | S | R | T |
| C | T | T | R |

**Exercise 2**

| | | | |
|---|---|---|---|
| 1. | M | 2. | S |
| 3. | U | 4. | U |
| 5. | S | 6. | U |
| 7. | M | 8. | M |
| 9. | U | 10. | S |

**Exercise 3**

| Number of Goods | Number of Prices in a Barter Economy | Number of Prices in a Money Economy |
|---|---|---|
| 5 | 10 | 5 |
| 25 | 300 | 25 |
| 50 | 1225 | 50 |
| 500 | 124,750 | 500 |
| 5000 | 12,497,500 | 5000 |

**Exercise 4**

| | | | |
|---|---|---|---|
| 1. | M1, M2, M3, L | 2. | L |
| 3. | M2, M3, L | 4. | M1, M2, M3, L |
| 5. | L | 6. | M2, M3, L |
| 7. | M2, M3, L | 8. | M3, L |
| 9. | M2, M3, L | | |

**Self-Test**
**Part A**

| | | | |
|---|---|---|---|
| 1. | T | 2. | F |
| 3. | F | 4. | T |
| 5. | F | 6. | T |
| 7. | T | 8. | T |
| 9. | T | 10. | F |

**Part B**

| | | | |
|---|---|---|---|
| 1. | a | 2. | b |
| 3. | c | 4. | b |
| 5. | d | 6. | c |
| 7. | d | 8. | d |
| 9. | d | 10. | a |
| 11. | b | 12. | b |
| 13. | b | 14. | d |
| 15. | d | | |

## ANSWERS TO CHAPTER 4

### Chapter Synopsis/Completions

| | | | |
|---|---|---|---|
| 1. | fixed payment | 2. | coupon rate |
| 3. | discount | 4. | present value |
| 5. | negatively | 6. | coupon |
| 7. | longer | 8. | rise |
| 9. | return | 10. | maturity |
| 11. | interest rates | 12. | credit market |

**Exercise 1**
1. $\$453.51 = \$500/(1 + .05)^2$
2. $\$413.22 = \$500/(1 + .10)^2$
3. $\$341.51 = \$500/(1 + .10)^4$
4. The present value falls.
5. The present value falls.

**Exercise 2**
**Part A**
1. $\$1,000 = \$600/(1 + i) + \$600/(1 + i)^2$
2. $1,041
3. Above
4. $975
5. Below

**Part B**
1. Below, because the price of the bond is above the par value.
2. $\$1,079 = \$100/(1 + i) + \$100/(1 + i)^2 + \$1,100/(1 + i)^3$
3. $1,052
4. Below
5. $1,136
6. Above

**Exercise 3**

| Price of the Discount Bond | Maturity | Yield on a Discount Basis | Yield to Maturity |
|---|---|---|---|
| $900 | 1 year (365 days) | 9.86% | 11.1% |
| $950 | 6 months (182 days) | 9.89% | 10.8% |
| $975 | 3 months (91 days) | 9.89% | 10.7% |

The table indicates that as the maturity of the discount bond shortens, the yield on a discount basis understates the yield to maturity by a smaller amount.

**Exercise 4**

| Coupon Rate | Maturity Date | Price | Yield to Maturity | Current Yield |
|---|---|---|---|---|
| 10 3/4s | May 2003 | 110 11/32 | 6.87% | 9.74% |
| 12 3/8s | May 2004 | 118 31/32 | 6.86% | 10.40% |
| 6 3/4s | May 2005 | 100 5/32 | 6.71% | 6.74% |
| 6 1/2s | Nov 2026 | 101 12/32 | 6.39% | 6.41% |
| 6 1/4s | May 2030 | 101 26/32 | 6.12% | 6.14% |

The 6 1/4 of May 2030, the 6 1/2 of November 2026, and the 6 3/4 of May 2005 are the bonds for which the current yield is a good measure of the interest rate. The reason for this is that all three are selling at a price close to par, while the 6 1/2 of November 2026 and the 6 1/4 of May 2030 both have long terms to maturity.

## Exercise 5

1. 110 percent, which is calculated as follows: The initial price of the consol is $1000 = $100/0.10 while next year the price is $2000 = $100/0.05. The return is therefore 110 percent = 1.10 = ($2000 - $1000 + $100)/$1000.

2. 14.8 percent, which is calculated as follows: The initial price of the coupon bond is $1000, since the interest rate equals the coupon rate when the bond is at par. Next year, when the bond has 1 year to maturity, the price is $1048 = $100/(1 + 0.05) + $1000/(1 + 0.05). The return is therefore 14.8 percent = 0.148 = ($1048 - $1000 + $100)/$1000.

The consol is a better investment because when the interest rate on two bonds has the same decline, the bond with the longer maturity--the consol--has a larger increase in its price.

## Exercise 6

1. 6%        2. -10%     3. 3%       4. 0%

You would rather be a lender in situation 1 because the real interest rate is the highest, while you would rather be a borrower in situation 2 because the real interest rate is lowest.

## Self-Test

### Part A
| | | | |
|---|---|---|---|
| 1. | T | 2. | F |
| 3. | F | 4. | F |
| 5. | F | 6. | T |
| 7. | F | 8. | F |
| 9. | T | 10. | F |

### Part B
| | | | |
|---|---|---|---|
| 1. | d | 2. | c |
| 3. | d | 4. | a |
| 5. | b | 6. | c |
| 7. | b | 8. | e |
| 9. | c | 10. | c |
| 11. | c | 12. | c |
| 13. | a | 14. | d |
| 15. | d | | |

## ANSWERS TO CHAPTER 5

### Chapter Synopsis/Completions

| | | | |
|---|---|---|---|
| 1. | demand | 2. | inversely |
| 3. | higher | 4. | down |
| 5. | lower | 6. | equilibrium |
| 7. | increases | 8. | increases |
| 9. | decreases | 10. | increases |
| 11. | increases | 12. | Fisher |
| 13. | increase | 14. | increase |
| 15. | declines | 16. | decline |
| 17. | opposite | 18. | higher |

### Exercise 1
| | | | |
|---|---|---|---|
| 1. | D → | 2. | ← D, S → |
| 3. | D → | 4. | S → |

5. S →
6. ← D
7. D →, S →
8. D →
9. D →
10. ← D

## Exercise 2

| Variable | Change in Variable | Change in Quantity Demanded |
|---|---|---|
| Wealth | ↓ | ↓ |
| Liquidity of asset | ↓ | ↓ |
| Riskiness of asset | ↓ | ↑ |
| Expected return of asset | ↓ | ↓ |
| Riskiness of other assets | ↓ | ↓ |
| liquidity of other assets | ↓ | ↑ |
| Expected return of other assets | ↓ | ↑ |

## Exercise 3

The new supply and demand curves are $B^s_2$ and $B^d_2$, and the market equilibrium moves from point 1 to point 2. As can be seen in Figure 5A the interest rate rises to $i_2$.

FIGURE 5A

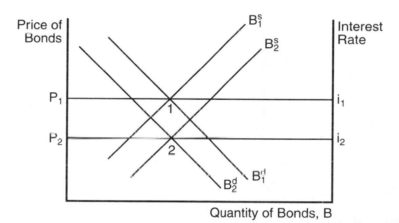

## Exercise 4

The new supply and demand curves are $M^s_2$ and $M^d_2$, and the market equilibrium moves from point 1 to point 2. As the figure is drawn, the interest rate rises, but if the shift of the demand curve is greater, then the interest rate could fall, instead of rise. What we are seeing here is a combination of the liquidity effect and the income effect of a money supply decrease. Since they have opposite effects the overall impact on the interest rate is ambiguous.

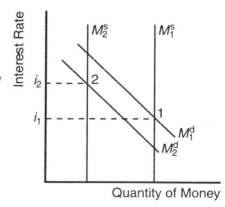

**Exercise 5**

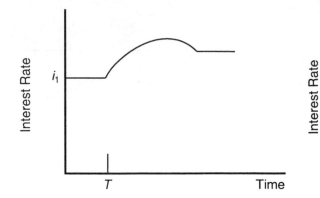

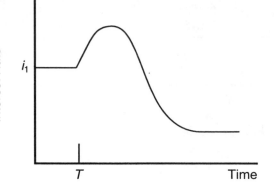

**Self-Test**

**Part A**

| | | | |
|---|---|---|---|
| 1. | T | 2. | F |
| 3. | F | 4. | F |
| 5. | T | 6. | F |
| 7. | T | 8. | F |
| 9. | T | 10. | F |

**Part B**

| | | | |
|---|---|---|---|
| 1. | b | 2. | a |
| 3. | b | 4. | b |
| 5. | b | 6. | c |
| 7. | a | 8. | d |
| 9. | d | 10. | d |
| 11. | c | 12. | d |
| 13. | a | 14. | a |
| 15. | d | | |

## ANSWERS TO CHAPTER 6

**Chapter Synopsis/Completions**

| | | | |
|---|---|---|---|
| 1. | risk | 2. | default risk |
| 3. | risk | 4. | liquidity |
| 5. | increases | 6. | lowers |
| 7. | term | 8. | yield curve |
| 9. | upward | 10. | segmented markets |
| 11. | risk | 12. | substitutes |
| 13. | higher | 14. | positive |
| 15. | rise | | |

**Exercise 1**

FIGURE 6A

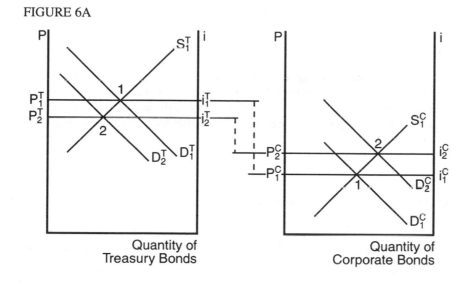

1. The interest rate on corporate bonds would probably rise. Both the demand and supply curves shift to the right. If the supply curve shifts out more than the demand curve, the interest rate rises.

2. The interest rate on Treasury bonds rises.

3. The risk premium depends on the size of the interest rate increase on corporate bonds relative to that on Treasury bonds. The analysis in the chapter suggests that the risk premium would probably fall.

**Exercise 2**
1. 8%                          2. $7.5\% = 10\% \times (1 - 0.25)$

You would prefer to hold the tax-exempt municipal bond because it has a higher after-tax return. Since you would prefer the municipal bond with a lower interest rate, this example indicates that municipal bonds will have lower market interest rates than                                                    they otherwise would because of their tax advantages.

**Exercise 3**

FIGURE 6B

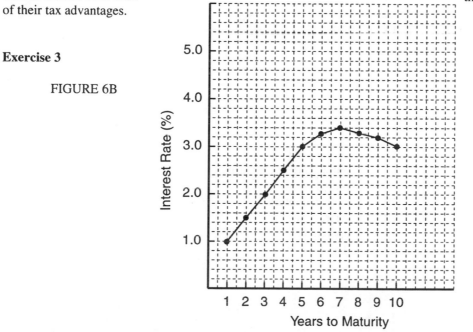

**Exercise 4**

1. $6\% = 0.06 = [0.06 + 0.06 + 0.06]/3$
2. $6\% = 0.06 = [0.07 + 0.06 + 0.05]/3$

The expected returns are identical. Our analysis of the expectations hypothesis indicates that when the 3 year interest rate equals the average of the expected future 1 year rates over the life of the 3 year bond, the expected returns on strategies 1 and 2 are equal. In our example here, the 3 year interest rate of 6% is the average of the 1 year rates over the life of the 3 year bond ($6\% = [7\% + 6\% + 5\%]/3$), so the expected return from the two strategies must be the same.

**Exercise 5**

A. The market is predicting that there will be a mild decline in short-term interest rates in the near future and an even steeper decline further out in the future.

B. The market is predicting that there will be a steep decline in short-term interest rates in the near future and a sharp increase further out in the future.

**Self-Test**
**Part A**

| | | | |
|---|---|---|---|
| 1. | F | 2 | T |
| 3. | F | 4. | F |
| 5. | F | 6. | T |
| 7. | T | 8. | F |
| 9. | T | 10. | F |

**Part B**

| | | | |
|---|---|---|---|
| 1. | c | 2. | c |
| 3. | d | 4. | a |
| 5. | a | 6. | e |
| 7. | d | 8. | b |
| 9. | d | 10. | b |
| 11. | d | 12. | a |
| 13. | a | 14. | a |
| 15. | b | | |

**ANSWERS TO CHAPTER 7**

**Chapter Synopsis/Completions**

| | | | |
|---|---|---|---|
| 1. | currency | 2. | deposits |
| 3. | forward | 4. | appreciated |
| 5. | more | 6. | purchasing power parity |
| 7. | depreciate | 8. | traded |
| 9. | tariffs | 10. | expected return |
| 11. | capital mobility | 12. | interest rate |
| 13. | rise | 14. | appreciate |
| 15. | appreciates | 16. | depreciation |

**Exercise 1**

1. 2 francs per dollar
2. $500

3. 200 francs
4. Depreciation of the franc; appreciation of the dollar
5. $250; less
6. 400 francs; more
7. When a country's currency appreciates, its goods abroad become more expensive and foreign goods in that country become cheaper (holding domestic prices constant in the two countries).

**Exercise 2**

| | | | |
|---|---|---|---|
| 1. | e | 2. | i |
| 3. | g | 4. | b |
| 5. | m | 6. | n |
| 7. | a | 8. | l |
| 9. | f | 10. | j |
| 11. | c | 12. | k |

**Exercise 3**

**Part A**
1. $10
2. 1800 zloties
3. None, because Polish wheat is more expensive in both countries and the goods are identical.
4. $5
5. 3600 zloties
6. None, because American wheat is more expensive in both countries and the goods are identical.
7. 500 zloties per dollar, because only at this exchange rate will both American and Polish wheat be purchased.
8. 300 zloties per dollar; a depreciation of the dollar

**Part B**
1. Tne value of the dollar will fall to 250 zloties per dollar.
2. The dollar will appreciate by 2%.

**Exercise 4**

| | Change in Factor | Response of the Exchange Rate |
|---|---|---|
| Domestic interest rate | ↓ | ↓ |
| Foreign interest rate | ↓ | ↑ |
| Expected domestic price level | ↓ | ↑ |
| Expected tariffs and quotas | ↓ | ↓ |
| Expected import demand | ↓ | ↑ |
| Expected export demand | ↓ | ↓ |
| Expected productivity | ↓ | ↓ |

**Self-Test**
**Part A**

| | | | |
|---|---|---|---|
| 1. | T | 2. | F |
| 3. | T | 4. | F |
| 5. | F | 6. | T |
| 7. | F | 8. | F |
| 9. | T | 10. | F |

**Part B**

| | |
|---|---|
| 1. c | 2. a |
| 3. b | 4. a |
| 5. c | 6. c |
| 7. a | 8. e |
| 9. a | 10. b |
| 11. d | 12. b |
| 13. a | 14. d |
| 15. c | |

# ANSWERS TO CHAPTER 8

## Chapter Synopsis/Completions

| | |
|---|---|
| 1. intermediaries | 2. adverse selection |
| 3. moral hazard | 4. bonds |
| 5. one-third | 6. financial |
| 7. external | 8. complicated |
| 9. information | 10. adverse selection |
| 11. worthiness | 12. equity |
| 13. restrictive covenants | 14. financial crises |

## Exercise 1

| | |
|---|---|
| 1. B | 2. B |
| 3. B | 4. B |
| 5. B | 6. B |
| 7. B | 8. M |

## Exercise 2

| | |
|---|---|
| 1. j | 2. i |
| 3. h | 4. g |
| 5. f | 6. e |
| 7. d | 8. c |
| 9. b | 10. a |
| 11. k | |

## Exercise 3

### Part A
1. sharp decline in the stock market
2. Unanticipated decline in the aggregate price level
3. Unanticipated depreciation of the domestic currency
4. A rise in interest rates that reduces cash flow

### Part B
1. Sharp increases in interest rates
2. Asset market effects on balance sheets (steep stock market decline)
3. An increase in financial market uncertainty
4. Problems in the banking sector

**Self-Test**

**Part A**

| | |
|---|---|
| 1. F | 2. T |
| 3. F | 4. T |
| 5. T | 6. T |
| 7. F | 8. T |
| 9. T | 10. T |

**Part B**

| | |
|---|---|
| 1. c | 2. e |
| 3. a | 4. d |
| 5. e | 6. e |
| 7. a | 8. d |
| 9. d | 10. b |
| 11. b | 12. a |
| 13. b | 14. c |
| 15. d | |

# ANSWERS TO CHAPTER 9

**Chapter Synopsis/Completions**

| | |
|---|---|
| 1. capital | 2. sources |
| 3. vault cash | 4. required reserves |
| 5. reserves | 6. outflows |
| 7. liquidity | 8. default |
| 9. diversifying | 10. federal funds |
| 11. dividends | 12. more |
| 13. gap | 14. mortgages |
| 15. loophole mining | 15. disintermediation |

**Exercise 1**

| | |
|---|---|
| 1. J | 2. d |
| 3. a | 4. f |
| 5. b | 6. g |
| 7. c | 8. i |
| 9. h | 10. e |

**Exercise 2**
**Part A**

First National Bank

| Assets | | Liabilities | |
|---|---|---|---|
| Reserves | + $2,000 | Checkable Deposits | + $2,000 |

**Part B**

| First National Bank | | | Second National Bank | |
|---|---|---|---|---|
| Assets | Liabilities | | Assets | Liabilities |
| Reserves<br>− $1,000 | Checkable Deposits<br>− $1,000 | | Reserves<br>+ $1,000 | Checkable Deposits<br>+ $1,000 |

**Part C**

Both banks end up with an increase of $1,000 in reserves.

**Exercise 3**

**Part A**

| Assets | | Liabilities | |
|---|---|---|---|
| Reserves | $19 million | Deposits | $94 million |
| Loans | $75 million | Bank capital | $10 million |
| Securities | $10 million | | |

No.  The bank does not need to make any adjustment to its balance sheet because it initially is holding $25 million of reserves when required reserves are only $20 million (20% of $100 million).  Because of its initial holding of $5 million of excess reserves, when it suffers the deposit outflow of $6 million it can still satisfy its reserve requirements: Required reserves are $18.8 million (20% of $94 million) while it has $19 million of reserves.

**Part B**

| Assets | | Liabilities | |
|---|---|---|---|
| Reserves | $15 million | Deposits | $90 million |
| Loans | $75 million | Bank capital | $10 million |
| Securities | $10 million | | |

Yes.  The bank must make an adjustment to its balance sheet because its required reserves are $18 million (20% of $90 million), but it is only holding $15 million of reserves.  It has a reserve deficiency of $3 million.

**Part C**

$3 million.  As we see above the bank has a reserve shortfall of $3 million, which it can acquire by selling the $3 million of securities.

**Part D**

| Assets | | Liabilities | |
|---|---|---|---|
| Reserves | $18 million | Deposits | $90 million |
| Loans | $75 million | Bank capital | $10 million |
| Securities | $ 7 million | | |

**Part E**

| Assets | | Liabilities | |
|---|---|---|---|
| Reserves | $15 million | Deposits | $80 million |
| Loans | $75 million | Bank capital | $10 million |
| Securities | $ 0 million | | |

The bank could fail. The required reserves for the bank are $16 million (20% of $80 million), but it has $15 million of reserves. The proceeds from the distress sale of loans could result in loss that exceeds bank capital, causing the bank to become insolvent.

**Exercise 4**

1. Finding borrowers who will pay high interest rates, yet are unlikely to default on their loans.
2. Purchasing securities with high returns and low risk.
3. Attempt to minimize risk by diversifying both holdings of loans and securities.
4. Manage the liquidity of its assets so that it can satisfy its reserve requirements without bearing huge costs.

**Exercise 5**

1. Banks now aggressively set target goals for asset growth and then acquire funds by issuing liabilities as they are needed.
2. Checkable deposits became a less important source of bank funds, while negotiable CDs and bank borrowings have increased in importance.
3. Banks have increased the proportion of their assets in loans.

**Exercise 6**

1. Screening good credit risks from bad
2. Specialization in lending
3. Monitoring and enforcement of restrictive covenants
4. Long-term customer relationships and lines of credit
5. Collateral and compensating balances
6. Credit rationing

**Exercise 7**

A. $30 million - 50 million = -$20 million.
B. Profits will decline.
C -$20 million × 0.02 = -$400,000.
D. Profits will increase by $600,000 (= $20 million × 0.03).

**Self-Test**
**Part A**

| | | | |
|---|---|---|---|
| 1. | F | 2. | T |
| 3. | F | 4. | T |
| 5. | F | 6. | T |
| 7. | F | 8. | T |
| 9. | F | 10. | T |

**Part B**

1.  d
3.  d
5.  e
7.  c
9.  c
11. a
13. d
15. a

2.  c
4.  d
6.  a
8.  b
10. a
12. b
14. b

## ANSWERS TO CHAPTER 10

### Chapter Synopsis/Completions

1.  Comptroller
3.  state
5.  small
7.  superregional
9.  Eurodollars
11. cost
13. junk

2.  national
4.  state
6.  branch banking
8.  international
10. 10%
12. commercial

### Exercise 1
1. Bank holding companies
2. Nonbank banks
3. Automated teller machines (ATMs)

### Exercise 2

1.  f
3.  a
5.  b
7.  c
9.  i

2.  e
4.  h
6.  d
8.  g

### Exercise 3
A.
1.  Money market mutual funds (decline in cost advantages in acquiring funds).
2.  Commercial paper market
3.  Junk bonds
4.  Securitization

B.  The junk bond market has allowed as traditional borrowers by-pass banks, thereby reducing the income advantages banks once had on uses of funds.

### Self-Test
**Part A**

1.  T
3.  F
5.  T
7.  T
9.  T
11. T

2.  T
4.  T
6.  T
8.  T
10. T
12. T

**Part B**

| | | | |
|---|---|---|---|
| 1. | d | 2. | d |
| 3. | d | 4. | a |
| 5. | b | 6. | c |
| 7. | d | 8. | a |
| 9. | c | 10. | c |
| 11. | b | 12. | d |
| 13. | e | 14. | e |
| 15. | d | | |

## ANSWERS TO CHAPTER 11

### Chapter Synopsis/Completions

| | | | |
|---|---|---|---|
| 1. | withdraw | 2. | moral hazard |
| 3. | adverse selection | 4. | moral hazard |
| 5. | examinations | 6. | financial |
| 7. | Regulation Q | 8. | interest |
| 9. | lowered | 10. | regulatory forbearance |
| 11. | moral hazard | 12. | Thrift Supervision |

### Exercise 1

1. Banks with deposit insurance are likely to take on greater risks than they otherwise would. This is the moral hazard problem.

2. Deposit insurance attracts risk-prone entrepreneurs to the banking industry. This is the adverse selection problem.

3. Deposit insurance reduces the incentives of depositors to monitor the riskiness of their banks' asset portfolios. This is the free-rider problem (see chapter 8).

### Exercise 2

### Part A

1. Adverse selection problems can be reduced through a chartering process that prevents crooks or risk-prone entrepreneurs from getting control of banks.

2. Moral hazard problems can be reduced through regulatory restrictions that prevent banks from acquiring certain risky assets such as common stocks or junk bonds.

3. High bank capital requirements raise the cost of a bank failure to the owners, thereby reducing the incentives of bank owners to take on too much risk, and reducing the moral hazard to depositors.

4. Regular bank examinations reduce moral hazard problems by reducing opportunities for bank owners to skirt regulations concerning asset holdings and minimum capital requirements.

### Part B

Regular bank examinations, restrictions on asset holdings, and minimum capital requirements help to reduce the adverse selection problem because, given fewer opportunities to take on risk, risk-prone entrepreneurs will be discouraged from entering the banking industry.

## Exercise 3

### Part A
1. The failure of a large bank could lead to greater uncertainty in financial markets, potentially causing a major financial crisis that could result in adverse macroeconomic consequences. The too-big-to-fail policy is intended to prevent greater financial market instability and adverse economic conditions.

### Part B
1. One implication is that individuals holding deposits in excess of the $100,000 insurance limit are fully protected. This suggests that depositors with uninsured deposits in large banks get a better deal than those in banks that are not-too-big-to-fail. It is also evident that the policy is not limited to the eleven largest banks, and may indicate that banks, which are even smaller than the Bank of New England, could be too-big-to-fail, no matter how poorly they are managed. Bank performance may suffer as a result of the increased incentives for moral hazard by big banks.

2. The alternative to the purchase and assumption method for dealing with failed banks is the payoff method.

3. These banks are liquidated, implying that uninsured depositors usually suffer some loss, as happened to depositors of Freedom National Bank (see Box 11.1 in text).

## Exercise 4

### Part A
1. A burst of financial innovation in the 1970s and early 1980s that produced new financial instruments and markets widened the scope for greater risk taking.

2. Financial deregulation opened up more avenues to savings and loans and mutual savings banks to take on more risk.

3. An increase in federal deposit insurance from $40,000 to $100,000, and the use of brokered deposits made it easier for high-rolling financial institutions to attract funds.

4. In the early stages of the 1980s banking crisis, financial institutions were harmed by the sharp increases in interest rates from late 1979 until 1981 and the severe recession in 1981-82.

### Part B
Regulators adopted a policy of regulatory forbearance toward insolvent financial institutions in the 1980s.

### Part C
1. The FSLIC lacked sufficient funds to cover insured deposits in the insolvent S&Ls.

2. The regulators were reluctant to close the firms that justified their regulatory existence.

3. The Federal Home Loan Bank Board and the FSLIC were reluctant to admit that they were in over their heads with problems.

## Exercise 5

1. The abolishment of the Federal Home Loan Bank Board and the FSLIC, both of which had failed in their regulatory tasks.

2. The transfer of the regulatory role of the Federal Home Loan Bank Board to the Office of Thrift Supervision, a bureau within the U.S. Treasury Department.

3. The expansion of the responsibilities of the FDIC, which is now the sole administrator of the federal deposit insurance system.

4. The establishment of the Resolution Trust Corporation to manage and resolve insolvent thrifts placed in conservatorship or receivership.

5. To replenish the reserves of the Savings Association Insurance Fund, the deposit insurance premiums for S&Ls were increased.

6. FIRREA imposes new restrictions on thrift activities. Under these restrictions, S&Ls can no longer purchase junk bonds, must limit their commercial real estate loans to four times capital, and must hold at least 70% of their assets in investments that are housing related.

**Exercise 6**

Regulators' desire to escape blame for poor performance, led them to adopt a perverse strategy of "regulatory gambling", whereby capital requirements were lowered and insolvent institutions were allowed to continue operating in the hope that conditions in the thrift industry would improve. Rather than mandate stricter controls, politicians encouraged lax monitoring and regulatory forbearance, even hampering regulatory efforts to close insolvent thrifts by cutting regulatory appropriations. Politicians, who were receiving generous campaign contributions from the savings and loan industry, like regulators, hoped that the industry would rebound.

**Exercise 7**

1. Recapitalizes FDIC.

2. Limits brokered deposits and the too-big-to-fail policy.

3. Sets provisions for prompt corrective action.

4. Instructs FDIC to establish risk-based deposit insurance premiums.

5. Increases examinations, capital requirements, and reporting requirements.

6. Includes the Foreign Bank Supervision Act which strengthens Fed's authority to supervise foreign banks.

**Self-Test**
**Part A**

| | | | |
|---|---|---|---|
| 1. | T | 2. | T |
| 3. | F | 4. | T |
| 5. | T | 6. | T |
| 7. | F | 8. | T |
| 9. | T | 10. | T |

**Part B**

| | | | |
|---|---|---|---|
| 1. | e | 2. | e |
| 3. | c | 4. | c |
| 5. | e | 6. | a |
| 7. | c | 8. | e |
| 9. | e | 10. | e |
| 11. | b | 12. | a |
| 13. | a | 14. | d |

15. b


# ANSWERS TO CHAPTER 12

## Chapter Synopsis/Completions

1. borrowers
3. moral hazard
5. casualty
7. underfunding
9. factoring
11. no-load
13. brokers

2. financial intermediation
4. long
6. income
8. consumer finance
10. money market
12. underwriters

## Exercise 1
1. Screening out bad risks
2. Risk-based premiums
3. Restrictive provisions
4. Prevention of fraud
5. Cancellation of insurance
6. Deductibles
7. Co-insurance
8. Limits on the amount of insurance

## Exercise 2
1. d
3. a
5. f
7. g
9. j
11. o
13. n
15. l

2. c
4. h
6. e
8. b
10. i
12. m
14. k

## Exercise 3
1. d
3. e
5. b
7. f
9. l
11. i

2. c
4. a
6. a
8. g
10. k
12. j

## Self-Test
### Part A
1. F
3. T
5. F
7. T
9. T

2. T
4. F
6. F
8. T
10. T

**Part B**

| | |
|---|---|
| 1. e | 2. b |
| 3. e | 4. a |
| 5. b | 6. b |
| 7. c | 8. d |
| 9. a | 10. d |
| 11. a | 12. b |
| 13. c | 14. c |
| 15. b | |

## ANSWERS TO CHAPTER 13

### Chapter Synopsis/Completions

| | |
|---|---|
| 1. hedge | 2. opposite |
| 3. short | 4. risk |
| 5. standardized | 6. reduces |
| 7. lowering | 8. right |
| 9. strike | 10. European |
| 11. sell | 12. long |

### Exercise 1
1. Futures are standardized contracts
2. Futures can be bought and sold up until maturity
3. Futures can be satisfied with any similar security
4. Futures are marked to market daily

### Exercise 2

| | |
|---|---|
| 1. d | 2. h |
| 3. f | 4. c |
| 5. g | 6. i |
| 7. j | 8. a |
| 9. e | 10. b |

### Exercise 3

| | |
|---|---|
| 1. j | 2. d |
| 3. f | 4. b |
| 5. h | 6. i |
| 7. c | 8. e |
| 9. a | 10. g |

### Exercise 4

| | |
|---|---|
| 1. selling | 2. short |
| 3. default risk | 4. arbitrage |
| 5. standardized | 6. reduce |

### Exercise 5

| | |
|---|---|
| 1. option | 2. call |
| 3. put | 4. strike |
| 5. European | 6. American |
| 7. swap | |

**Self-Test**
**Part A**

| | | | |
|---|---|---|---|
| 1. | F | 2. | T |
| 3. | T | 4. | F |
| 5. | T | 6. | T |
| 7. | F | 8. | T |
| 9. | T | 10. | T |

**Part B**

| | | | |
|---|---|---|---|
| 1. | d | 2. | a |
| 3. | c | 4. | a |
| 5. | c | 6. | a |
| 7. | d | 8. | e |
| 9. | a | 10. | d |
| 11. | a | 12. | c |
| 13. | c | 14. | c |
| 15. | a | | |

## ANSWERS TO CHAPTER 14

### Chapter Synopsis/Completions

| | | | |
|---|---|---|---|
| 1. | panic | 2. | last resort |
| 3. | Board of Governors | 4. | New York |
| 5. | independence | 6. | appropriations |
| 7. | Treasury securities | 8. | fourteen |
| 9. | interest | 10. | bureaucratic |
| 11. | increasing | 12. | inflationary |
| 13. | undemocratic | | |

### Exercise 1

| | | | |
|---|---|---|---|
| 1. | c | 2. | c |
| 3. | a | 4. | a |
| 5. | a | 6. | b |
| 7. | b | 8. | a, c |
| 9. | a | 10. | a |

### Exercise 2

Two explanations seem possible. First, the Fed may have feared that Congress would overreact and set Regulation Q ceilings much too low for too long, causing severe economic harm to affected groups. Thus the Fed may have felt that its action was a least worst strategy. Second, the Fed may have feared losing permanent control over Regulation Q. The Theory of Bureaucratic Behavior suggest that bureaucracies want to maximize their power and prestige. The potential loss of power over Regulation Q would diminish the overall power of the Fed and might encourage Congress to usurp other duties from the Fed. Additionally, since lower Regulation Q ceilings allow the Treasury to borrow more cheaply, the Fed may have been attempting to avoid a potential conflict with the executive branch as well.

### Exercise 3

Making the Fed a branch of the U.S. Treasury would eliminate the Fed's current source of revenue. The Treasury Department would allocate part of its annual budget to Fed activities, but presumably this allocation would not vary from changes in money growth. If inflationary expansions in the money supply result from the Fed's desire to increase the revenue available for expenditures on its activities, then making the Fed a branch of the Treasury eliminates the incentive to overly expand the money supply.

**Exercise 4**

**Part A**
1. Greater focus on long-run objectives.
2. Less pressure to finance deficits and less pressure to pursue inflationary policies.
3. More likely to pursue policies in the public interest even if politically unpopular.

**Part B**

1. Greater accountability. If Fed policymakers make mistakes there is no way of voting them out, thus system is undemocratic.
2. Coordination of fiscal and monetary policy would be easier.
3. President is ultimately held responsible for economic policy, yet he does not have control over monetary policy, an important element determining economic health.
4. Lack of evidence indicating that an independent Fed performs well.

**Self-Test**
**Part A**

| | | | |
|---|---|---|---|
| 1. | T | 2. | F |
| 3. | F | 4. | T |
| 5. | F | 6. | T |
| 7. | T | 8. | F |
| 9. | T | 10. | T |

**Part B**

| | | | |
|---|---|---|---|
| 1. | a | 2. | c |
| 3. | d | 4. | c |
| 5. | c | 6. | c |
| 7. | b | 8. | c |
| 9. | d | 10. | d |
| 11. | b | 12. | a |

## ANSWERS TO CHAPTER 15

**Chapter Synopsis/Completions**

| | | | |
|---|---|---|---|
| 1. | central | 2. | banks |
| 3. | Federal Reserve System | 4. | reserves |
| 5. | monetary base | 6. | open market |
| 7. | identical | 8. | currency |
| 9. | declines | 10. | deposits |
| 11. | multiple | 12. | simple deposit multiplier |
| 13. | excess | 14. | smaller |

**Exercise 1**

**Part A**

Banking System

| Assets | | Liabilities |
|---|---|---|
| Securities | + $100 | |
| Reserves | − $100 | |

### The Fed

| Assets | | Liabilities | |
|---|---|---|---|
| Government Securities | − $100 | Reserves | − $100 |

Change in the monetary base = -$100
Change in Reserves = -$100.

**Part B**

### Nonbank Public

| Assets | | Liabilities |
|---|---|---|
| Securities | + $100 | |
| Checkable deposits | − $100 | |

### Banking System

| Assets | | Liabilities | |
|---|---|---|---|
| Reserves | − $100 | Checkable deposits | − $100 |

### The Fed

| Assets | | Liabilities | |
|---|---|---|---|
| Government Securities | − $100 | Reserves | − $100 |

Change in the monetary base = -$100
Change in Reserves = -$100.

**Part C**

### Nonbank Public

| Assets | | Liabilities |
|---|---|---|
| Securities | + $100 | |
| Currency | − $100 | |

### The Fed

| Assets | | Liabilities | |
|---|---|---|---|
| Government Securities | − $100 | Currency in circulation | − $100 |

Change in the monetary base = -$100
Change in Reserves = 0.

In all cases, the open market sale leads to a $100 decline in the monetary base. In part C, however, reserves do not change, while they decline by $100 in parts A and B.

**Exercise 2**
**Part A**

| First National Bank | | | The Fed | |
| Assets | Liabilities | | Assets | Liabilities |
| --- | --- | --- | --- | --- |
| T-bills<br>  + $100,000<br>Reserves<br>  - $100,000 | | | T-bills<br>  + $100,000 | Reserves<br>  - $100,000 |

Reserves in the banking system have fallen by $100,000.

**Part B**

| First National Bank | | | The Fed | |
| Assets | Liabilities | | Assets | Liabilities |
| --- | --- | --- | --- | --- |
| Reserves<br>  - $100,000 | Discount Loans<br>  - $100,000 | | Discount Loans<br>  - $100,000 | Reserves<br>  - $100,000 |

Reserves in the banking system have again fallen by $100,000.

**Exercise 3**

A. $100
B. $100, the amount of its excess reserves.
C.

| Panther State Bank | | |
| Assets | | Liabilities |
| --- | --- | --- |
| Reserves |   - $100 | |
| Loans |   + $100 | |

**Exercise 4**
**Part A**
A. The deposit liabilities of Bank A increase by $1000, implying that required reserves increase by $200 (20 percent of $1,000). Bank A can safely lend $800. In the process of lending $800, checkable deposits increase by $800. Thus checkable deposits at Bank A are $1,800 higher than before the Fed open market purchase.

**Part B**

| Bank | Change in Deposits | Change in Loans | Change in Reserves |
|---|---|---|---|
| A | + $1000.00 | + $800.00 | + $200.00 |
| B | + 800.00 | + 640.00 | + 160.00 |
| C | + 640.00 | + 512.00 | + 128.00 |
| D | + 512.00 | + 409.60 | + 102.40 |
| . | . | . | . |
| . | . | . | . |
| . | . | . | . |
| Total All Banks | + $5000.00 | + $4000.00 | + $1000.00 |

**Exercise 5**

1. The simple deposit multiplier formula is $D = (1/r_D)R$.

2. The $10 billion dollar sale of government bonds causes bank reserves to fall by $10 billion. This is partially offset by the $5 billion in discount loans that increase bank reserves by $5 billion. Thus on net, bank reserves fall by $5 billion.

3. The change in checkable deposits is calculated by multiplying the $5 billion decline by 5 ( = 1/0.20). Checkable deposits fall by $25 billion in the simple model.

**Self-Test**
**Part A**

| | | | |
|---|---|---|---|
| 1. | F | 2. | F |
| 3. | F | 4. | F |
| 5. | T | 6. | F |
| 7. | T | 8. | F |
| 9. | F | 10. | F |

**Part B**

| | | | |
|---|---|---|---|
| 1. | c | 2. | c |
| 3. | b | 4. | c |
| 5. | d | 6. | a |
| 7. | c | 8. | d |
| 9. | e | 10. | c |
| 11. | e | 12. | b |
| 13. | c | 14. | a |

**ANSWERS TO CHAPTER 16**

**Chapter Synopsis/Completions**

| | | | |
|---|---|---|---|
| 1. | reserves | 2. | currency |
| 3. | checkable deposits | 4. | monetary base |
| 5. | overstates | 6. | increase |
| 7. | decline | 8. | interest rate |
| 9. | positively | 10. | multiplier |
| 11. | increases | 12. | negatively |
| 13. | nonborrowed | | |

**Exercise 1**

A. $m = [1 + \{C/D\}]/[r_D + \{ER/D\} + \{C/D\}]$

B. $\{C/D\} = \$280b/\$800b = 0.35$
$\{ER/D\} = \$40b/\$800b = 0.05$
$m = 1.35/0.5 = 2.7$

C. $MB = C + R = \$280 + 80 + 40 = \$400$ billion
$R = MB - C = \$400 - \$280 = \$120$
$R = RR + ER = \$120$
$RR = r_D(D) = 0.10(800) = \$80$
$ER = R - RR = \$120 - \$80 = \$40$

D. $m = 1.35/0.48 = 2.8125$
$M = \$400 \times 2.8125 = \$1125$

E. $M = C + D$
$M = [\{C/D\}]D + D$
$M = 1.35 \times D$
$D = \$1125/1.35 = \$833.33$
$C = \$833.33 \times 0.35 = \$291.67$

F. $RR = 0.08(833.33) = \$66.67$
$ER = \$120 - \$66.67 = \$53.33$

**Exercise 2**

A. $m = 1.4/0.5 = 2.8$
$M = m \times MB = 2.8 \times \$400 = \$1120$

B. $C + D = 0.4D + D = 1.4D = \$1120$
$C = \$320$
$D = \$1120/1.4 = \$800$
$RR = 0.1(800) = \$80$
$R = MB_n - C = 400 - 320 = \$80$

C. $m = 1.4/0.56 = 2.5$
$M = 2.5 \times \$400 = \$1000$
$D = \$1000/1.4 = \$714.29$
$C = 0.4 \times \$714.29 = \$285.71$
$RR = 0.1(714.29) = \$71.43$
$ER = MB - C - RR = \$400 - \$285.71 - \$71.43 = \$42.86$
$ER = \{ER/D\} \times D = 0.06 \times \$714.29 = \$42.86$

**Exercise 3**

| Change in Variable | | Money Supply Response |
|---|---|---|
| $r_D$ | ↓ | ↑ |
| $Mb_n$ | ↓ | ↓ |
| $i_d$ | ↓ | ↑ |
| $\{C/D\}$ | ↓ | ↑ |
| Expected deposit outflows | ↓ | ↑ |
| $i$ | ↓ | ↓ |

**Self-Test**
**Part A**

| | | | |
|---|---|---|---|
| 1. | T | 2. | F |
| 3. | T | 4. | F |
| 5. | T | 6. | F |
| 7. | T | 8. | F |
| 9. | T | 10. | F |

**Part B**

| | | | |
|---|---|---|---|
| 1. | e | 2. | c |
| 3. | a | 4. | b |
| 5. | d | 6. | d |
| 7. | a | 8. | c |
| 9. | b | 10. | a |
| 11. | d | 12. | c |
| 13. | a | 14. | a |
| 15. | b | | |

## ANSWERS TO CHAPTER 17

**Chapter Synopsis/Completions**

| | | | |
|---|---|---|---|
| 1. | discount rate | 2. | reserve requirements |
| 3. | securities | 4. | dynamic |
| 5. | purchase | 6. | reserve repos |
| 7. | flexible | 8. | liquidity |
| 9. | extended | 10. | lender of last resort |
| 11. | money multiplier | 12. | 100% |

**Exercise 1**

1. Starting from point 1, if the Fed purchases U.S. Treasury securities, the <u>supply</u> curve shifts to the <u>right</u>, and the federal funds interest rate <u>declines</u>.

2. Starting from point 1, if the Fed lowers the discount rate, the <u>supply</u> curve shifts to the <u>right</u>,  ,and the federal funds interest rate <u>declines</u>.

3. Starting from point 2, if the Fed raises the discount rate, as it did on May 16, 2000, the <u>supply</u> curve shifts to the <u>left</u>, and the federal funds interest rate <u>rises.</u>

4. Starting from point 4, if the Fed sells U.S. Treasury securities, the <u>supply</u> curve shifts to the <u>left</u>, and the federal funds interest rate <u>rises</u>.

5. Starting from point 3, if the Fed lowers reserve requirements, the <u>demand</u> curve shifts to the <u>left</u>,  and the federal funds interest rate <u>declines</u>.

6. Starting from point 2, if the Fed raises reserve requirements, the <u>demand</u> curve shifts to the <u>right</u>, and the federal funds interest rate <u>rises.</u>

7. Starting from point 3, if the Fed purchases U.S. Treasury securities, the <u>supply </u>curve shifts to the <u>right</u>, and the federal funds interest rate <u>declines.</u>

**Exercise 2**

1. g
3. d
5. c
7. e
9. j

2. a
4. h
6. b
8. i
10. f

**Exercise 3**
**Part A**
The Federal Reserveuses open market operations to target the federal funds interest rate.

**Part B**
1. Dynamic open market operations
2. Defensive open market operations

**Part C**
1. Open market operations occur at the initiative of the Fed.
2. Open market operations can be used to any degree.
3. Open market operations are easily reversed.
4. Open market operations can be implemented quickly.

**Exercise 4**
**Part A**
1. Adjustment credit
2. Seasonal credit
3. Extended credit

**Part B**
Many deposits exceed the $100,000 limit that the FDIC promises to pay. Thus the lender of last resort prevents bank failures due to large depositor withdrawals. In addition, the FDIC contingency fund is limited and a wave of bank failures could seriously jeopardize the solvency of the system leading to a severe financial panic that only a lender of last resort might prevent.

**Exercise 5**
**Part A**
1. Small changes in reserve requirements are too costly to administer, so it is too blunt a tool to be used effectively.
2. Raising reserve requirements can cause immediate liquidity problems for banks with small amounts of excess reserves.

**Part B**
1. The main advantage is that the narrowly defined money would be controlled exactly because the money multiplier would exactly equal one.
2. The main disadvantage is that there would surely be financial innovation that would create money substitutes. Thus the narrowly defined money supply would probably cease to be the economically relevant measure of the money supply.

**Self-Test**
**Part A**

1. F
3. T
5. F
7. T
9. T

2. F
4. F
6. T
8. T
10. T

**Part B**

| | |
|---|---|
| 1. d | 2. a |
| 3. a | 4. c |
| 5. c | 6. d |
| 7. a | 8. b |
| 9. b | 10. b |
| 11. c | 12. d |
| 13. c | 14. a |
| 15. c | 16. c |

## ANSWERS TO CHAPTER 18

### Chapter Synopsis/Completions

| | |
|---|---|
| 1. high employment | 2. economic growth |
| 3. price stability | 4. interest rate stability |
| 5. financial market stability | 6. foreign exchange market stability |
| 7. natural rate | 8. higher |
| 9. operating | 10. open market |
| 11. money | 12. controllable |

### Exercise 1

**Part A**
1. monetary aggregates such as M1, M2, or M3
2. short- or long-term interest rates
3. inflation rate

**Part B**
1. reserve aggregates such as reserves, nonborrowed reserves, or the monetary base
2. interest rates such as the federal funds rate or the T-bill rate

### Exercise 2
1. Measurability
2. Controllability
3. The ability to predictably affect goals

### Exercise 3: The Taylor Rule for the Federal Funds Rate

| Inflation Rate | Equilibrium Federal Funds Rate | Inflation Target | Percentage Deviation of Real GDP from Potential GDP | Federal Funds Rate |
|---|---|---|---|---|
| 3% | 2% | 2% | 1% | 6.0% |
| 4% | 2% | 2% | 1% | 7.5% |
| 4% | 2% | 2% | 2% | 8.0% |
| 4% | 2% | 2% | −1% | 6.5% |
| 4% | 2% | 2% | −2% | 6.0% |
| 5% | 2% | 2% | 1% | 9.0% |
| 1% | 2% | 2% | −2% | 1.5% |
| 1% | 2% | 2% | 1% | 3.0% |

**Self-Test**
**Part A**

| | | | |
|---|---|---|---|
| 1. | T | 2. | F |
| 3. | F | 4. | T |
| 5. | F | 6. | F |
| 7. | F | 8. | T |
| 9. | T | 10. | F |

**Part B**

| | | | |
|---|---|---|---|
| 1. | a | 2. | c |
| 3. | e | 4. | b |
| 5. | c | 6. | e |
| 7. | e | 8. | b |
| 9. | a | 10. | b |
| 11. | a | 12. | c |
| 13. | b | 14. | c |
| 15. | d | | |

# ANSWERS TO CHAPTER 19

## Chapter Synopsis/Completions

| | | | |
|---|---|---|---|
| 1. | dirty | 2. | increase |
| 3. | credits | 4. | trade balance |
| 5. | reserve currency | 6. | fixed |
| 7. | fixed | 8. | managed float |
| 9. | exchange rate | 10. | gains |
| 11. | reserve currency | 12. | contractionary |
| 13. | increase | 14. | depreciation |
| 15. | devalue | | |

**Exercise 1**

U.S. Balance of Payments in 2001 (billions of dollars)

|  | Receipts | Payments | Balance |
|---|---|---|---|
| Current account: |  |  |  |
| 1. Merchandise exports | +500 |  |  |
| 2. Merchandise imports |  | -600 |  |
| 3. Trade balance |  |  | -100 |
| 4. Net investment income |  | -40 |  |
| 5. Net services | +20 |  |  |
| 6. Net unilateral transfers |  | -15 |  |
| 7. Current Account Balance |  |  | -135 |
| Capital account: |  |  |  |
| 8. Capital outflows |  | -50 |  |
| 9. Capital inflows | +100 |  |  |
| 10. Statistical discrepancy | +60 |  |  |
| 11. Official reserves transactions balance |  |  | +110 |
| Method of financing: |  |  |  |
| 12. Increase in U.S. official reserve assets |  | -5 |  |
| 13. Increase in foreign official assets | +25 |  |  |
| 14. Total financing of surplus |  |  | +25 |

**Exercise 2**

| | | | |
|---|---|---|---|
| 1. | b | 2. | e |
| 3. | d | 4. | g |
| 5. | a | 6. | j |
| 7. | I | 8. | f |
| 9. | c | 10. | h |

**Exercise 3**

**Part A**

| Mexican Central Bank | | Mexican Public | |
|---|---|---|---|
| Assets | Liabilities | Assets | Liabilities |
| U.S. dollars + $1 billion | Mexican pesos + $1 billion | Mexican goods and assets - $1 billion U.S. dollars 0 Mexican pesos + $1 billion | |

The effect of the Mexican central bank's intervention in the foreign exchange market is a $1 billion increase in the Mexican monetary base and a $1 billion increase in the Mexican central bank's holdings of international reserves (dollar-denominated assets).

**Part B**

| Mexican Central Bank | | American Public | |
|---|---|---|---|
| Assets | Liabilities | Assets | Liabilities |
| U.S. dollars 0 U.S. securities + $1 billion | Mexican pesos + $1 billion | Mexican goods and assets + $1 billion U.S. dollars 0 U.S. securities - $1 billion | |

Since there is no change in the American public's holdings of dollars, the U.S. monetary base is unaffected. In the U.S. balance of payments, the foreign official assets entry is + $1 billion.

**Exercise 4**

**Part A**

1. purchase; selling
2. reducing; rise; right

**Part B**

FIGURE 19A

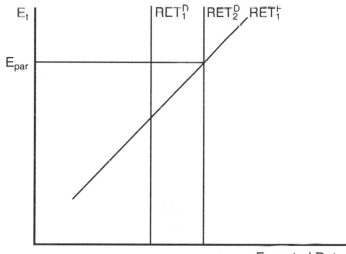

**Exercise 5**

**Part A**.

1. An international lender of last resort can provide liquidity without the undesirable side effect of raising inflation expectations.

2. An international lender of last resort may be able to prevent contagion.

**Part B**.

1. The existence of an international lender of last resort creates the moral hazard problem in that irresponsible financial institutions may take excessive risks that make financial crises more likely.

2. The IMF as lender of last resort may feel forced to come to the rescue, even if the emerging market country resists adopting necessary reforms.

3. The IMF has been criticized for imposing austerity programs on the East Asian countries, rather than microeconomic policies to fix the crisis-causing problems in the financial sector.

4. The IMF may take too much time to provide sufficient funds to keep the crisis from becoming worse.

**Self-Test**

**Part A**

| | | | |
|---|---|---|---|
| 1. F | | 2. | F |
| 3. F | | 4. | F |
| 5. T | | 6. | F |
| 7. F | | 8. | T |
| 9. T | | 10. | T |

**Part B**

| | | | |
|---|---|---|---|
| 1. | c | 2. | b |
| 3. | a | 4. | d |
| 5. | d | 6. | c |
| 7. | e | 8. | c |
| 9. | c | 10. | a |
| 11. | a | 12. | b |
| 13. | c | 14. | a |
| 15. | a | 16. | a |

**ANSWERS TO CHAPTER 20**

**Chapter Synopsis/Completions**

| | | | |
|---|---|---|---|
| 1. | nominal anchor | 2. | time-inconsistency problem |
| 3. | expansionary | 4. | distrust |
| 5. | exchange rate | 6. | shocks |
| 7. | speculative | 8. | currency board |
| 9. | last resort | 10. | domestic |
| 11. | inflation targeting | 12. | New Zealand |
| 13. | transparent | 14. | accountability |
| 15. | output | 16. | implicit |

## Exercise 1

| | |
|---|---|
| 1. b | 2. c |
| 3. f | 4. g |
| 5. e | 6. a |
| 7. h | 8. d |

## Exercise 2

### Part A

1. It directly keeps inflation under control by tying the inflation rate for internationally traded goods to that found in the anchor country to which its currency is pegged.

2. It provides an automatic rule for the conduct of monetary policy that helps mitigate the time-inconsistency problem.

3. It has the advantage of simplicity and clarity.

### Part B

1. It results in a loss of independent monetary policy and increase the exposure of the economy to shocks from the anchor country.

2. It leaves the currency open to speculative attacks.

3. It can weaken the accountability of policymakers because the exchange rate signal is lost.

## Exercise 3

### Part A

1. It enables monetary policy to focus on domestic considerations.

2. Stability in the relationship between money and inflation is not crucial to its success.

3. Its readily understood by the public and is highly transparent.

4. It increases the accountability of the central bank.

5. It appears to ameliorate the effects of inflationary shocks.

### Part B

1. An inflation target does not send immediate signals to both the public and markets.

2. It might impose a rigid rule on policymakers.

3. Sole focus on the inflation rate could mean larger output fluctuations.

## Exercise 4

### Part A

1. It enables the central bank to adjust its monetary policy to cope with domestic considerations.

2. Information on whether the central bank is achieving its target is known almost immediately.

### Part B

1. It works well only if there is a reliable relationship between the monetary aggregate and inflation.

**Exercise 5**

**Part A**

1. It enables monetary policy to focus on domestic considerations.

2. Stability in the relationship between money and inflation is not crucial to its success.

3. It has had demonstrated success.

**Part B**

1. It has a lack of transparency.

2. It is strongly dependent on the preferences, skills, and trustworthiness of the individuals at the central bank.

3. It has some inconsistencies with democratic principles because the central bank is not highly accountable.

**Self-Test**

**Part A**

| | | | |
|---|---|---|---|
| 1. | T | 2. | T |
| 3. | T | 4. | F |
| 5. | F | 6. | T |
| 7. | F | 8. | T |
| 9. | T | 10. | F |

**Part B**

| | | | |
|---|---|---|---|
| 1. | e | 2. | d |
| 3. | b | 4. | d |
| 5. | d | 6. | e |
| 7. | a | 8. | a |
| 9. | c | 10. | d |

## ANSWERS TO CHAPTER 21

**Chapter Synopsis/Completions**

| | | | |
|---|---|---|---|
| 1. | velocity | 2. | exchange |
| 3. | money | 4. | flexible |
| 5. | price level | 6. | interest rates |
| 7. | liquidity preference | 8. | speculative |
| 9. | decline | 10. | negatively |
| 11. | positive | 12. | procyclical |

**Exercise 1**

**Part A**

1. transactions motive
2. precautionary motive
3. speculative

**Part B**

Speculative motive

**Part C**
  Risk

**Exercise 2**

1. 600
3. 2
5. 800

2. 1000
4. 4

**Exercise 3**

1. Q
3. C
5. F
7. K
9. Q
11. K

2. C
4. K
6. F
8. K
10. Q
12. F

**Self-Test**
**Part A**

1. T
3. T
5. F
7. T
9. T

2. T
4. F
6. T
8. T
10. T

**Part B**

1. d
3. a
5. c
7. b
9. a

2. a
4. d
6. b
8. b
10. b

# ANSWERS TO CHAPTER 22

**Chapter Synopsis/Completions**
1. aggregate demand
3. income
5. autonomous
7. planned
9. employment
11. higher

2. investment spending
4. marginal propensity
6. inventory investment
8. multiplier
10. IS
12. income

**Exercise 1**
1. g
3. i
5. a
7. j
9. k
11. d
13. c
15. n

2. h
4. b
6. l
8. o
10. m
12. f
14. e

**Exercise 2**
**Part A**

| Point | Disposable Income (DI) | Change in DI | Change in C | Autonomous Consumption | Total Consumption |
|-------|------------------------|--------------|-------------|------------------------|-------------------|
| A | 0 | | | 50 | 50 |
| B | 100 | 100 | 75 | 50 | 125 |
| C | 200 | 100 | 75 | 50 | 200 |
| D | 300 | 100 | 75 | 50 | 275 |
| E | 400 | 100 | 75 | 50 | 350 |
| F | 500 | 100 | 75 | 50 | 425 |

**Part B**

FIGURE 22A

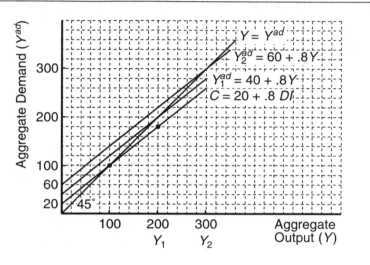

**Exercise 3**
**Part A**

FIGURE 22B

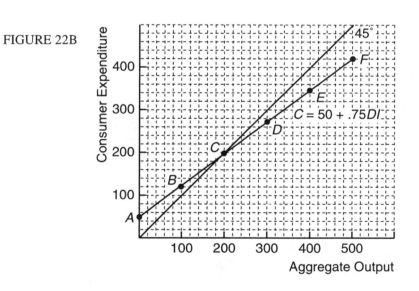

B. $Y_1 = 200$
C. $Y_2 = 300$
D. 5

**Exercise 4**

A. $Y^{ad} = 100 + 0.9Y + 100 + 200 = 400 + 0.9Y$

B. Inventory investment = $-100 = (Y - Y^{ad}) = 3000 - 400 - 0.9(3000)$

C. Output will increase since business will expand production in the second time period.

D. 4000: Because $Y - Y^{ad} = 0 = Y - 400 - 0.9Y$; $0.1Y = 400$; $Y = 4000$

E. 4000: The same level where unplanned inventory investment is zero.

**Exercise 5**

|  | Consumer Expenditure | | Planned Investment Spending | Government Spending | Equilibrium Aggregate Income |
|---|---|---|---|---|---|
|  | Autonomous | Induced | | | |
| Decrease in interest rate | 0 | + | + | 0 | + |
| Decrease in mpc | 0 | - | 0 | 0 | - |
| Decrease in tax rate | 0 | + | 0 | 0 | + |
| Increase in planned investment spending | 0 | + | + | 0 | + |
| Increase in autonomous consumer expenditure | + | + | 0 | 0 | + |
| Decrease in mps | 0 | + | 0 | 0 | + |
| Decrease in government spending | 0 | - | 0 | - | - |

**Exercise 6**

A. $5 = 1/(1 - 0.8)$

B. $-4 = -0.8(5)$

C. Change in $G = 40$

   Change in $T = 50$

**Exercise 7**

(b) The *LM* Curve

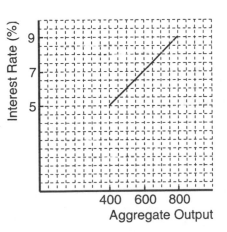

**Exercise 8**

(c) The *IS* Curve

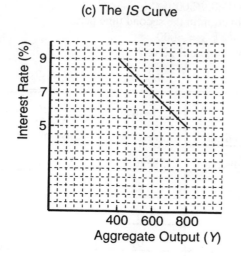

**Self-Test**
**Part A**

| | | | |
|---|---|---|---|
| 1. | T | 2. | F |
| 3. | T | 4. | F |
| 5. | F | 6. | T |
| 7. | T | 8. | F |
| 9. | T | 10. | T |

**Part B**

| | | | |
|---|---|---|---|
| 1. | d | 2. | b |
| 3. | a | 4. | c |
| 5. | b | 6. | d |
| 7. | a | 8. | a |
| 9. | b | 10. | e |
| 11. | a | 12. | b |
| 13. | a | 14. | b |
| 15. | c | | |

# ANSWERS TO CHAPTER 23

**Chapter Synopsis/Completions**

| | | | |
|---|---|---|---|
| 1. | fiscal | 2. | IS |
| 3. | investment | 4. | right |
| 5. | LM | 6. | excess |
| 7. | income | 8. | fall |
| 9. | right | 10. | rightward |
| 11. | rise | 12. | IS |
| 13. | ineffective | 14. | downward |
| 15. | right | | |

**Exercise 1**

**Part A**
1. increase in autonomous consumer expenditures
2. increase in autonomous investment

3. increase in government spending
4. decline in taxes

**Part B**
1. increase in                                          autonomous consumer expenditures
2. increase in                                          autonomous investment
3. increase in                                          government spending
4. decline in taxes

**Part C**
1. increase in the money                          supply
2. decline in money                               demand

**Part D**
1. decline in the money                            supply
2. increase in the money                         demand

**Exercise 2**

FIGURE 23A

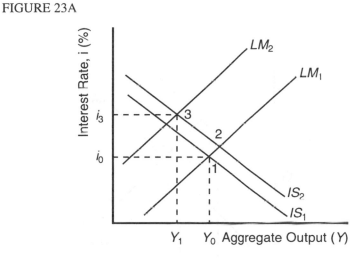

The LM curve must have shifted to the left (to $LM_2$), moving the economy to point 3. The leftward shift in the LM curve is best explained by the combination of two factors. First, the Fed, in an attempt to slow inflation which had reached double-digit levels in 1979 and 1980, slowed money growth. Second, people's concerns about recession and rising unemployment led to an increase in money demand. Both of these factors cause the LM curve to shift to the left and thus reinforce each other. Some economists have argued that the Fed was slow to realize the increase in money demand. Had the Fed known earlier, it is possible that the Fed would not have slowed money growth so sharply.

Note that the contractionary monetary policy explains the decline in real GDP, while the combination of an expansionary fiscal policy and contractionary monetary policy pushed interest rates up. In 1982, these interest rates adjusted for inflation (real interest rates) proved to be very high, leading to concerns that the fiscal-monetary policy mix of the Reagan administration would prove harmful to investment.

**Exercise 3**

FIGURE 23B

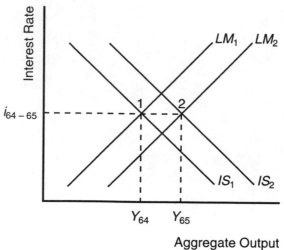

**Exercise 4**

FIGURE 23C

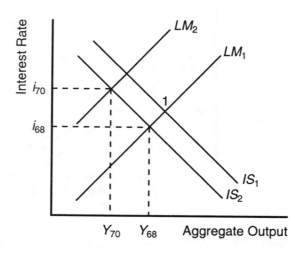

The prime rate of interest rose from 6.3% in 1968 to 7.91% in 1969 and 1970, while the unemployment rate rose from 3.6% in 1968 to 4.9% in 1970.

**Exercise 5**

1. M
3. F
5. M
7. B

2. F
4. M
6. F

**Exercise 6**

1. F
3. M
5. M

2. M
4. F

**Exercise 7**

A. →
B. ←
C. ←

D. ←
E. →
F. ←

**Self-Test**
**Part A**

| | | | |
|---|---|---|---|
| 1. | F | 2. | T |
| 3. | F | 4. | T |
| 5. | T | 6. | F |
| 7. | F | 8. | F |
| 9. | F | 10. | T |

**Part B**

| | | | |
|---|---|---|---|
| 1. | a | 2. | d |
| 3. | d | 4. | b |
| 5. | c | 6. | c |
| 7. | b | 8. | b |
| 9. | a | 10. | a |
| 11. | c | 12. | b |
| 13. | d | 14. | a |
| 15. | d | | |

## ANSWERS TO CHAPTER 24

### Chapter Synopsis/Completions

| | | | |
|---|---|---|---|
| 1. | price | 2. | money supply |
| 3. | increase | 4. | money |
| 5. | right | 6. | right |
| 7. | fixed | 8. | expand |
| 9. | rise | 10. | aggregate output |
| 11. | aggregate suppy | 12. | price level |
| 13. | shocks | 14. | stagflation |

### Exercise 1

#### Part A

1. increase in the money supply
2. increase in government spending
3. increase in net exports
4. reduction in taxes
5. improved consumer optimism
6. improved business optimism

#### Part B

1. decline in the money supply
2. decline in government spending

3. decline in net exports
4. increase in taxes
5. increase in consumer pessimism
6. increase in business pessimism

**Exercise 2**

**Parts A and C**

FIGURE 24A

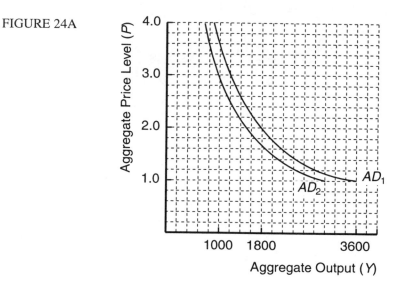

**Part B**
Aggregate spending will fall from 3600 to 3000

**Exercise 3**

| | |
|---|---|
| 1. ← | 2. ← |
| 3. → | 4. ← |
| 5. ← | 6. → |

**Exercise 4**

FIGURE 24B

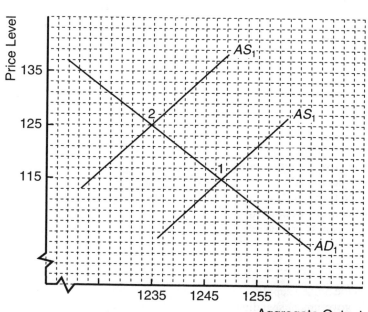

Since the actual unemployment rate exceeds the natural unemployment rate in 1974, the labor market was slightly "easy" at this time, suggesting that the aggregate supply curve would have shifted out, all else constant. Most of the blame for the shifting of the aggregate supply curve must go to OPEC which had significantly raised the price of oil in 1974, crop failures, and the lifting of wage and price controls.

## Exercise 5

The large decline in aggregate demand from 1929 to 1933 is clearly evident in the data as both real GNP and consumer prices fall significantly. It appears that between 1933 and 1936 that the aggregate demand curve had shifted out due to more expansionary monetary and fiscal policy. The aggregate supply curve appears to have shifted out. This is also consistent with the theory presented in Chapter 23, which indicates that when unemployment is above the natural rate there will be downward pressure on wages. Thus the behavior of aggregate demand and supply during the Great Depression is consistent with our more modern theory.

FIGURE 24C

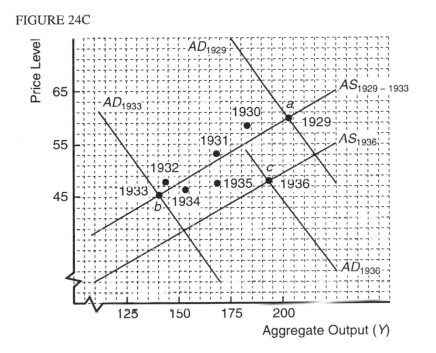

## Exercise 6

| | | | |
|---|---|---|---|
| 1. | B | 6. | K |
| 2. | N | 7. | K |
| 3. | K | 8. | M |
| 4. | M | 9. | B |
| 5. | M | 10. | B |

## Self-Test
### Part A

| | | | |
|---|---|---|---|
| 1. | T | 2. | T |
| 3. | F | 4. | T |
| 5. | F | 6. | T |
| 7. | F | 8. | T |
| 9. | T | 10. | F |

**Part B**

| | |
|---|---|
| 1. c | 2. c |
| 3. b | 4. c |
| 5. e | 6. d |
| 7. d | 8. a |
| 9. c | 10. b |
| 11. a | 12. c |
| 13. d | 14. d |
| 15. e | |

## ANSWERS TO CHAPTER 25

### Chapter Synopsis/Completions

| | |
|---|---|
| 1. monetarists | 2. evidence |
| 3. reduced form | 4. structural |
| 5. forecasts | 6. specified |
| 7. reverse causation | 8. third |
| 9. real | 10. statistical |
| 11. historical | 12. price level |
| 13. stock | 14. worth |
| 15. cash flow | |

### Exercise 1

| | |
|---|---|
| 1. R | 2. S |
| 3. R | 4. K |
| 5. R | 6. S |
| 7. S | 8. S |
| 9. R | |

### Exercise 2

| | |
|---|---|
| 1. K | 2. M |
| 3. M | 4. S |
| 5. M | 6. M |
| 7. K | 8. K |
| 9. K | |

### Exercise 3

1. If workers and other resource suppliers anticipate future price increases, they may attempt to hedge against inflation by increasing their prices now, especially if longer term contracts are prevalent.

2. When parties enter into longer term agreements they will have expectations of what the future will be like. If high rates of inflation are anticipated, wages will tend to reflect these anticipations. Thus, it is possible that wages rise in anticipation of higher prices rather than cause higher prices.

3. Many economists would argue that changes in monetary growth drive both input costs, such as wages, and prices.

### Exercise 4

| | |
|---|---|
| 1. d | 2. e |
| 3. f | 4. a |
| 5. g | 6. b |
| 7. c | |

**Self-Test**

**Part A**

| | | | |
|---|---|---|---|
| 1. | F | 2. | T |
| 3. | T | 4. | T |
| 5. | T | 6. | F |
| 7. | T | 8. | F |
| 9. | T | 10. | T |

**Part B**

| | | | |
|---|---|---|---|
| 1. | b | 2. | e |
| 3. | b | 4. | d |
| 5. | b | 6. | d |
| 7. | c | 8. | b |
| 9. | d | 10. | a |
| 11. | a | 12. | c |
| 13. | b | 14. | c |
| 15. | b | | |

## ANSWERS TO CHAPTER 26

### Chapter Synopsis/Completions

| | | | |
|---|---|---|---|
| 1. | monetary | 2. | temporary |
| 3. | accommodation | 4. | compatible |
| 5. | supply shocks | 6. | unemployment |
| 7. | cost push | 8. | low |
| 9. | hyperinflation | 10. | constraint |
| 11. | cost push | 12. | stable |
| 13. | time lags | 14. | crowding out |
| 15. | activist | | |

### Exercise 1

1. Concern over unemployment. Expansionary macropolicies reduce unemployment in the short run, but raise the price level in the long run. Such policies may prove inflationary if the unemployment target is set too low. Alternatively, monetary authorities may expand the money supply in response to cost-push pressures that threaten to raise unemployment.

2. Budget deficits. If deficits push interest rates upward, the Fed may automatically accommodate them if it pursues an interest-rate targeting strategy. Even if the Fed does not attempt to peg interest rates, the Fed may feel pressure to expand the money supply to keep interest rates from rising.

**Exercise 2**

FIGURE 26A

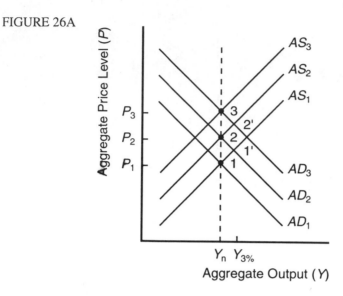

The target level of unemploymnent is below the natural rate level so $Y_{3\%}$ is above $Y_n$, as is drawn in the figure. Hence in trying to reach an output level of $Y_{3\%}$, the government will shift the aggregate demand curve to $AD_2$. Because the resulting level of output at point 1' is above the natural-rate level, the aggregate supply curve shifts in to $AS_2$ and output falls to the natural-rate level. To raise aggregate output to $Y_{3\%}$, the government again pursues expansionary policy to shift the aggregate demand curve to $AD_3$. The aggregate supply curve again shifts up to $AS_3$ because $Y > Y_n$. The outcome of this process is that the price level continually rises from $P_1$ to $P_2$ to $P_3$ and so on. The result is a demand-pull inflation.

**Exercise 3**

U.S. govemment budget deficit does not necessarily lead to monetary expansion because the Fed is not obligated to monetize the debt.
1. The budget deficit must lead to upward pressure on interest rates.
2. The Fed will try to prevent any rise in interest rates.

Although the Fed may have tried to prevent interest rate rises in the 1960-1980 period, the budget deficits could not have led to upward pressure on interest rates since the debt-to-GNP ratio did not rise in this period. Thus the budget deficits in this period could not have been the source of higher money growth.

**Exercise 4**

A comparison of the Argentine experience with that of post-World War I Germany suggests that changing the person in charge and issuing new currency may be insufficient by itself to rid a country of inflation. The German government constrained itself by limiting currency issue and moving toward a balanced budget. The deflation proved costly as the German economy went into recession. However, one can reasonably assume that the recession would have been longer and deeper had their policies not been viewed as credible by the citizenry. Especially important to achieving credibility is the reduction of budget deficits, since many people associate large deficits with inflation. Unfortunately, the failure of past reforms probably means that even serious reforms may, at first, be regarded with skepticism. Thus one might anticipate that deflationary policies will prove relatively more costly in Argentina than they did in 1920s Germany. The initial success of the Argentine anti-inflation program differed from previous attempts by addressing the problem of government budget deficits. Reducing the budget deficit likely changed inflationary expectations, contributing to the dramatic drop in the Argentine inflation rate in 1986. The government's failure to constrain budget deficits explains, in part, the return of triple-digit inflation rates.

**Exercise 5**

The rate hike appears to have been important in changing expectations. The Fed wanted to get inflation under control but feared that a deflationary monetary policy would cause high unemployment. Therefore, the Fed wanted its new strategy to be regarded as credible. It believed that the discount rate increase would signal to financial market participants its concern over inflation. The switch to reserve targeting was probably aimed at economists. Few others would understand the distinction between reserve targeting and interest-rate targeting. News reports following the announcement confirms this impression. The financial pages of most newspapers emphasized the discount-rate increase, while discussions among economists focused on the change in the targeting procedure.

**Exercise 6**

A.
1. The government can increase taxes.
2. The government can borrow from the public.
3. The government can borrow from the Fed.

B. When the government borrows from the Fed, the monetary base increases.

C. Monetizing the debt or it is sometimes called printing money.

D. No, because the Fed does not have to monetize it--that is, buy the Treasury debt. On the other hand, if the Fed wants to prevent a rise in interest rates, then it will purchase bonds to keep interest rates low and the result will be expansion of the monetary base.

**Self-Test**

**Part A**

| | | | |
|---|---|---|---|
| 1. | T | 2. | F |
| 3. | F | 4. | F |
| 5. | F | 6. | F |
| 7. | T | 8. | T |
| 9. | T | 10. | F |

**Part B**

| | | | |
|---|---|---|---|
| 1. | c | 2. | b |
| 3. | d | 4. | a |
| 5. | a | 6. | b |
| 7. | c | 8. | d |
| 9. | d | 10. | d |
| 11. | c | 12. | a |
| 13. | b | 14. | d |
| 15. | c | 16. | c |

## ANSWERS TO CHAPTER 27

### Chapter Synopsis/Completions

1.  adaptively
2.  past
3.  rational expectations
4.  predictions
5.  optimal forecasts
6.  efficient capital markets
7.  prices
8.  equilibrium
9.  financial analysts
10. random walk
11. expected
12. hold
13. brokerage
14. insider information

### Exercise 1

1.  c
2.  f
3.  d
4.  b
5.  c
6.  g
7.  h
8.  a
9.  a
10. c

### Exercise 2

A. If the Federal Reserve action was widely anticipated, long-term interest rates are likely to be unaffected. Since asset prices, and hence financial market yields, reflect currently available information, efficient markets theory suggests that the anticipated Federal Reserve action will not change long-term interest rates.

B. If the policy, once it is implemented, changes expectations so that people become convinced that the slower growth of money will be permanent, long-term interest rates might fall as people revise their expectations of inflation downward.

C. Finally if the policy should come as a surprise but expected inflation is not reduced, then long-term interest rates are likely to rise as the excess demand for money leads to failing bond prices (see Chapter 6).

D. Thus, when the Fed slows the growth of the money supply, predicting the interest-rate outcome requires some knowledge of people's expectations. While there is dispute as to whether or not unexpected money growth influences long-term interest rates, this example illustrates that expectations can play an important role in determining the effectiveness of monetary policy.

### Self-Test

#### Part A

1.  T
2.  F
3.  T
4.  T
5.  T
6.  T
7.  F
8.  F
9.  F
10. F

#### Part B

1.  c
2.  a
3.  d
4.  c
5.  c
6.  b
7.  c
8.  b
9.  a
10. c
11. c
12. b
13. d
14. c
15. d

## ANSWERS TO CHAPTER 28

### Chapter Synopsis/Completions

1. expectations
2. constant
3. new classical
4. flexible
5. supply
6. price level
7. ineffectiveness proposition
8. rigidities
9. anticipated
10. new Keynesians
11. policy critique
12. activist
13. credible
14. budget deficits

### Exercise 1

In the new classical model, the aggregate supply curve shifts out to $AS_{NC}$ and the economy goes to point NC. Aggregate output does not fall, while the price level falls to $P_{NC}$.

In the new Keynesian model, the aggregate supply shifts out but only to $AS_{NK}$ and the economy goes to point N. Aggregate output falls below $Y_N$ and the price level falls to $P_{NK}$, which is higher than that found in the new classical model.

In the traditional model, the aggregate supply curve does not shift out at all and the economy goes to point T. Aggregate output falls to $Y_T$, which is lower than in the other models, and the price level falls to $P_T$, which is higher than in the other models.

FIGURE 28A

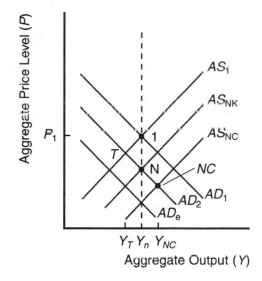

294

**Exercise 2**

FIGURE 28B

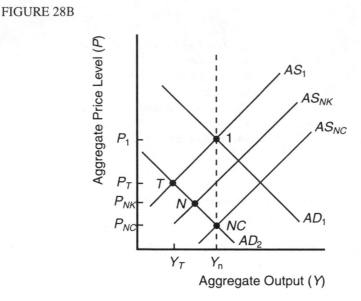

In the new classical model, the aggregate supply curve shifts out to $AS_{NC}$ (where output would equal $Y_n$ if the realized aggregate demand curve were $AD_e$). The economy goes to point NC, at which point aggregate output has risen to $Y_{NC}$. Aggregate output does not fall but rather rises.

In the new Keynesian model, the aggregate supply curve shifts out by less than in the new classical model. As drawn, the aggregate supply curve shifts to $AS_{NK}$ and the economy is at point N with the level of output unchanged. Thus aggregate output need not fall. However, the new Keynesian aggregate supply curve can lie above or below the $AS_{NK}$ drawn in the figure, and output could fall as well as rise in the new Keynesian model.
In the traditional model, the aggregate supply curve does not shift, so the economy ends up at point T. Only the traditional model gives the unequivocal result that output falls from the contractionary policy (to $Y_T$).

This example illustrates that in either the new classical or new Keynesian model a contractionary policy does not necessarily lead to a decline in output and can even lead to a rise in output if the policy is less contractionary than expected.

**Exercise 3**

The Fed will buy securities, but if expectations are rational, then the Fed's efforts in stabilizing nominal interest rates will be hampered. People realizing that higher rates of money growth will eventually prove inflationary, will bid up nominal interest rates further. (Recall that the nominal interest rate is the sum of the real interest rate and the expected rate of inflation, so that if inflation expectations rise by more than the real interest rate falls, the nominal rate rises.)

**Exercise 4**

1. NC
3. K
5. NC
7. NK

2. NC
4. M, NC
6. NC
8. K, M, NK

**Exercise 5**

| | |
|---|---|
| 1. NC, NK, T | 2. T |
| 3. T | 4. NK, NC |
| 5. T | 6. NC |

**Exercise 6**

In the traditional model, your announcement will not effect the aggregate supply curve; expectations about the Fed's policy will not effect the outcome. In the new classical model, your announcement will shift up the aggregate supply curve if it is believed and so the Fed's policy will not be as expansionary as the chairman of the Fed hopes. The chairman would prefer that you keep quiet about his intentions. The new Keynesian model leads to a similar conclusion as the new classical model. The Fed's policy will not be as expansionary as the chairman hopes; again, he would prefer you to keep quiet. However, the announced policy is likely to be more expansionary in the new Keynesian model than in the new classical model. If no one believes you when you make your announcement, then the aggregate supply curve will not shift even in the new classical or new Keynesian model.

**Self-Test**

**Part A**

| | |
|---|---|
| 1. T | 2. T |
| 3. F | 4. F |
| 5. T | 6. F |
| 7. T | 8. T |
| 9. F | 10. F |

**Part B**

| | |
|---|---|
| 1. a | 2. c |
| 3. d | 4. e |
| 5. e | 6. b |
| 7. c | 8. a |
| 9. c | 10. b |
| 11. c | 12. d |
| 13. c | 14. a |
| 15. b | |